D0016598

GROUP HOMES FOR TEENAGERS
A Practical Guide

GROUP HOMES FOR TEENAGERS
A Practical Guide

Albert L. Shostack, Ph.D.

HUMAN SCIENCES PRESS, INC.
72 FIFTH AVENUE
NEW YORK, N.Y. 10011-8004

Copyright © 1987 by Albert L. Shostack
Published by Human Sciences Press, Inc.
72 Fifth Avenue, New York, New York 10011

All rights reserved. No part of this work may be reproduced
or utilized in any form or by any means, electronic or
mechanical, including photocopying, microfilm and recording,
or by any information storage and retrieval system without
permission in writing from the author and publisher.

Printed in the United States of America
987654321

Library of Congress Cataloging-in-Publication Data

Shostack, Albert L.
  Group homes for teenagers.

  Includes index.
  1. Group homes for youth—United States—Planning.
2. Group homes for youth—United States. 3. Social
work with youth—United States. I. Title.
HV1431.S47 1987   362.7'32'088055   86-15349
ISBN 0-89885-323-0

CONTENTS

5

INTRODUCTION

Over the last two decades community-based group homes have gained wide acceptance as a resource for the care and treatment of troubled youths. Today thousands of homes care for dependent, disturbed, retarded, maladjusted, and physically handicapped youngsters. Although comparatively new and still evolving, the homes have earned an important place in the spectrum of residential care.

Group homes are residential care facilities in which a number of residents live under the supervision of staff members. They are distinguished from other residential care facilities by (a) small size—usually from 6 to 12 occupants; (b) few restraints on the movement of residents and on their interaction with the surrounding community; and (c) reliance on community resources such as public schools and recreation facilities to provide essential services (which is why group homes are termed community-based programs).

What accounts for the growing popularity of group homes? One reason is the movement to deinstitutionalize youths in residential care. The result has been the transfer of many young people to group-home and foster-family settings. Recent criticism of the mingling of "status" offenders (youths charged with antisocial behavior that is not technically a crime) with juvenile delinquents in correctional and detention facilities also has led to the placement of many status offenders in group homes. They may remain there briefly until their cases are processed, or they may be placed in a home for long-term care.

11

Some state and local governments have stimulated the development of group homes. They have provided financial incentives to private operators or set up government-owned facilities. Zoning restrictions have been eased to permit homes to locate in residential neighborhoods. School authorities have accepted responsibility for educating out-of-area youngsters assigned to local group homes.

Group homes also have expanded to serve new populations. Specialized facilities now shelter runaways, serve as halfway houses, and care for youths addicted to drugs. There are homes for blind, retarded, autistic, and other handicapped young people.

Most important, there is growing awareness of the potential advantages of group homes. They provide a placement alternative for youths who are unlikely to adapt to life with a foster family but who do not need the intensive services and controls of closed treatment institutions. They enable troubled youngsters to remain in a community setting. The group home milieu encourages supportive relations between staff and residents and among the residents themselves. It offers excellent opportunities to employ group work as a treatment tool. Admission to and departure from a home are less traumatic than the transition into or out of a larger facility. Finally, a stay in a group home is less likely to label youths adversely as delinquents or psychological deviants.

Responding to the mounting interest, numerous private and public agencies, as well as altruistic individuals, have set up group homes. However, few had any previous experience with such facilities. Older models of residential care proved to be inappropriate. Replication of the emotionally charged relations of family life, with its ambivalent undercurrents of love, anger, rejection, dependence, and domination is not therapeutic for troubled youngsters who have been removed from their homes. Nor are the roles of parents, grandparents, older siblings, aunts, and uncles appropriate for staff members. As child care professionals, they must attend to their jobs in a technical and neutral way, adjusting their relations with the youngsters to the requirements of a systematic therapeutic program.

The institutional model also does not fit a group home. A home's staff is not in a position to exert 24-hour supervision over the activities of the residents. The young people are free to come and go most of the day and spend a good deal of their time unobserved by the staff. They choose their own friends in school and neighborhood and are influenced by peer groups outside the home. Lacking specialized staffs of their own, group homes must depend for services on public schools, recreation facilities, and other agencies that are not under their direct control. Because of such differences they can no more copy large institutions than the traditional family.

Group homes have had to adopt distinctive approaches geared to their special circumstances. In the absence of intensive supervision and a controlled physical environment, they must rely on indirect, nonauthoritarian ways of influencing residents. They try to create a therapeutic social milieu in which everyday life and relationships contribute to character growth. Through group work, residents are encouraged to exert a positive influence on the attitudes and values of their peers. Personalized staff relations and nondirective counseling reduce the need for disciplinary measures. Often the young people are consulted in designing the home's rules, activities, and treatment plans.

This nonauthoritarian approach does not represent weakness or permissiveness. It reflects instead a realistic recognition of the special conditions under which group homes operate and the characteristics of the residents they serve. Rigid demands for obedience to rules prescribed by adults are simply impractical and self-defeating in community-based residential programs.

Not all homes have been successful. A substantial number have been troubled by rapid turnover of residents, high vacancy rates, staff "burnout," and complaints from parents, teachers, and neighbors. Financial hardship, conflict with child-placement agencies, and community hostility are additional hardships. Some homes, overwhelmed by administrative and treatment problems, have gone out of business.

Fortunately, home operators and child welfare agencies have accumulated valuable experience in recent years. Knowledge is being shared in professional publications, child care conferences, and informal interaction among group home personnel. This book represents an effort to distill that experience as a basis for practical recommendations on how to plan and operate group homes. Following are some of the questions that will be considered:

1. Who operates group homes? How can a home get started?
2. What children are served? Where do they come from?
3. How are homes financed?
4. What physical facilities does a home need?
5. Where should homes be located? How can they gain community acceptance?
6. What kinds of staffs do group homes need?
7. How should everyday life be structured in a home?
8. What services should homes provide for their residents?
9. How can a therapeutic social milieu develop in a home?
10. When are residents terminated? Where do they go?

The intention is to help group home operators evaluate their resources realistically, assemble a sound therapeutic program, develop supportive relations with community and government agencies, and anticipate the difficult problems that have threatened group homes in the past. The information also should assist child welfare and regulatory agencies in developing policies for financing, evaluating, and supervising group homes. Finally, persons preparing for or engaged in a career in residential child care will find this publication a worthwhile addition to their training program.

The book will focus on homes that serve teenagers who fall into three categories:

1. Dependent youths—who are victims of parental neglect, abuse, incapacity, or abandonment or who cannot live with parents or relatives for other reasons. Some of those youngsters are not psychologically disturbed themselves but have come under the supervision of child welfare agencies as orphans or victims of disordered family members.

2. Mildly disturbed youths—who require services in a structured group setting but are not in need of continuous supervision, intensive psychotherapy, drug therapy under close medical care, and highly specialized education. The psychologically disturbed youths assigned to group homes exhibit abnormal feelings and behavior patterns that impair their functioning in everyday life. They are unable to sustain positive relations in family, school, peer group, or work situations. They may display distressing psychosomatic symptoms.

3. Socially maladjusted youths—who have engaged in socially unacceptable or self-endangering behavior but who are able to interact with others in a rational fashion and are not in substantial psychological distress. Such youngsters may have a history of fighting, sexual promiscuity, drug abuse, curfew violations, chronic truancy, or even petty crimes like trespassing and shoplifting. Rebellion against parental, school, and other authority is a typical characteristic; some of the youths are characterized as "uncontrollable" by parents and teachers.

The three categories are overlapping. It is likely, for example, that an abused and neglected youth will display symptoms of social maladjustment. Similarly, the behavior of a socially maladjusted youth may reflect psychological illness. Young people in any of the categories are suitable for placement in a community-based group home if they are capable of living in a group setting; do not require intensive, continuous supervision; can utilize school, recreation, health, and other community facilities; and do not require intensive psychiatric or drug therapy.

There were some 175,000 dependent, disturbed, or socially maladjusted young people in residential facilities in 1981. Of those almost 20,000 lived in group homes with from 7 to 12 beds. Group homes are the fastest-growing component of residential care for such youths, increasing almost 900 percent, to 2,066 facilities, between 1966 and 1981. Closely related facilities that accommodate 13 to 20 residents more than doubled, to about 700, during the period (Dore, Young, & Pappenfort, 1984, pp. 489–490).[1]

---

[1]The figures exclude homes serving mentally retarded, physically handicapped, and chronically ill youth.

Chapter 1

GROUP HOMES AND THEIR RESIDENTS

Approval by the Placement Agency

Most of the homeless, psychologically disturbed, and socially maladjusted youths in group homes have been placed there by state or local government child welfare agencies. Such placement agencies assume the guardianship of youths whose families are unable to provide them with adequate care in their own homes. They determine which residential facilities will be authorized to care for children under their supervision, and they designate the facilities to which each youth will be referred. The placement agency reimburses group homes, in whole or part, for the costs of care.

Most placement agencies issue detailed manuals that prescribe how residential facilities must operate. A manual is likely to require certain physical facilities, staffing patterns, and treatment services. Applicable state/local health, safety, and fire regulations are usually identified. There are financial regulations as to record keeping, allowable costs, and reimbursement procedures. To ensure compliance, provision is made for monitoring and evaluation of programs by placement agency staff.

Some child placement agencies issue licenses to new homes; others rely on less formal procedures. If a facility draws residents from several placement agencies, it may have to satisfy different requirements imposed by each of them.

The approval process can be complex and can take a long time. Home operators may be required to submit applications that describe their ownership, structure, financial resources, staff, proposed services, and target populations. There will be preliminary talks with agency personnel, a review by various offices, inspections, and negotiations about reimbursement. Modification of the home's quarters and proposed services may have to be made to meet agency standards. Sometimes applications are held up by budget uncertainties, reorganizations, poor coordination, and staff turnover in the placement agency. All of those activities and potential obstacles can delay final approval for a year or more.

Once a new group home gains the placement agency's approval, it is usually required to enter into a written agreement with the agency. The agreement specifies the number and type of youngsters to be served, placement procedures, services to be provided, the home's rights and obligations, and the rate of reimbursement for the home's services.

An agreement may be for a definite period, such as a year, with renewal subject to an evaluation of the home's performance and the availability of funds. Alternatively, the agreement may be open-ended, continuing in effect until the placement agency or group home requests a change. An important section of the agreement describes the conditions under which it may be canceled by either party, the notice of cancellation required, and any rights of appeal available to adversely affected group homes.

Monitoring and Evaluation of Homes

Child placement agencies use several methods of keeping watch on the residential facilities that care for their children. First, an agency is likely to assign a member of its staff to monitor each home on a continuing basis. The monitor visits the home from time to time, talks to staff and residents, checks various records, and tries to ensure that the facility is adhering to all relevant standards.

A second form of supervision is exercised by the placement agency's finance office. That office checks claims for reimbursement submitted by group homes to make sure that they cover only allowable expenditures.

A third method of supervision is an in-depth evaluation of each facility, conducted when a facility's license or contract comes up for renewal or at other intervals. Some placement agencies send a team of evaluators who spend several days at a group home examining financial records, checking services, and inspecting the home's quarters. Team members interview staff members and residents. After such a visit the evaluators prepare a report with recommendations for improvements. Those recommendations are taken into account during negotiations on the renewal of the home's contract.

Periodic evaluations help to strengthen group home programs. They serve as occasions for the home's staff and residents to review its goals and policies and to take a fresh look at what it is doing.

Inevitably, there are complaints about the evaluation process. Some home operators argue that placement agency evaluators have never worked in a residential care facility and do not understand its needs and realities. They say that evaluations take too much of the staff's time and focus only on quantifiable aspects of group home operation. The recommendations of successive evaluation teams are often inconsistent and bear no relation to the availability of funds. Sometimes group homes are not afforded a timely opportunity to respond to unfavorable findings.

Despite such problems close supervision of residential facilities is a necessary function of placement agencies. Home operators are well advised to become familiar with evaluation procedures and to learn how to use the system in a positive way.

Private versus Government Operation

Government child welfare, mental health, corrections, and related agencies have established numerous group homes for troubled youths. A much larger number, however, are owned by private organizations that are paid to care for young people assigned to them by the government agencies.

Why do not government agencies themselves operate all of the group homes? One reason is to save money. Private homes generally have lower costs than government facilities. That is particularly true of labor costs. The homes are rarely unionized, do not have to pay high civil service salaries and fringe benefits, and can impose flexible work schedules on their employees. They can hire or fire workers with a minimum of red tape.

Not only are their costs lower, but the homes are often required to share the costs of caring for their residents. Such reliance on private resources conforms to an honored American tradition of altruism, voluntarism, and pluralism in the social services.

Government facilities do have financial advantages that are the envy of private facilities. Once their annual budget has been approved, they can count on a definite amount of money for the upcoming year regardless of fluctuations in the number of occupants. Predictable financial resources permit long-term planning and encourage the staff to feel secure in their jobs. The staff does not have to devote time to fund-raising and has access to government training, technical assistance, and other services.

There are pros and cons to both private and government facilities, and the existence of a mix of both types is probably beneficial.

Nonprofit and For-Profit Homes

Private group homes are either operated on a nonprofit basis or seek a financial profit. Most are of the nonprofit type.

The reason so few homes for troubled youth are profit-seeking is that it is very difficult to earn money in such enterprises. They require a substantial capital investment and are subject to strict regulation by the placement agencies. They are reimbursed only for the bare essentials of child care and must cope with unpredictable year-to-year fluctuations in funding and occupancy.

Nonprofit status has some positive advantages. It makes group homes eligible for tax-exempt donations from individuals and corporations. It increases the chances of receiving grants from foundations and governments. Nonprofit homes also may be exempt from certain taxes in their states and localities.

Nonprofit homes have a greater likelihood of gaining community acceptance than do for-profit facilities. They are in a better position to draw on the resources of local service agencies, to elicit cooperation from neighbors, and to recruit volunteer workers. It is possible, too, that both staff members and residents may form more positive attitudes toward their group home if they perceive it as an altruistic enterprise.

Affiliation with Parent Agencies

Private group homes also can be separated into independent entities and those that belong to larger parent organizations. An independent home may be an outgrowth of an older institution that has encountered a reduced demand for its services. For example, some traditional orphanages and shelters for unwed pregnant girls have been transformed into group homes as demand for their services dwindled. Occasionally, one or more concerned individuals may set up an independent home.

Private organizations that operate group homes include community youth agencies, church groups, YM–YWCA's, mental health and family service agencies, and civic bodies. Many large residential treatment facilities also have established group homes to help recovering residents make a transition to noninstitutionalized life.

Group homes affiliated with parent agencies have important advantages, including:

a. Readier acceptance by placement agencies;

b. Greater acceptance by the neighboring community;

c. More adequate financial resources;

d. Expert legal, accounting, grant-seeking, and other services;

e. Sharing of clerical and maintenance services with the parent agency;

f. More effective staff utilization—staff members can transfer from one job to another within the organization to prevent burnout, expand their skills, and move up a career ladder.

g. Access to the parent agency's learning-disability specialists, family therapists, and other experts;

h.   Access by residents to more appropriate forms of care as their needs change.

Despite the advantages of affiliation, it would be wrong to discourage unaffiliated group homes. Their dedication and creativity can lead to innovative and effective programs.

Incorporation

Whether nonprofit or for profit, virtually all private organizations operating group homes take the form of corporations. Incorporation is useful to acquire nonprofit status with the Internal Revenue Service and state authorities. It limits the personal liability of the group home operators for financial claims filed against their facility—by injured residents, irate parents, or people with whom the home does business. Corporate status also lends continuity to the organization; it is less likely to be disrupted by the departure of an officer or even of a founding member.

How Do Youngsters Find Their Way into Group Homes?

Placement Agencies

Because placement agencies play a crucial role in funding, setting standards for, and monitoring group homes, as well as serving as their source of residents, it is important to understand their structure and procedures.

The structure of child placement agencies varies from state to state. In New York, for example, a state agency sets overall standards and provides partial funding, but autonomous local governments conduct the day-to-day operations of the placement program. Pennsylvania has a similar system, but the state child welfare agency is in charge of correctional facilities for juvenile delinquents as well as residential care for homeless, disturbed, and maladjusted youths. In New Jersey a state placement agency works directly with troubled families through its own district offices, eliminating the role of local government.

Often local placement offices have considerable latitude in deciding where to place youngsters. Some offices may go to special lengths to keep a troubled youth at home; others may emphasize foster family placements. A local office may utilize group homes or remain skeptical about their effectiveness. An office may give priority to local residential facilities, or it may prefer to place youngsters in distant institutions that are deemed to provide better care. The local office can therefore play a major role in the survival of group homes.

Voluntary and Involuntary Placements

Essentially, group home placements can be divided into two categories: voluntary and involuntary. Involuntary placements are those ordered by a court or another government agency that has mandatory powers. A juvenile court may have the authority to order the placement of a juvenile delinquent or status offender in a group home in lieu of a correctional facility. The court may be authorized to specify the facility to which the youth is to be assigned, or it may simply refer the youth to a state or local child welfare agency for placement. In either case there is an element of compulsion: the offender enters residential care as a condition of probation, the dropping of charges, or escape from more stringent penalties.

In some circumstances child welfare agencies are authorized to make short-term involuntary placements on their own. They may, for example, have to remove abused youngsters from their homes and find them a safe place to live on an emergency basis. Agencies have to assume responsibility for lost children or those left without parental care by an accident. Generally, however, involuntary placements by child welfare agencies are only temporary and require court approval for extended stays.

Voluntary placements are those in which parents agree to permit a placement agency to assume the temporary supervision of their child and to place him in residential care. Court action is not normally required. Probably most group home placements are voluntary.

Youths who are placed with the voluntary consent of their parents come to the attention of child welfare agencies in several ways. Very often the parents themselves turn to the agency for assistance with a disturbed or incorrigible child. They may be unable to cope with the child's problems because of their own psychological tensions or physical incapacity, the breakup of the family, or inability to afford private treatment services. They may fear that their child's behavior and association with disreputable acquaintances are beyond their control and are adversely affecting his education and daily life. Not infrequently, the family is referred to the child welfare agency by a therapist, school counselor, or public assistance worker who has become aware of the family's needs.

With another group of parents who agree to voluntary placements it is the child welfare agency that has taken the initiative. Agencies authorized to investigate and remedy child abuse or neglect may identify families in trouble and persuade them to accept corrective services.

Youths who have been charged with status offenses are a third source of voluntary placements. Court officials generally try to resolve such cases informally in a way that is therapeutic for the young offender. If there are no serious criminal charges, the family is likely to be referred to the local child welfare office for remedial services, which might include residential care. Probably some parents agree to a placement to help their child escape charges of juvenile delinquency and potential confinement in a correctional facility.

Independent Review of Placements

The need to limit residential placements to cases of real necessity is a continuing concern of child advocates and child care professionals. Some think that more youngsters could probably remain at home if community services for troubled families were expanded. Some question whether youths are being placed in the least restrictive environment consistent with their needs. There are fears that some parents may have been pressured to agree to inappropriate placements by court or child welfare agency personnel. There are also parents who agree to a placement as an easy way of evading their parental responsibilities. Because of such concerns, new procedures are emerging to double-check the assignment of young people in residential care.

A number of states now require an independent review of all placements made by government child welfare agencies. The review systems vary greatly. Generally, all new placements are reviewed shortly after each youth enters residential care. Follow-up reviews of each youngster's status are conducted annually or at other intervals thereafter to determine whether placements should be altered or terminated by the child welfare agency. Depending on the content of state laws, the reviews may be conducted by juvenile court judges, social workers employed by the court, citizen panels appointed by judicial or executive departments, or combinations of those.

Of necessity, the independent reviewers must rely heavily on data furnished for each youth by the placement agency. However, they are usually permitted to meet with parents, youngsters, and residential care staffs to obtain additional information. Hearings and appeals by interested parties may be permitted.

Group homes are likely to find that independent reviews of the status of their residents demand a considerable amount of staff time. There are reports to be prepared and hearings to attend. The staff loses valuable time traveling to and from review sessions or waiting about for postponed or canceled hearings. Still, independent review systems have a beneficial effect in drawing attention to the needs of individual youths and ensuring that each will receive appropriate attention from the placement agency. Overall descriptions and appraisals of independent review systems are given in Cutler and Bateman (1980), McLaughlin (1981), and Chappell and Hevener (1977).

Two comprehensive reports on review systems in operation are found in Festinger (1976) and Association for Children of New Jersey (1979).

CHOOSING A TARGET POPULATION

From the universe of homeless, psychologically disturbed, and socially maladjusted young people in need of residential care, a group home must select the types of youngsters it will serve. There are many alternatives. Should the home serve boys or girls? Teenagers or ten-year-olds? Short- or long-term residents? Should the home admit only local youths? Should it accept those with records of juvenile delinquency or serious mental illness? What kind of psychological disorders should the home attempt to treat? Obviously, the answers to such questions strongly influence the structure and content of the home's program.

Not all homes have made their decisions in an informed, systematic way. Facilities have been started in the wrong places, for the wrong kinds of youngsters, for the wrong reasons. An altruistic individual may donate funds to start a facility for teenage girls only because his teenage daughter had emotional problems. Organizations have started homes in localities served adequately by existing facilities merely because they owned vacant buildings there. Untested preconceptions, such as "Younger children are easier to manage than older ones" and "Life on a farm is just what delinquent kids need," have influenced the choice of a target population.

This section discusses some important issues in deciding which youths to serve. It suggests the kind of information that home operators should have and the advantages and disadvantages of alternative admissions policies.

Information Requirements

As a first step in selecting a target group, prospective group home operators should discuss the matter wtih administrators of placement agencies, residential child care facilities in the area, and other local agencies serving youth. They should inquire about the number and characteristics of youths placed in group homes, their length of stay, and procedures for assigning youths to particular homes. They should determine whether there is a shortage or surplus of beds, for what types of youths, and in what area.

Not only present needs but the future supply and demand for residential care are relevant in choosing a target population. The use of group homes may be affected by changes in government policies and appropriations. Emerging trends in child care, such as the deinstitutionalization movement of recent years, affect the utilization of facilities. The uncoordinated establishment of new homes may create a surplus of accommodations for some types of troubled youth in the future. Such areas should be explored with placement agencies and other informed sources.

Choosing a Service Area

A group home may admit only youths who live in its own locality or it may admit youths from anywhere in the state. It may even receive referrals from other states. Homes affiliated with an intensive treatment or correctional facility, on the other hand, may limit admissions to youths referred by their parent agency.

Group homes serving only local youths have important advantages:

1. They can develop close working relations with the local office of the placement agency. Caseworkers supervising their residents are readily available, familiar with the home, and held to consistent policies.

2. The home need only adhere to a single set of standards and reporting requirements imposed by a single placement agency.

3. Families of residents live nearby and are easily available for counseling and therapeutic visits to or from their children.

4. If indicated by their treatment plans, residents can remain in the same school and retain old friends after entering the group home.

5. Local schools and community elements are more likely to support the home if it serves only local youths.

There are also disadvantages in limiting admissions to a small geographic area. The supply of local youngsters in need of residential care may be too small to keep the home at full occupancy. The very existence of the home comes to depend on the cooperation of a single office of the placement agency, which can withhold potential residents if it is dissatisfied with the home's performance.

Residential facilities that serve a statewide clientele are more likely to receive an adequate number of residents and to avoid dependence on a single placement office. They perform an essential social service in accepting youths from areas lacking adequate facilities of their own. They are a haven for young people who need to be removed from harmful family and peer group influences, and who need a "fresh start" in a new school. Drawing from a large area, statewide homes can specialize in caring for small, widely dispersed problem groups such as children with both physical and psychological handicaps and those with language difficulties.

Age

A group home may choose to serve a narrow range of ages; e.g., fourteen to sixteen. The assumption here is that youths of the same age share similar experiences and levels of maturity. As a result, they are more likely to benefit from group work and to form a therapeutic social milieu.

Other homes prefer a wider age range in the belief that this encourages the emergence of supportive and noncompetitive relationships among residents. Also, with a wide age range a home can accommodate siblings who prefer to stay together while in residential care.

A wide age range creates some practical difficulties:

1. The home must deal with not one but several public schools, i.e., a high school, junior high school, and even an elementary school.

2. There must be different rules for younger and older residents, which creates resentment and friction. For that reason Rabinow (1964) suggests a maximum age range of 3 years so that a single set of rules can be applicable to all residents.

3. Separate recreational activities must be arranged for residents of disparate ages. They will favor different television programs, sports, games, and outings.

4. The effectiveness of group counseling and group therapy may be impaired if participants have greatly different interests, experiences, and levels of maturity. Vocational choices, life-styles, sexuality, and family ties mean different things to a twelve-year-old than to an eighteen-year-old.

Boys or Girls

The decision to serve boys or girls should be based on information about which of the sexes is most in need of group home openings. The placement agency is the best source of information on this matter.

Some group home operators are experimenting with coeducational populations. Their intention is to create a more natural, family-like environment in which residents can learn to relate to the opposite sex in a realistic way consistent with their level of physical and psychological maturity. As an added benefit, coed homes make it possible to keep brothers and sisters together during their placement.

Probably coeducation for teenagers works better in large, self-sufficient residential facilities than in group homes. Teenage residents of group homes have daily opportunities for spontaneous interaction with the opposite sex in public schools, local places of recreation, and elsewhere in the community. They make neighborhood friends of both sexes, receive and make frequent visits with boy and girl friends, and are free to go out on "dates" under most circumstances. Group homes for older youths have no need, therefore, to risk the tensions, temptations, and testing of staff that may occur when troubled boys and girls are thrown together in confined quarters.

At present most coed group homes serve children below the ages of twelve or thirteen. A coed environment seems most feasible for that population.

Race and Ethnic Groups

Placement agencies supported by public funds are not permitted to assign youngsters to residential facilities on the basis of race, ethnic group, or religion. In practice, however, some homes do have a predominantly white, black, Hispanic, or other distinctive population.

The location of a home—in a racially segregated urban area, an ethnic enclave, an affluent white suburb, or an integrated neighborhood—affects its population mix. So do the objectives and reputation of its parent organization. A placement agency's policy of placing children in their own communities or of distributing children on a statewide basis affects the mix of residents in each facility. Sometimes the preferences of anxious parents result in the assignment of their child to a home in which most residents are of their own racial or ethnic group. In such ways an unintended pattern of segregation may emerge.

Once a racial/ethnic group becomes a majority of a home's residents, the segregation process tends to accelerate. Potential residents are attracted to homes serving youths of similar backgrounds, and they reject placements elsewhere. Prejudiced parents withdraw residents who belong to the home's minority group. Even the placement agency's caseworkers may stereotype the group home as one that serves a single racial/ethnic group, and they may become reluctant to refer other youngsters to the facility.

Integration is feasible even in facilities operated by organizations identified with a specific racial/ethnic/religious group. Catholic, Protestant, and Jewish service organizations have long cared successfully for youngsters of backgrounds different from their own. To make integration work, their staff members try to learn about the dynamics of prejudice and discrimination. They acquire appropriate language skills and information about the distinctive family relations and social attitudes of each group. Role models can be provided by employing multiracial/ethnic staffs and by involving volunteers from all segments of the community.

Legal Status

In deciding which youths to serve, some group homes take account of their legal status and previous contacts with the law. A home may prefer to accept only voluntary placements, or it may mix youths placed with parental consent with those placed involuntarily under court orders. It may be in a position to accept or exclude youths convicted of crimes and those on probation or parole. Where such choices are available to a home, they pose a significant issue in selecting a target population.

The trouble is that legal labels worn by potential residents, such as "juvenile delinquent," status offender, probationer, parolee, or voluntary placement do not necessarily predict how they will adapt and progress in a group home program. Youngsters with the same label have different psychological characteristics, family and school problems, and needs for services. Their legal labels change frequently as they pass through successive contacts with the juvenile justice and child welfare systems. A wild youth may be processed as a status offender one month but, after shoplifting or smoking a "joint," become a delinquent the next. For those reasons, the legal status of youths is not in itself a reliable guide for deciding whom to admit to a home.

One sound rule can be suggested. Community-based group homes are not appropriate places for youths who have committed violent crimes. The facilities cannot provide the intensive supervision required to manage such individuals. Hardened delinquents may exert a negative influence on other residents and create a threatening atmosphere that disrupts the home's program, causes frightened youths to run away, and leads parents to withdraw their children. The admission of violent delinquents also undermines the home's acceptance by the surrounding community.

Psychological Characteristics

The most difficult decision in selecting a target population concerns the types and degree of psychological disorder—from mild maladjustment to severe disturbance—that will be accepted for treatment. This decision affects the entire group home program. It influences the way quarters are arranged and furnished, the number and kind of staff members employed, and the services provided for residents. It determines the number of potential residents who will be referred by the placement agency, their length of stay, and the cost of care. The psychological characteristics of residents also affect the home's relations with the school and the community.

Before making a decision it is important to learn how the placement agency evaluates the psychological characteristics of children and what criteria are used in assigning them to group homes. Does the agency classify children in some standard way? If so, what categories are employed? How many youths fall into each category?

One also should ask whether the placement agency requires different services and pays different rates for youths in each psychological category. It is useful to know whether area homes specialize in treating specific types of psychological disorders and whether there are shortages or supluses of facilities for particular kinds of disorders.

Unfortunately, information on the psychological characteristics of youngsters referred to group homes is often vague. The placement agency may describe them in broad categories such as "emotionally disturbed," "socially maladjusted," or "predelinquent." They may be said to suffer from a "situational neurosis" or "character disorders of adolescence"—categories too general for planning an admissions policy. Psychological labels may be assigned inconsistently by school psychologists, psychiatric consultants, therapists in community service agencies, placement agency caseworkers, or others.[1]

In deciding which types of psychological disorders to accept for treatment, the most important rule is that a home should admit only those youths

---

[1] An effort to systematize the classification of troubled youths is reflected in the *Diagnostic and Statistical Manual of Mental Disorders* (third edition, 1980) prepared by the American Psychiatric Association. The categories appear somewhat broad for selecting a group home target population, however.

for whom it can provide adequate care. The skills and experience of the staff, the physical quarters, and the therapeutic services must meet the residents' treatment needs. Second, residents must be able to participate in and benefit from group living. In a group home, peer group relations, informal staff–resident relations, cooperative activities, group decision-making, group counseling, and other aspects of the social milieu are essential treatment tools.

There are other guidelines. Residents must be able to attend and benefit from public schools; do personal shopping on their own; use community health, transportation, and recreation facilities; and move about the neighborhood with a degree of self-reliance. Their behavior must not arouse fear or hostility in the community. Nor can their disturbance be so severe that it endangers the safety or disrupts the treatment of other residents. Violent youths, chronic runaways, fire setters, and compulsive thieves require more structured settings than group homes. Youths requiring intensive psychotherapy or drug therapy also need closer supervision and access to specialized health personnel than are possible in group homes.

The exclusion of serious psychological disorders does not imply that group homes can serve only well-adjusted, healthy youngsters. There remains a substantial intermediate category of mildly disturbed and socially maladjusted young people who can benefit from group home care.

Chapter 2

FINANCING GROUP HOMES

Financial problems have driven some group homes out of business. In others they have led to curtailed services and insecurity among staff members and residents. It is important, therefore, to operate homes on a sound financial basis.

Home operators are concerned about such basic questions as (a) how much does it cost to start a group home? (b) where can I raise money to acquire and prepare a facility? (c) who will pay my expenses during periods of low occupancy? (d) how will I be reimbursed by the placement agency(ies)? (e) which expenses are reimbursable, and which are not? (f) do I have to share the cost of caring for the placement agency's children? These and related matters will be discussed in this chapter.

At the outset it is necessary to distinguish the capital costs of group homes from their operating costs. The former represent the home operator's long-term investment of capital—to buy and/or rehabilitate a building, pay for equipment, and cover start-up costs of various kinds. Operating costs, on the other hand, represent the day-to-day expenses of conducting the program. They include payments for food, clothing, supplies, transportation, repairs, salaries, utility and insurance bills, and related items. Generally, funds to meet capital and operating costs come from different sources and are subject to different policies. They will therefore be discussed separately below.

Capital Costs—Can We Afford to Start a Group Home?

Starting a group home requires a substantial investment of money. Efforts to stint on the quality of facilities, staff, and services simply lead to failure and to the loss of some invested funds as well. The large amount of capital required reflects the rising cost of buildings and services and the need to cover heavy costs during a long planning and start-up period before the home begins to pay its way.

Individuals or organizations planning a group home are usually expected to furnish all or most of the necessary capital from their own resources. Home operators are unlikely to recover their initial investment from the payments they receive from placement agencies. Even a limited recovery will take a very long time.

Four activities that require capital expenditures by new group homes—activities in the planning period, acquiring a physical facility, buying equipment, and operating the home below its full capacity in the start-up period—are described below.

Activities in the Planning Period

Expenses during the long planning and get-ready period are rarely reimbursed by placement agencies. One substantial expense is the salary of a director employed to develop the home's policies and procedures, negotiate with the placement agency and local school and community agencies, and to recruit and train junior staff members. Toward the end of the planning period a social worker, child care workers, and others also must be available to serve new residents.

Office space is another expense. Individuals planning a home need a place where they can prepare written materials, use the phone, meet business visitors, and keep the project's files. A typewriter, file cabinet, desk, table, and chairs must be obtained. Clerical services, telephone, stamps, and office supplies are necessities. There also may be printing costs for a descriptive brochure and resident handbook. Finally, with the cost of operating a car nowadays at more than 25 cents per mile, transportation can be a heavy drain on capital.

The legal costs incurred by new homes can require a substantial investment, depending on the complications they encounter. A home that faces community opposition, zoning conflicts, real estate tangles, and the need to borrow some of its capital will incur more legal costs than, say, a home that quietly occupies a building owned by its parent agency. An unaffiliated home will have the expense of incorporating and seeking tax-free status, whereas a unit of an existing agency will not.

Acquiring Quarters for a Home

If a group home must buy a building for its program, that is its largest capital expense. Generally, placement agencies do not provide buildings or funds with which to buy one.

The cost of a facility depends on its size, condition, and accommodations. The level of real estate prices in the area is an important factor. The cost of renovating and converting a building for group living can be substantial, particularly when the building was formerly a single-family residence. Fire escapes, sprinkler systems, fire walls, extra bathrooms, remodeling of kitchens, and electrical rewiring may be required to meet health and safety standards. Closets may have to be added, a basement converted to recreation use, or a porch enclosed.

Some group homes have had the good fortune of receiving a building free of charge from their parent organization, well-to-do individuals, or a government agency. Before accepting a donated building, however, home operators should be sure that it is in a suitable location and has adequate facilities.

Renting quarters for a home reduces initial capital costs. A significant proportion of all homes occupy rented quarters (Citizens Committee for Children of New York, 1976, Supplement, p. 11). Among the economic considerations that influence a decision to rent or buy quarters are (a) the availability of mortgages at a reasonable rate of interest; (b) the availability of cash for a down payment; (c) the availability of funds to rehabilitate a purchased building; (d) the willingness of a landlord to invest his own funds in rehabilitating or converting a rented building; (e) opportunities for appreciation of the value of a purchased property; (f) the duration of leases offered by landlords; and (g) the placement agency's reimbursement policies.

Generally, agencies will not reimburse a home for down payments and mortgage payments required to purchase quarters, reasoning that the home operator is compensated by the accumulation of equity in the property. Instead, group homes are likely to receive a fee for the use and/or depreciation of their facilities.

Rent paid by group homes, on the other hand, is likely to be a reimbursable cost. Some placement agencies may, however, refuse to reimburse a home that rents quarters from its own parent organization or from one of its own officers.

Equipment Costs

Equipping a group home requires another substantial expenditure of capital. Institutional-size sinks, stoves, refrigerators, and water heaters are needed. So are large pots and pans and an ample supply of dishes and silverware. Group homes require sturdy but comfortable furnishings capable of hard use by active teenagers. A van or station wagon is a necessity for shopping trips; delivering residents to medical appointments, the bus station, and elsewhere; recreational outings; trips to the placement agency; and many other purposes. A large-screen television set is found in virtually all group homes.

Other necessities are washing machines, dryers, blankets, sheets, and towels. If closets are inadequate, individual lockers must be purchased for the clothing and valuables of residents. Lawnmowers, gardening tools, simple "fix-it" tools, and flashlights must be available.

Capital to Cover Operating Deficits

Although the day-to-day cost of operating a group home is reimbursed in whole or in large part by the placement agency, home operators must have a reserve of capital to cover operating costs during periods when payments are delayed or inadequate. Operating deficits are more pronounced during the start-up period of a new home, when it may have a high vacancy rate. Until most of its beds are filled, the home's income is inadequate to cover its fixed costs, such as rent, salaries, insurance, maintenance, and utility bills. New homes, therefore, may have to draw on their capital to survive until full occupancy is attained.

Long-established facilities also have to dip into their capital from time to time. Reimbursement of their operating costs can be delayed by bureaucratic bottlenecks. Disputes with the placement agency over the terms of next year's contract can reduce a home's income temporarily. Occupancy may decline during the summer months. Quarters and equipment may require repairs or replacement. A capital reserve for such contingencies is a "must" for group homes.

Total Capital Requirements

How much capital does it take to start a group home? No single estimate is accurate for all facilities. Capital needs depend on whether quarters are rented, purchased, donated, and/or renovated. They reflect the level of salaries, the availability of volunteer workers, and the amount of free services provided by other organizations. Among other factors are regulatory agency requirements, community acceptance, the characteristics of a home's target population, and the time required to reach full occupancy.

A very generalized example of the investment required for a 10-bed home is presented below. The example is based on the assumption that costs are above average; capital needs may be much higher under some common circumstances.

Cost of purchasing a physical facility (includes a down
  payment of one-third on price of $180,000; $10,000
  for rehabilitation; and $10,000 for legal, brokerage,
  and settlement fees) $ 80,000

Costs in planning period (assumes that most preliminary planning and other support will be provided by volunteers or parent agency employees)	10,000
Cost of furniture, equipment, and a van/station wagon.	20,000
Reserve for operating deficits during start-up period.	20,000
Reserve for deficits after full operation has begun	5,000
Total	$135,000

Sources of Capital

Organizations and individuals planning a group home should review their resources realistically to make sure they have adequate capital. The assistance of a competent accountant is an asset during the planning period.

Some sources of funds for group homes are noted below:

1. Donations and endowments by charitable individuals have helped some homes get started and stay in business.

2. Some placement agencies may provide capital for limited purposes, such as correction of building defects or staff training during the start-up period. Government agencies concerned with juvenile justice, mental health, economic development, community action, and urban renewal also have provided grants for limited objectives.

3. Private foundations concerned with the needs of troubled youth have made some grants.

4. Community, church, service, business, and professional groups may "adopt" a facility and raise funds to get it into operation. The local United Way is more likely to help with the operating costs of existing facilities than with the capital needs of new ones.

5. Some group homes undertake fund-raising "drives" to collect money from the public. Activities range from garage sales and raffling off an automobile to sponsoring fairs and shows.

If a business firm that specializes in conducting fund-raising drives is retained, care must be taken to select a reliable and ethical company. The group home should monitor the firm's work to ensure that its program is described accurately, that all receipts and expenses are accounted for, that government regulations are satisfied, and that all collected funds are turned over to the home.

6. Many group homes borrow money to get started. Mortgage loans are common. Money is often borrowed to pay for a van or station wagon. Home operators should contact their placement agencies concerning their policies on reimbursing homes for interest payments.

FINANCING DAY-TO-DAY OPERATIONS

Once a group home is established, it begins to incur operating costs—expenses for food, utilities, supplies, salaries, services, repairs, rent, depreciation, and other items. These amount to substantial sums. The scattered data available indicate that operating costs probably average from $1,200 to $1,600 per month for each resident, amounting to as much as $190,000 or more per year for a facility serving 10 young people. Health care covered by Medicaid and education in the public schools are not included in these figures.

Wide differences exist among the financial needs of individual facilities. Homes serving more seriously disturbed youths incur higher costs than those providing mainly custodial care. Homes employing houseparent couples have lower salary costs than those relying on shift workers. Variations in the standards of different placement agencies also create differences in costs.

Although almost all private group homes rely on their placement agency-(ies) for at least partial reimbursement of operating costs, the degree of dependence varies. For many facilities, placement agencies are the sole source of funds. Others draw on independent sources, such as their parent agencies and private donors, to meet some portion of their operating costs.

There are also wide differences in the way that placement agencies calculate and reimburse operating costs. Rules may be statewide or vary from locality to locality. In some jurisdictions (New York and Pennsylvania, for example) reimbursement rates are the subject of negotiations between government placement agencies and associations of residential care facilities. Elsewhere, each group home negotiates the amount of reimbursement on its own. Placement agencies may limit their reimbursement by imposing "ceilings," "freezes," and uniform cost-of-living adjustments. These heterogeneous practices have evolved in piecemeal fashion. They have never been completely compiled and evaluated, and they deserve more intensive study.[1]

Operating Costs in Placement Agency Contracts

Typically, the written agreement between the placement agency and the home specifies the amount of money the home will receive for its services and the manner in which it will be paid. Expenses that are reimbursable and those that will be disallowed by the placement agency are listed. Accounting, record-keeping, and reporting procedures are prescribed. With attachments and finely printed "boiler plate," the financial section of an agreement can reach formidable size.

The process by which agreements are revised and renewed can be cum-

[1] Interesting discussions of reimbursement concepts and practices can be found in Leeman (1978) and Child Welfare League of America (1980).

bersome and time-consuming. There are so many steps to complete that the renewal process must start months in advance of the expiration date. The home may be required to submit annually a description of its program, summarize the previous year's operations, provide detailed financial data, and estimate its financial needs for the next contract period. The document may have to be reviewed by several offices in the placement agency; e.g., the finance, contracts, operations, and evaluation units. Intensive audits of the home's expenses and fiscal procedures can be expected, as well as an on-site inspection of the facility.

There may be protracted negotiations about the rate of reimbursement and required services. If the home is required to correct some deficiencies or modify its program, disputes may arise over the need for changes and who is responsible for paying for them. Negotiations may be further retarded by the placement agency's uncertainty about the size of its own budget for the next fiscal year.

The placement agency is willing to reimburse only expenses that are necessary for the care of the young people. As one may expect, decisions on which costs are necessary are often the subject of disputes. Following are examples of costs that are usually reimbursable:

1. Personnel costs: salaries, fringe benefits, staff training, bonding of staff members, and the services of lawyers, accountants, and consultants.

2. The cost of shelter, including rent or, if the quarters are owned by the home, a sum to cover their depreciation or use value over the contract period.

3. Utility costs—heat, light, water, telephones, etc.

4. Premiums for fire, theft, accident, workmen's compensation, and other insurance. Recently it has been suggested that facilities insure themselves against claims of improper care that violates the civil rights of their residents (Leahy & Barnes, 1977).

5. Maintenance of the property, including painting, repairs, lawn care, automotive repairs, and cleaning supplies.

6. Subsistence costs: food, clothing, personal care items, allowances.

7. Recreation and cultural activities, including admission fees, athletic gear, materials for arts and crafts, and transportation costs.

8. Administrative expenses such as the cost of office supplies and equipment, subscriptions to professional periodicals, and association dues.

Some costs may be reimbursed only up to a specified maximum amount. For example, a placement agency may set a maximum figure for staff salaries and the number of child care workers who can be employed. It may restrict the use of consultants. When a home shares clerical, maintenance, social work, or other services with its parent agency, elaborate rules govern the allocation of the cost of those services between the parent organization and its affiliate.

Agreements with group homes also identify operating costs that the placement agency will not reimburse. Those vary from one agency to another, so the fine print requires careful study. Typically, homes are not compensated directly for capital expenditures to improve their physical facilities; e.g., the cost of installing a recreation room, a garage for the van, or a new furnace. Those are excluded because they add to the value of the home operator's property. Payments on the principal of a mortgage, and often the interest, fall into the same category. However, compensation is usually provided for the gradual depreciation of physical property.

The purchase of a new vehicle is a capital expenditure. Placement agencies usually pay for automotive repairs, depreciation, and use.

Expenses incurred before the signing of an agreement with the placement agency are likely to be nonreimbursable; for example, the cost of training and paying staff members during the preparatory stage of a new facility. Similarly, costs incurred after the expiration of a contract may never be recovered. An example is a penalty paid by a group home for the premature termination of the lease on its quarters.

The Amount of Reimbursement

How do placement agencies decide how much money they will pay to residential facilities caring for their children? Several common approaches, and their advantages and disadvantages, are discussed below.

Full reimbursement for all allowable costs.   Under this approach, the placement agency pays, in full, all allowable costs incurred by a group home. The financing of group homes owned and operated by the placement agency itself furnishes the simplest example.

Full reimbursement of privately operated homes is far less common. Where it exists, homes may bill their placement agencies periodically for all of their allowable operating expenses. Or they may submit a proposed budget for placement agency review in advance of each contract period and receive the full amount of money in monthly or other periodic installments.

Full reimbursement of all allowable costs encourages group homes to provide high-quality services. It enables organizations with limited resources to operate group homes. However, full-funded homes have no incentive to economize, and their placement agencies may insist that they give up the right to be selective in choosing their residents.

In a variation of the full-reimbursement approach, the placement agency may pay all allowable costs but only up to a specified maximum. For example, homes exceeding a cost of $50 per day per child might have to make up the difference from their own resources. Obviously, this variation provides some incentive for economy, but it also reduces the incentive to enrich and intensify group home programs.

Cost-sharing. Another approach to reimbursement is cost-sharing, a policy that requires group homes to meet at least some of their operating costs from their own resources, with the placement agency paying the remainder. A substantial proportion of group homes do in fact have independent financial resources.

Placement agencies implement cost-sharing in different ways. Under one policy each home is required to use all of its own financial resources to meet as much of the cost of care as possible. The placement agency then reimburses a home only for allowable costs that exceed its own resources. Thus, a wealthy facility has to meet most of its operating costs from its own independent income, whereas a home with only minimal outside income will have all or most of its expenses reimbursed.

In a variation of that form of cost-sharing, homes are required to contribute all of their own funds but not more than a specified proportion of the cost of care; e.g., one-fourth of the total. Alternatively, all facilities may be required to cover a *uniform* proportion of their costs (e.g., 20 percent) from their own resources. Once it has contributed its required share, the home is free to use its remaining resources for other purposes.

Cost-sharing conserves the placement agency's funds so that it can serve more youngsters. It also serves as an incentive for homes to operate in an economical fashion. As financial partners, residential facilities benefit from a stronger voice in shaping placement agency policies and in deciding which youths should be assigned to them for care.

The policy has disadvantages as well. To begin with, where residential facilities are required to spend all of their own money before the placement agency will defray any of their operating costs, the facilities are left with no incentive to engage in fund raising. Potential donors have no incentive to contribute funds if their gifts will simply result in a corresponding decrease in reimbursement by the placement agency.

Another problem: cost-sharing imposes a need for placement agencies to determine each home's independent income. Such audits are time-consuming and contentious, and they invite evasion. The separation of a home's financial resources from those of its parent organization or individual owner can raise complex legal and accounting problems.

Finally, privately operated homes that are required to use all of their financial resources to care for the placement agency's children are unable to accumulate surplus funds to expand, enrich, or experiment in their programs, which inhibits improvements in the quality and capacity of residential facilities.

Reimbursement at uniform rates. Before it can reimburse a group home under either the full-reimbursement or cost-sharing methods, the placement agency must determine what the home's operating costs have been during the fiscal period. An alternative approach is to pay all group homes at a uniform rate, regardless of their actual costs. For example, a placement agency might simply pay $50 per day or $1,500 per month for each youth in residence. The uniform rate may cover the costs of some facilities and it may fall short in others.

Uniform rates have the advantage of administrative simplicity. However, those homes that are willing to accept hard-to-place, seriously troubled youths may find that the uniform rate does not cover the full cost of care.

Some of the difficulties are eased by grouping residential facilities into categories, which are reimbursed at different uniform rates. Group homes, for example, might be categorized on the basis of the types of psychological problems they are prepared to treat, the intensity of their services, and the age of their residents. Homes serving the most difficult youngsters can be paid the highest rate, whereas homes that merely provide custodial care end up in the lowest-paid category.

Supplemental payments by placement agencies.   In addition to regular payments to cover the operating costs of group homes, many placement agencies provide supplemental funds to meet specific operating needs. A common supplement is the clothing allowance, a sum of money paid to the home for each resident to defray clothing costs. Staff training is another supplemental resource provided by many placement agencies. The training may be conducted by the agency itself, or homes may be given extra funds to pay for training conducted by outside organizations.

Serving multiple placement agencies.   Homes that serve more than one placement agency encounter special reimbursement problems. If the agencies use different methods of reimbursement, the group home is burdened with inconsistent bookkeeping requirements, differing financial reports, and multiple audits. Each placement agency conforms to its own schedule, conducts its own inspection, applies its own special standards, and computes costs and reimbursement its own way. Each agency will want to know how much the home is paid by the others and is likely to refuse to pay more than any other agency.

How Funds Are Disbursed

Homes that provide services in return for a prespecified annual payment may receive that amount in monthly installments. However, the most common method of reimbursing group homes is to pay them a specified sum per day, month, or other period for each youth in residence. In some jurisdictions, that sum is termed the board rate. In a typical procedure the home submits a monthly list of its residents. After the list is checked, the home receives its payment, which represents the board rate multiplied by the number of residents. Adjustments are made for youths who were not present for the full payment period.

If a placement agency pays a uniform rate to all group homes (e.g., $40 per day for each resident), that is its board rate. On the other hand, if it is an agency's policy to reimburse group homes for all or a proportion of their actual costs, a separate board rate must be determined for each facility. That requires the agency to estimate what each facility's operating costs, occupancy, and perhaps independent income will be during the contract period. The agency then tries to set a board rate that, over the year or other contract period, is likely to yield the required reimbursement. Often year-end adjustments have to be made to compensate for overpayments or underpayments.

There are some problems associated with the board-rate method of payment. In some areas reimbursement may be delayed a month or more while the placement agency verifies each home's periodic occupancy report. Such delays are most likely where a home's residents are supervised by numerous caseworkers in scattered local offices. A second difficulty arises when a resident is temporarily hospitalized or absent without leave. During the temporary absence the placement agency may suspend the payment of board rates for the missing individual; yet the home cannot replace that income by admitting a new resident because the missing youth is expected to return.

But the most serious problem is the adverse effect of board rates on homes that unexpectedly develop high vacancy rates. Receiving payments for fewer residents than had been predicted when their board rates were determined, such homes may be forced to operate at a loss or even to close their doors. This problem is discussed in Simone (1985, p. 362).

Homes with high vacancy rates are tempted to borrow money, lower their admission standards, reduce services, and prolong the stay of residents. That starts a vicious cycle in which placements decrease still further and losses continue to mount. To alleviate the problem, it has been suggested that placement agencies commit themselves to meeting the fixed costs of all group homes, regardless of the number of youths in residence.

Chapter 3

APPROPRIATE QUARTERS FOR GROUP
HOMES

All home operators face critical decisions on where to locate their facilities, what kinds of buildings and furnishings to acquire, and how many residents to accommodate. This chapter discusses some alternatives and principles to help group homes resolve those issues.

CHOOSING A LOCATION

The location of a group home is a critical factor in its success or failure. A home located in a community with good educational, health, recreation, and cultural facilities is off to a good start. A home's location determines the health, safety, and zoning requirements it has to meet. Location determines the kind of neighborhood influences that its residents will encounter, the friends they will make, and the places they will go in their spare time. Depending on where it is located, a group home may encounter supportive, neutral, or hostile community attitudes. Clearly, great care must be taken to ensure that a home's location will contribute to a therapeutic program. The following guidelines are suggested.

1. Group homes should be in residential neighborhoods where their occupants can find friends among local youths and have access to parks, swimming pools, libraries, and other public facilities. Dismal factory areas,

39

isolated houses surrounded by overgrown lots, and seedy rooming-house zones are not therapeutic settings.

2. To reduce the likelihood of community opposition, new homes should avoid neighborhoods that are already "saturated" with residential facilities for troubled people (Citizens Committee for Children of New York, 1976, pp. 13–14).

3. Racially integrated neighborhoods are best for group homes.

4. Preferably, group homes should not be located in high- or low-income areas. Residents may feel at a disadvantage among high-income peers who live in expensive houses, travel widely during vacations, can afford expensive clothing and hobbies, and drive their own cars. At the other extreme, group home youths may be affected adversely by the pathological conditions commonly found in poverty-stricken areas.

5. Homes should be located in areas where youths can come and go safely without continuous staff supervision. They should not be near shady "hangouts" that exert a negative influence.

6. Homes should be within walking distance of shopping, recreation, and snack-bar facilities to afford residents a chance to stroll, buy needed items, and be on their own without relying exclusively on activities and transportation arranged by the staff.

7. Homes should have access to public transportation so that residents can keep medical/dental appointments and participate in extracurricular activities without having to be chauffeured by the staff. Public transportation also facilitates visits to and from family members.

8. Since group homes are dependent on the public school system to educate their residents, it is essential to locate in a community with effective schools.

9. If possible, group homes should be within walking distance of schools. That facilitates participation in extracurricular activities and permits the residents to carry their school friendships into after-school hours.

Group homes face this dilemma: they would like to locate in a family-oriented residential area, but they are more akin to small institutions than to families. Frequently, therefore, they run afoul of local zoning restrictions. Some facilities have had to give up proposed locations and settle for less desirable sites because of that problem.

Many homes have fought vigorously, and often successfully, to overcome zoning barriers. That might involve appeals to zoning boards, the courts, and legislatures. Unfortunately, zoning conflicts can be expensive and time-consuming.

Some homes have rented or purchased rooming houses or inns that were previously approved for non-family use. Such buildings can be quite suitable. They probably have large common rooms and multiple bathrooms, fire escapes and other required safety equipment, institutional-type kitchens, parking facilities, and other suitable characteristics. Home operators utilizing such quarters should make sure, however, that the neighborhood is consistent with a therapeutic program.

Plans to open a group home are often greeted by heated opposition from the local community. Neighbors fear a decline in property values, loss of privacy, parking congestion, and thefts or violence. Racial prejudice contributes to fears that group home residents will be a bad influence. It may be alleged that a group home will create problems for the local school.

There are some things that group homes can do to reduce the likelihood of community opposition. The following preventive measures deserve consideration because once opposition emerges, it is difficult to control:

1. Communities with a history of opposition to facilities for problem groups should be avoided.

2. Homes should be located in racially integrated neighborhoods if possible.

3. The chance of opposition is reduced if homes are not immediately adjacent to a family dwelling. Rather than invite confrontations, it makes sense to choose a site bordered by a church, park, street, or wide lawn on one or all sides.

4. Group homes should keep their houses and grounds attractive and well maintained.

5. Sites should include adequate parking for the staff and visitors.

6. It helps to have a porch or gazebo at the rear of the building so that residents need not spend their free time lounging around the front entrance.

7. At group meetings residents of the home should be asked to wear acceptable clothing, hold down noise, resist whistling at passing members of the opposite sex, and observe other rules of courteous behavior.

Other measures to minimize community opposition have been proposed, but there is far less consensus on their effectiveness. Some of the approaches may be applicable within the circumstances of particular homes. (See Weber, 1978, for a thoughtful and practical discussion of other strategies to overcome neighborhood opposition; also Pierce & Hauck, 1981, and Solomon, 1983.) It has been suggested that persons planning a new group home discuss their plans in advance with neighbors and community leaders. The problem with this approach, obviously, is that those contacted may mobilize an adverse public reaction before the facility can even get started. For that reason some group home operators suggest that new facilities get started without notifying anybody except trusted supporters and responsible authorities.[1]

---

[1]Almost half of the 17 New York home operators commenting on this matter in a 1975 survey maintained that view (Citizens Committee for Children of New York, 1976, p. 14).

Some advise that homes should be initiated in gradual stages to avoid up-setting hostile neighbors. For example, a pair of houseparents might live in the home for a month before any youths arrive. After that period youths might be admitted one or two at a time. Such a gradual start may prevent the emergence of opposition, but it gives hostile neighbors more time to organize and it drains the capital of the home.

It is usually a good idea to notify the local public schools, police, and fire department when a group home is opened. Those agencies will be providing services to the home. If the police are familiar with the home's program, they are less likely to stereotype its residents as "wild kids." Protection may be pro-vided in a sympathetic, unobtrusive manner. For example, officers may agree to use unmarked cars when visiting the home. Runaways and youths picked up for minor offenses may be returned to the home without excessive for-mality.

Once a home is established, efforts to build goodwill among the neigh-bors are worth a try. The director should accept invitations to address com-munity groups. The home might participate in neighborhood fairs and block parties. Some facilities set aside "open house" days for visits by local leaders and neighbors. Group home youths can be encouraged to participate in civic enterprises such as drives to collect paper for recycling. There is a danger, however, that such activities will label a home's residents as different from other young people, retarding their acceptance in school and neighborhood.

On the face of it a rural location might seem to solve some of the prob-lems described in the preceding sections. Out in the country a home is away from restrictive zoning and neighbors. No need for manicured lawns and pol-ished doorknobs out there! There are no evil hangouts around the corner. The location provides opportunities for adventure and sports like canoeing and riding that are wholesome alternatives to antisocial behavior.

There are, however, reasons why a rural location is not generally advan-tageous. The most telling reason is that isolation of youths from the give-and-take of the community reduces their opportunities to develop the judgment and social skills they will need after leaving the group home. Transportation presents another problem. The home's staff has to chauffeur the young peo-ple to and from the store, bus stops, medical appointments, and the movies. It is hard for family members to visit and participate in counseling programs.

Some rural schools are less sophisticated than urban or suburban ones. They may lack learning-disability specialists, special classes, and counselors. There may be a tendency to handle disciplinary problems simplistically. Of course, in these days of consolidated rural schools, many do have up-to-date policies and resources.

It is important to keep in mind that disturbed youngsters, mainly from urban areas, may have unreasonable fears of animals, snakes, insects, and the sounds of the night. Fears of getting lost, being alone, or being attacked may be overwhelming. Teasing by fellow residents and facile reassurances by staff members are not likely to help the situation.

THE RIGHT SIZE FOR A GROUP HOME

Sometimes the maximum number of residents for a group home is dictated by placement agency rules or the capacity of the home's quarters. For home operators who can decide for themselves, some guidelines may be suggested.

To begin with, group homes must not be so large as to develop an institutional ambience. Staff members must be familiar with each resident's personality and treatment needs. The home must be able to blend into a residential neighborhood with a minimum of visibility and traffic. An upper limit of 12 beds is, therefore, recommended.

There is also a minimum number of beds below which the effectiveness of a home is impaired. The number of residents must be large enough to permit therapeutic group work. Probably a reasonable minimum for group work is five. Taking into account the likelihood that one or two beds will be vacant from time to time, it is suggested that homes should have accommodations for no less than six youths. (For comments supporting this view on group home size, see Hirschbach, 1975, p. 3; Jewett, 1973).

Financial considerations influence group size. In a home reimbursed on the basis of the number of youths in residence, the number of residents must be sufficient to produce an income large enough to cover the facility's costs, even if one or two beds are vacant for a period.

In practice, facilities calling themselves group homes range in capacity from 5 to 14 or more residents. Most, however, have from 6 to 12 beds. Group home operators themselves often recommend 8 to 10 residents as the best size.

INSIDE THE GROUP HOME—THE PHYSICAL ENVIRONMENT

The physical surroundings affect the feelings of residents about themselves, the staff, and the group home. They expand or curtail opportunities for recreation, study, and cooperative relationships. Even small housing defects such as inadequate closet space and a cramped dining room can create human relations problems. This section suggests some considerations in selecting and equipping an effective facility.

Health and Safety

Because most homes are in buildings that were formerly single-family dwellings, they are usually faced with the expense of remodeling to meet state and local health and safety standards. Examples of renovation that might be necessary are the enclosure of stairwells, electrical rewiring, installation of interior sprinkler systems and smoke alarms, and the addition of exterior fire escapes. Kitchens, too, often have to be remodeled.

Unless the renovation of a building is planned carefully, it can have an adverse effect on the program. Repairs may consume the home's capital and delay the opening date. The beauty of an old mansion may be destroyed by outdoor fire escapes, the enclosure of a delicate stairway, and the hanging of sprinkler pipes from the ceiling to conform to local codes.

Good ventilation and comfortable temperatures in the group home are important for the health and disposition of the residents. Air conditioning has major advantages. It reduces the irritability and emotional boiling points of troubled youths and facilitates sound sleep. The youngsters will be more likely to stay close to the home during their free time. Facilities located in areas with warm climates and those occupying poorly ventilated row houses or apartments should certainly consider air conditioning. At the very least, homes should have adequate fans to help residents and staff through the summer.

Accident hazards should be eliminated. Loose steps, poorly lit stairwells, sharp edges on kitchen equipment, and exposed wires are things to look for.

Kitchen and Dining Facilities

Kitchens in group homes require oversize stoves, sinks, and refrigerators. Adequate storage and work space is essential. It is a good idea to have two refrigerators: one for general food storage that is off-limits to the residents and a smaller one in which residents can forage for snacks as in a normal family setting.

The dining area must be roomy and airy. There should be plenty of room at the dinner table, which is often a good place to do homework, play quiet games, and write letters between meals. The dining room is also a gathering place for group discussions, tutoring, sewing, and visits with family members.

Common Rooms

There will be times when residents will prefer to study, read, listen to music, or talk with friends in their own rooms. Most of the time, however, the common rooms of the group home are heavily used for recreation, organized group activities, or just "hanging around."

It is recommended that at least two common rooms be provided. One should be available for noisy and physical activities: Ping-Pong, listening to records, dancing, tumbling, or just "fooling around." Here the young people can "work off steam" without creating staff confrontations and friction with other residents. This room should be furnished inexpensively and informally. Cushions and mats on the floor are as inviting as fancy armchairs—and they last much longer.

The second common room is a "quiet room" for passive activities. The television set is likely to be the centerpiece here. Other uses of the quiet room are reading, sewing, chatting, having a snack, and entertaining visitors. At a designated hour the room may become a study hall for homework and tutoring.

Bedrooms

Appropriate sleeping areas contribute to a therapeutic milieu. It is particularly important for troubled youths to get all the sleep they need and to feel secure at night. Their bedrooms serve as private retreats from the tensions of group life. In addition, the choice of roommates influences a youth's adaptation to the home.

Bedrooms should be well ventilated, lighted, and cool in hot weather. Overcrowding should be avoided; beds that are too close and rooms that are cramped evoke tension between the occupants.

The staff may worry about what is going on in the bedrooms when the doors are closed. Although some commonsense restrictions can be applied, staff members should be aware that young people do feel a need for privacy and solitude occasionally. If they believe that they have no space of their own and are being spied on all of the time, they will be resentful, evasive, and secretive.

An issue confronting group homes is whether to distribute their residents in single- or multiple-occupancy rooms. Single rooms provide the privacy and quiet that individuals need from time to time. For some a private room reduces feelings of insecurity. Separating troubled youths may prevent conflicts over cleaning the room, borrowed clothing, and missing bracelets. Temptations and anxiety about nudity and sexuality are minimized. Some youths have a special need for privacy until they can overcome physical and psychological problems such as bed-wetting, snoring, deformities, and skin infections that affect their acceptance by fellow residents.

Putting two or more youths in a room has advantages, too. The most obvious is lower costs, but there can also be therapeutic gains. Pairing a new resident with a long-term resident may help the former adapt to the group home and imbue the latter with a sense of responsibility and self-esteem. Youths from different racial and ethnic groups can be paired to combat prejudice and encourage good relations. Residents who are afraid of the dark or of being alone may benefit from shared rooms.

The staff should be alert to potential problems. Long-term residents may haze new roommates or initiate them into negative behavior. Friends rooming together may form cliques that mar the cohesion of the group. There may be frequent requests for changes in room assignments.

The best approach is probably a combination of single- and multiple-occupant rooms. Single rooms can be assigned to older or long-term residents, to residents who earn their own room as a reward for progress in the program, and/or to youths with special needs. If there are enough bedrooms to go around, it is a good idea to allow residents to decide for themselves whether they will live in a single or shared room. Perhaps their preferences will change as they benefit from the home's services, gain acceptance from peers, and make special friends.

Bathrooms

An adequate number of bathrooms reduces conflict in a group home. That is particularly true in the morning when residents are rushing to prepare for school, around bedtime, and prior to a mass departure for some outing.

One way to make more efficient use of bathrooms is to utilize other space for personal care activities. Extra mirrors and vanity tables enable female residents to dry and set their hair elsewhere in the house. A separate laundry room frees the bathroom from use as a place to wash and dry clothes.

There are good reasons for ensuring bathroom privacy. Troubled youths often have distorted feelings about their bodies, nudity, and sexuality. Obese or disfigured youngsters are likely to be particularly reluctant to show their bodies to peers. In the absence of privacy, bathrooms can become sites for hazing and sexual harassment. For those reasons bathrooms should have doors. If they include more than one toilet or shower, those should be separated by partitions.

Furnishings

When furnishing a home, "the institutional look" should be avoided. Beds should not be of the institutional type. Closets or wooden wardrobes for storing clothes are preferred over metal lockers. Bedrooms should differ somewhat even though this costs a bit more. Residents should be allowed to individualize their rooms; e.g., by hanging posters or bringing inexpensive objects from home.

Furnishings should be as attractive as possible so that residents can identify proudly with the home, develop an appreciation for aesthetic surroundings, and feel good about inviting friends and relatives to visit. Simple curtains, scatter rugs, and a few pictures on the wall make a big difference at low cost.

Furniture must be sturdy, ready to take abuse. One must expect it to be carved and kicked. There will be feet on the coffee table, and it will be used as a bench. Low-cost secondhand furniture is appropriate. The less fragile the furniture, the less need to watch and nag the young people. That, in turn, reduces their temptation to challenge and test the staff and the staff's need to invoke disciplinary authority.

Regardless of its appearance, furniture must meet basic health and comfort requirements. Beds must have firm mattresses for restful sleep. Chairs should be consistent with good posture. Dressers and/or foot lockers are needed for adequate storage space. There should be sufficient desks and lamps to encourage reading and study.

In selecting furniture the effect on interpersonal relations must be kept in mind. The dining room table should be large enough to avoid crowding that evokes bickering and mischief. The availability of two or more dining tables permits the separation of incompatible youths at mealtimes. There should be enough chairs and tables in the common rooms to avoid territorial arguments. In bedrooms a separate closet or locker for each occupant will cut down bickering, borrowing, and theft.

The presence of a piano, however battered, may encourage someone to take music lessons, stimulate an interest in group singing, and even permit some adult volunteer to give an informal concert once in a while. Desks in the bedrooms facilitate schoolwork that would otherwise be done perfunctorily on the bed or floor. A bookcase filled with recent issues of magazines and donated paperbacks may encourage a youth to read.

OUTDOOR AREAS

The property surrounding the home's building is a place where residents can enjoy noisy "rough and tumble" activity. In the backyard a youth can be alone for a while when the unceasing interaction in the house gets on his nerves. The availability of a backyard for play encourages residents to spend free time around the group home, where they can be observed and supervised by the staff. It offers an alternative to congregating on the front steps —a habit that irritates passersby. For those reasons homes occupying apartments or town houses lacking outdoor space are missing a useful program tool.

The outdoor area can be equipped simply with sturdy benches and tables for picnics, games, and passive relaxation. Young people are likely to make use of a basketball hoop over the paved driveway. A net across the lawn can be used for volleyball and badminton. Croquet on a level lawn is also likely to be popular.

If the yard is not very large, it is useful to surround it with high hedges to protect the privacy of both the neighbors and the home's residents. A birdhouse and/or bird feeder is an inexpensive way of stimulating interest in the natural world. A staff member or volunteer may even enlist the help of residents in some gardening.

QUARTERS FOR THE STAFF

Some group homes have staff members who live in the facility; others do not. For live-in staff, adequate quarters are an absolute necessity if they are to perform their tension-filled roles effectively over a prolonged period of time. Their quarters must be a comfortable, private haven where they can recuperate from the stresses of child care, pursue their private interests, and nurture their relationships with family and friends.

The kind of staff quarters needed depends on several factors: whether the home is managed by a married houseparent or by unrelated child care workers; whether live-in staff members utilize an outside residence on their days off or remain in the facility 7 days a week; and whether houseparent couples have children of their own. As a minimum, live-in workers should have a private bedroom and bathroom. If they are raising children of their own, the children should have their own sleeping rooms, as in most private family dwellings.

It is strongly recommended that staff members who live in the home 7 days a week be provided with a kitchen where they can prepare and eat meals in privacy on their days off. They will also benefit from a private sitting room where they can relax, watch their own favorite adult television programs, and entertain personal friends.

In many group homes live-in child care workers leave for the weekend and are replaced by relief workers. It is a good idea to respect the privacy of the live-in workers by providing a separate sleeping room for the persons who relieve them. Some individuals feel uncomfortable about having a relief worker occupying their quarters one or more days each week and using their bed, bath, and closets.

OFFICE SPACE

Staff members need private office space. Requirements vary, depending on the staffing pattern of each home and whether the home's director and/or social worker have offices at some outside location. If they are headquartered at the home, they require, as a minimum, a room for counseling youngsters and their parents, making confidential telephone calls, preparing correspondence, filing records, and conferring with staff members and placement agency caseworkers. Child care workers may have to share this space for individual counseling, confidential telephone calls, and storing valuables.

Chapter 4

STAFFING PATTERNS FOR GROUP HOMES

What staff members and how many are needed to run a group home? Oddly enough, despite the small size and apparent uniformity of the homes there are striking differences in their staffing patterns. Staff roles are combined in many ways, and a staffing pattern that works in one home may be a disaster in another (see Shostack, 1978).

Some tasks are essential in a group home. Someone must plan and direct the home's program. There must be at least one person qualified to evaluate the treatment needs of residents, arrange necessary services, serve as liaison with outside agencies, counsel parents and youths, and manage each resident's "case." Trained professionals must be available to provide psychiatric treatment and evaluations if required. Paraprofessional child care workers are essential to supervise residents on an everyday basis. And one or more persons must take on educational, recreation, housekeeping, maintenance, clerical, and other support tasks. Those are universal requirements.

This chapter discusses the issues faced in staffing a group home, alternative staffing patterns, and the duties of group home employees. Covered in turn are the positions of director, social worker, psychologist, child care worker, and several types of support staff. Staffing is also the subject of the following chapter, which discusses the qualifications of staff members, staff turnover, and burnout among child care workers.

THE GROUP HOME DIRECTOR

The director of a group home designs its program, selects and trains its staff members, and decides who will be admitted for care. He represents the home in relations with the placement agency and the surrounding community. Home operators have a number of alternatives in deciding how to structure the director's position. These are explored below.

Full-time versus Part-time Directors

One issue to be resolved is, should the director's position be full- or part-time? During the start-up period of a new home, the director may have more than a full-time work load. Once in operation, however, many homes find a part-time director sufficient. That reduces a home's salary costs and makes it possible to employ as directors psychologists and others who are available only for part-time work.

In some smaller homes full-time directors are required to assume the duties of child care workers. Obviously, that is an economical approach, and it ensures that the director will be well informed about the needs and progress of the residents. However, there are serious drawbacks. Interacting intensively with the residents day after day, the director tends to lose objectivity and a long-range view of the program. His relations with the residents come to resemble the emotionally charged role of a foster parent rather than the role of a detached, treatment-oriented professional.

Combining the Positions of Director and Social Worker

Should the director serve as the home's social worker? There are differences of opinion among knowledgeable persons. Some of the factors that influence a decision are very practical; e.g., whether the director has enough time to handle detailed casework and whether he has the requisite skills. Practical considerations, however, are not the most compelling reasons for separating the roles of director and social worker. More important is the fact that the director is the final authority in the home. As a result he cannot easily establish the neutral and confidential relationships that are essential for effective social work. At the least some residents will hesitate to discuss openly their feelings and behavior with the director. Similarly, child care workers who might feel comfortable discussing their problems with and seeking advice from a neutral social worker are likely to be much more constrained in meetings with "the boss" (see Gula, 1965, p. 25).

Locating the Director's Office

Still a third issue is, should the.director's office be in the group home or at a separate, perhaps distant location? A substantial proportion of directors have their offices outside the home—in the parent agency's headquarters, a downtown office building, another residential facility, or elsewhere. The office may be in a distant location because the director is responsible for several homes or conducts a part-time private practice. A distant office.may be preferred because it is accessible to public transportation, facilitates private meetings with parents, and is in a community from which the home draws financial support and adult volunteers. Some directors feel that distance sustains their objectivity, reduces burnout, and lends them an aura of authority that helps to maintain discipline in the facility. Finally, a group home may simply lack space for a private office, forcing the director to seek an office elsewhere.

A director who works out of a distant office surrenders a measure of knowledge and control. He is more likely than an in-home director to keep regular 9:00 a.m. to 5:00 p.m. hours—a period when residents are mainly in school and there is not much opportunity to observe and develop close relationships with them. The distant director also must delegate more authority to the staff. The home's social worker may supervise the child care workers or they may be allowed to work with little direct supervision of any kind. With the boss too far away to monitor their activities closely, houseparents may deviate from program policies and concepts, falling back on their own ideas, folk wisdom, expediency, and impulse to guide their interaction with residents.

Regardless of the location of their offices, all directors are well-advised to spend a considerable portion of their time in the home, time needed to deepen a director's familiarity with daily operations and lend credibility to his efforts to guide the child care workers and develop rapport with the young people.

Duties during the Planning Stage

It is advisable to employ a director well before a new home opens for business. A salaried director can give more attention to the multitude of pressing details than can a committee of volunteers or a busy executive of the home's parent agency. He can apply professional skills in recruiting staff members and planning the home's program.

The director's duties during the planning period are suggested below.

Self-training.   New directors with only limited group home experience should visit other group homes to learn their procedures and share their experience. It is sometimes a good idea to work as a volunteer in another home for a few weeks. Directors also should familiarize themselves with the juvenile justice system in the state and area.

Coordination with the placement agency.   The director must learn as much as possible about the placement agency's responsibilities and procedures, including (a) the origin and legal status of children under the agency's supervision; (b) procedures for purchasing group home services; (c) standards that group homes are expected to meet; (d) procedures for review, selection, and licensing of homes; (e) placement procedures and the termination of placements; (f) monitoring and evaluation of group homes; (g) policies for compensating group homes; and (h) resources available to group homes.

Contact with local placement offices.   Group home directors must develop working relationships with the staff members of local offices responsible for placing youths.

Program design.   The director needs to design a program. There are a thousand issues, such as the following:

> What types of youths will be admitted?
>
> How will they be evaluated and selected?
>
> What services will be provided, by whom, how often, when and where?
>
> What will be the duties of each staff member?
>
> How will finances be managed?
>
> How will everyday life be structured?
>
> What will be the home's policy on curfews, family visits, room assignments, telephone use, allowances, chores, incentives, and a multitude of other items?

It is suggested that a plan for the facility be prepared in written form. That would help the home conduct its program in a systematic manner, rather than "shooting from the hip" in response to crises and unanticipated requirements. A written design can be submitted for review to the home's governing board, advisory groups, the placement agency, and knowledgeable specialists. It helps to maintain a continuity of services when staff members are replaced, and serves as a basis for staff training and periodic evaluation of the program.

Hiring a staff.   The recruitment and training of a staff, and the collection of information about salaries and fringe benefits paid to comparable workers in other facilities are duties of the director.

Coordination with the school system.   As new residents must be enrolled in the local public schools, planning with school officials is required to arrange appropriate services and good communication.

Preparation of a brochure.   It is helpful to prepare a brief brochure, describing the home's objectives, facilities, and services. Finances permitting, the brochure should be printed in an attractive format, including photographs. The brochure might be distributed to offices of the placement agency, prospective residents and their families, potential givers of financial support, community organizations, schools, local government officials, neighbors, the police and fire departments, and juvenile justice personnel.

Handbook for residents. A handbook for residents is necessary to provide a framework of shared information and expectations for staff and residents. A handbook informs residents about their legal status, the role of the placement agency and its caseworkers, the services and policies of the home, and the responsibilities of both staff and residents. Useful items to include are:

> A welcome to new residents;
>
> The history affiliations, and objectives of the home;
>
> The address and phone number of the facility;
>
> The name, address, and phone number of the placement agency and a brief statement of its responsibilities and procedures;
>
> The names, titles, and duties of the staff;
>
> A description of the home's treatment and support services, recreation and educational opportunities, and family services;
>
> Rules for everyday life, such as the sharing of chores, proper dress, visiting privileges, allowances, use of the telephone, and curfews;
>
> The locations of community facilities that residents will be using, such as the local school, library, YMCA, bus terminal, shopping areas, and places of recreation.

It is not recommended that the handbook be burdened with long lists of rules, penalties, and rewards. These stimulate anxiety among newcomers while simply challenging youths who come to the facility with hostile attitudes. If the home has a formal behavior modification system, the details are best distributed in a separate document at a time when they can be explained to new residents in a reassuring way.

Miscellaneous tasks. During the planning stage directors often find themselves fighting zoning restrictions, supervising the renovation of a building, arguing with the fire marshal, buying furniture, shopping for a passenger van, raising funds, arranging for medical care, setting up a bookkeeping system, and performing many other tasks.

Responsibilities after the Group Home Is Activated

Once the group home is in full operation, the director's principal task is to weld the human beings who live and work in the facility into a therapeutic social milieu. The mere issuance of rules is insufficient. Successful directors learn that the supervision of staff and residents is as much an art as a bundle of technical skills. Life in the home must be influenced flexibly and subtly, in close touch with the feelings and opinions of the staff, placement agency officials, residents, and the parents of residents.

The most common functions of the director in a fully operating home include the following:

Relations with the home operator.   The director must maintain a supportive working relationship with the home's board of directors, parent agency executives, and others who oversee the home. Directors should meet with the home operator at frequent intervals and submit monthly and annual reports. The preparation of an annual budget for the facility also gives the home operator an opportunity to evaluate program needs and plans. Some suggestions for relations between the directors and governing boards of child welfare agencies can be found in Herstein (1983).

Relations with the placement agency.   The director prepares annual budgets and represents the home in negotiating the periodic renewal of its contract. He must prepare for periodic agency evaluations, submit required reports, and meet monitors and caseworkers.

Administrative responsibilities.   In a larger facility administrative responsibilities might be shared with a bookkeeper, an administrative assistant, a health director, chief of maintenance, and cafeteria supervisor. In a group home the director is likely to handle all administrative matters himself.

Continuous refinement of the home's policies.   The director must revise the home's policies continuously in the light of experience and changing needs. Policies must be adapted as the home's population changes, school lets out in the summertime, old rules are outworn, and new standards are imposed by placement agencies.

Supervision of staff.   The director recruits and trains paid staff and volunteers. The counseling of staff members is a distinctive feature of the director's role because of the tensions experienced by employees and the crucial importance of self-awareness, emotional stability, and objectivity in dealing with troubled youths.

Selecting residents for the home.   The director reviews the files of potential residents, interviews youngsters and their parents, observes them in preplacement visits, and consults caseworkers and other staff members concerning possible admission.

The purchase of treatment services.   The director selects, monitors, and pays doctors, dentists, psychologists, mental health clinics, family planning clinics, and others who provide services to the home.

Relations with community agencies.   Relations with public schools, police, recreation facilities, shelters for status offenders, and other service agencies must be maintained. The director also nurtures good relations with neighbors, civic groups, the news media, and other community elements. He may accept speaking engagements, attend community functions, prepare press releases, organize public relations activities, and represent the facility in associations.

Termination of residents.   The decision to terminate a resident is made by the director in conjunction with the placement agency caseworker.

Miscellaneous tasks.   It would be unrealistic to ignore a host of odd jobs that are assumed by the director because there is nobody else around to do them. When all else fails, it is the director who substitutes for an absent child care worker and social worker. He may have to unclog the kitchen sink, cook dinner, or repaint a room for a new resident. The director is likely to spend a midnight hour on the phone with a hysterical parent or drive around town looking for a youth who missed the evening curfew. When the residents are bored and listless, it is an alert director who suggests a camping trip or a visit to the airport to dispel their depression.

The director exerts a subjective influence by being easy to talk to, glad to lend a hand, fair, trustworthy, and a role model for staff and residents. He uses authority with judgment and restraint to minimize the grievances and paranoia that fester in institutional settings. Yet there is a need for strength to say no where necessary, to maintain discipline, to correct staff members— even when such actions evoke anger and complaints.

THE SOCIAL WORKER

The roles assigned to social workers in group homes also vary widely. The small size of the staffs and the difficulty in recruiting qualified workers compel most homes to be flexible, crossing occupational boundaries to take into account the strengths and limitations of individual staff members.

Duties commonly assigned to social workers in group homes are indicated below:

1.   Helping the director design services and everyday routines for the home.

2. Training and advising the child care workers and other paraprofessionals.

3. Counseling staff members to help them cope with personal and work tensions.

4. Evaluating potential residents.

5. Developing and updating treatment plans for individual youths.

6. Counseling the families of residents.

7. Conducting individual and group counseling.

8. Liaison between the group home and school(s).

9. Liaison with placement and juvenile justice agencies.

10. Arranging hospital admissions for residents who develop a need for intensive medical or psychiatric treatment.

11. Advising the director concerning the readiness of residents for termination.

12. Planning "aftercare" services for departing residents.

Whereas there is a consensus on the preceding duties, there is a great deal of variation with respect to other responsibilities assigned to social workers. Some alternative ways of structuring the role of social workers are evaluated below.

The Director as Social Worker

In some group homes, particularly those of small size, the director may serve as the social worker. The first section of this chapter suggested that, because directors exercise authority over staff and residents, they cannot assume the neutral and confidential posture required for effective social work.

Full-time versus Part-time Social Workers

A decision on whether to employ a full- or part-time social worker depends in part on the duties assigned to the worker, the size and turnover of the home's population, the severity of its problems, the full- or part-time status of the director, and other work-load indicators. It is probable that homes accommodating more than eight residents require a full-time social worker if their directors work only part-time. Small homes with a full-time director are likely to find a part-time social worker adequate, unless residents are seriously disturbed and the social worker serves as the home's psychotherapist.

The Social Worker as a Supervisor

In some homes the social worker supervises the child care workers and other paraprofessional staff members. Elsewhere social workers advise the director but have no direct authority over their co-workers. There is something to say in behalf of both approaches.

Designating the social worker as a supervisor gives the director time to focus on administrative matters, program design, and community relations. Supervisory social workers become familiar with the activities of staff and youngsters, and can ensure adherence to treatment plans. On the other hand, a supervisory social worker can no longer serve as a neutral, confidential counselor to staff members and residents.

Close versus Limited Contact

In some homes the social worker has only limited contact with the residents. His office may be in a remote location; e.g., the parent agency's headquarters, where residents can be seen only by appointment. The social worker may be on duty only on weekdays, from 9:00 a.m. to 5:00 p.m., when the youngsters are mainly at school. A large part of that time may be spent at meetings, in travel, and in preparing reports, rather than in interaction with residents and staff.

In other homes the social worker has an on-site office and is expected to develop a close relationship with residents. The worker spends one or more evenings each week and occasional weekends at the home, mingling informally with the population, sharing a meal, joining recreational outings occasionally, observing group interaction, and providing a little "curbstone" counseling along the way.

Some social workers argue that their 9-to-5 hours are necessary because it is only in that interval that placement agency, court, school, and other contacts can be made. A remote office is justified by the need for confidentiality in meeting with youths, parents, and officials. However, those workers must give up the deeper understanding of the dynamics of the group home that comes from more intensive contact with residents and staff.

Fragmented versus Integrated Social Work

There are a few homes in which required social work is not assigned to a single person but is parceled out among a number of professionals. That may happen, for example, where a large parent agency employs several social workers, to each of whom only one or two group home youths are assigned. Or one social worker may conduct group counseling; another, family counseling; a third, staff training, and so on.

Although that approach may help the parent agency equalize the case loads of its staff, it severely limits the effectiveness of social work. The workers are unable to compare the youngsters' perceptions and experiences, nor to grasp their relations with the peer group. They gather only a fragmented impression of the attitudes and practices of the child care workers and of the overall social milieu. Serving only one or two residents, social workers are not in a strong position to influence the policies of the home or to adjust the treatment of other youths whose behavior affects those assigned to them (see Gula, 1965, p. 28; and Seidman, 1965).

The Social Worker as Psychotherapist

In a few group homes the social worker provides individual and/or group psychotherapy for the residents. That practice has advantages. Interacting frequently with youths and staff in the home, the social worker learns more than an outside psychotherapist about their relationships and daily behavior. Hirschbach (1973) points out that the home's social worker is in a position to use the events of daily life as "grist for his mill" in therapy sessions — as starting points for discussions of deeper concerns, feelings, and behavior patterns (p. 31). The home's social worker is in a better position than an outside therapist to initiate changes in the social milieu surrounding each resident and can influence the relations between parents and child.

Doubtless, most social workers currently in group homes have not had adequate training for psychotherapy. Group therapy with mildly disturbed youths, however, should be within the capabilities of many workers who hold an M.S.W. degree. If necessary, a psychiatric consultant can be employed for several hours each month to evaluate difficult cases and to provide supervision and training.

PSYCHIATRISTS AND PSYCHOLOGISTS

Psychiatrists and psychologists are utilized by most homes, but their roles vary. The home's treatment concepts, the capabilities of its own social worker, the severity of the psychological disturbances treated by the home, its financial resources, and placement agency requirements are among factors considered in planning psychological services.

Typical duties of psychiatrists and psychologists include advising on the content of the home's program, evaluation of potential and current residents, advising on individual treatment plans, individual and group psychotherapy, treatment of residents requiring psychotropic drugs, training staff members, and counseling them concerning work-related and personal problems.

Group homes procure the services of psychiatrists and psychologists in various ways. Some employ specialists in private practice who charge a fee for each hour of therapy, staff training, or consultation. Other homes contract with mental health centers, family service agencies, or a group practice to furnish all needed services for a prespecified total sum. Homes affiliated with a parent organization often have access to its specialists.

The qualifications and efficient utilization of psychotherapists and psychological consultants are discussed in more detail in Chapter 10.

CHILD CARE WORKERS

Administrators and social workers are essential in group homes, but none exceed in importance the child care workers who supervise the residents 24 hours a day. Because of their continuous and close contacts, they exert a very deep influence on the young people and on the overall social milieu. The manner in which they implement policies and treatment plans vitally affects the outcome of the program.

Although child care workers are generally classified as paraprofessionals, and almost always earn less than professionally trained staff, they bear complex and heavy responsibilities. Their roles combine parenting, counseling, and teaching with physical work such as cooking, housekeeping, chauffeuring, and maintenance. While performing these tasks, the workers are on their own most of the time. There is usually no other adult to turn to for advice on how to respond therapeutically to the troubled youngsters. The job calls for resourcefulness, self-confidence, and strength of character.

The duties of child care workers vary somewhat from home to home, depending on their status as houseparents or shift workers, the severity of the psychological disturbances they deal with, and the extent to which they are assisted by housekeepers and other auxiliary personnel. The following duties are most common.

Physical Care

Child care workers plan nutritious meals, shop for food, and either cook or supervise cooking tasks. They make sure that the young people wear proper clothing, that clothes are laundered, and that baths are taken at appropriate intervals. They arrange for medical attention in cases of illness or accident and make sure that residents keep their medical appointments and take their medicine on time.

Child care workers are usually responsible for the cleanliness of the quarters. In addition to their own efforts they supervise the residents and housekeepers (if any) in cleaning chores.

Providing Security

Child care workers protect the young people from the aggressive behavior of fellow residents. They prevent fights, theft, bullying, extortion, sexual harassment, and hazing. Their responsibilities also include fire prevention, the exclusion of unauthorized persons from the premises, monitoring the behavior of visitors, and guarding against the introduction of alcohol and illegal drugs.

Chauffeuring and Maintenance

Youths must be driven to extracurricular school activities, doctors, stores, recreational facilities, and bus terminals—and picked up again at those places. In some homes child care workers may mow the lawn, trim shrubs, replace filters and light bulbs, paint a room, and repair leaky faucets.

Fostering Positive Behavior

In everyday interaction with the young people, child care workers model and teach constructive ways of responding to people and situations. On a more formal level they enforce the home's rules for cooperative group living by doling out incentives and sanctions with good judgment, fairness, and consistency.

Helping to Implement Individual Treatment Plans

Child care workers play an indispensable role in implementing individual treatment plans. A plan may prescribe withdrawal of privileges from an offending youth, praise for a timid youngster, drawing an isolate into group activities, encouraging a friendship between two lonely residents, or keeping a close watch on a potential runaway. Perhaps an aggressive youth is to be diverted into athletics, a talented youth encouraged in a hobby, or an anxious individual offered some "curbstone" counseling each day. Achievement of those objectives depends on the skill of child care workers.

Informal Counseling

"Curbstone" counseling is a universal function of child care workers. Informal talk around the dinner table, in the home's station wagon, or on the front porch provides valuable moments for influencing young people.

Leading Group Meetings

In many homes workers and residents meet once or more each week at scheduled times. Other homes rely on their workers to convene group meetings sporadically whenever a need arises. Group meetings are convened to issue instructions, share information, and make group decisions on rules, outings, and other matters. They may discuss problems of group living such as thefts, monopolization of the phone, and conflicts over television use. They explore grievances expressed by the residents or staff members.

Supporting Progress at School

Child care workers encourage school attendance, foster good study habits, tutor slow learners, and facilitate extracurricular school activities.

Encouraging Wholesome Recreation

Workers plan and lead group outings, stimulate recreation activities in the home, and model good use of spare time. The worker who suggests a game of charades or the baking of cookies on a dull rainy day, who joins the youngsters in shooting baskets on the parking lot, leads a camping trip, or drives some youths to the local library is making a significant contribution to the treatment program.

Evaluation of Residents

Child care workers are responsible for observing the behavior of residents, reporting their progress, and bringing their needs to the attention of the professional staff.

Miscellaneous

There are dozens of other important duties, depending on the policies of the group home, the training and personality of the child care worker, and the roles assigned to other staff members. For example, a child care worker who develops good rapport with parents of the residents may be helpful in reassuring and counseling them. Workers who enjoy arts and crafts may give instruction in those fields. Workers serve as models of decent, caring, and reasonable adults—a category that may have been scarce in the lives of some residents.

Group home operators must make a key decision: should their child care workers be houseparents or shift workers? That decision has a major impact on their program.

Typically, houseparents are a married couple who live in the home, where they supervise and care for the residents. In some cases both husband and wife are regarded as full-time employees of the home, even expected to be on duty or on call around the clock like parents in a family setting. In a large proportion of facilities, however, only one member of the married pair is considered to be an employee. The spouse is free to take an outside job, attend school, or do whatever he wishes. Nonetheless, either by prearrangement with the director or by an unavoidable involvement in the home's social milieu, the nonemployed individual is likely to interact with the youths intensively during his "free time," and even to be pressed into service as a substitute maintenance worker, relief child care worker, recreation aide, cook, and chauffeur when necessary.

Shift workers are simply those who work a scheduled number of hours each day or week and then are off duty. That arrangement, common in large residential care facilities, is also found in many group homes. Shift hours vary from place to place, depending on treatment concepts, the personal convenience of the workers, the availability of support staff, and other factors.

Eight hours per day, 5 days per week, with some overlap of shifts to provide time for the exchange of information and staff meetings, is probably the most common work schedule. However, there are many other arrangements, such as (a) 4 10-hour days on duty and 3 days off during the first week, followed by 3 days on and 4 days off during the second week; (b) 4 24-hour days per week, including nights spent at the home "off duty" but on call; (c) 2 24-hour days on duty each week.

Homes that employ houseparents believe that they help to create a family-type setting in the facility. Interacting with houseparents and fellow residents, the young people may learn how to adjust to their own parents and siblings. It is also believed that houseparents develop more intimate relations with the residents because they are on duty or on call in the home most of the time. That may be particularly therapeutic for younger children in need of emotional nurturing. There is also a very practical reason for employing houseparents: they cost less than shift workers. They are on duty or on call for very long hours; sometimes 7 days per week. In most cases the home receives the services of both spouses for the price of one. In contrast, a minimum of four shift workers is required for round-the-clock care of residents.

Some homes employing houseparents have run afoul of federal and state wage and hour laws. Long hours on the job (from wakeup to bedtime), midnight hours on call or consoling, tending, and checking the youngsters, and 6- or 7-day work weeks exceeded the number of hours per day and week that can be compensated on a straight-time basis under the law. In a few facilities the average hourly wage of houseparents fell below the national or state minimum hourly wage when their long work weeks were taken into account. It is important to check the relevant laws and regulations before setting working hours and compensation for live-in staff.

Home operators who prefer shift workers see little value in replicating a conventional family setting when a large proportion of group home youths come from, and will return to, families headed by only one parent. They contend that some residents are likely to transfer hostile feelings from their parents to the houseparents, contributing to rebellious and disruptive behavior.

Shift workers are said to be more receptive to teamwork and direction by the professional staff. They do not become as emotionally involved with the residents and are therefore more likely to deal with them in a therapeutic manner. Since at least four shift workers are required for a home, the residents have a good chance of finding at least one adult with whom they can develop an especially trusting relationship. If a shift worker's employment is terminated, other workers familiar to residents remain on the job, whereas the departure of a houseparent can be shattering. Moreover, shift workers may be less likely than houseparents to experience burnout because they spend fewer hours with residents and bear less individual responsibility for the program.

Despite the lack of consensus about the advantages of houseparents versus shift workers, experience suggests some guidelines for making a choice between them. Generally, houseparents seem most suitable for small homes, with no more than six or seven residents. Many small facilities are unable to afford round-the-clock shift workers. More important, houseparents in charge of only a few youths experience less stress than those in larger homes and are more likely to develop intimate relationships with the residents. It also has been suggested that houseparents are particularly advantageous for young children of preteen age. Such youngsters may have a special need for intimate and personalized care.

Employment of shift workers is likely to be most advantageous in group homes with eight or more beds. They are also the best choice for homes serving young people with comparatively severe psychological disturbances and adjustment problems.

To some extent the role of shift workers can be structured to provide some of the continuity and personalized care attributed to houseparents. One approach is to have one or more shift workers live in the facility. Such workers are encouraged to maintain informal contact with the residents during off-duty hours—joining in games, eating with the group, and serving as role models and informal counselors. Or each shift worker may be designated as a "personal counselor" for two or three youths in addition to his standard child care duties. To develop close relationships the personal counselor may join an overweight youth in a diet program, tutor a slow learner, jog daily with a lonely resident, accompany an anxious boy or girl to the doctor, or cut red tape to arrange piano lessons, part-time jobs, or a visit by family members.

Support Staff

In addition to the director, social worker, and child care workers, many group homes employ auxiliary workers. Such workers free other staff members from routine tasks; give them time to plan, evaluate, and recuperate; and improve security in the home. In some homes support workers help to balance the age, sex, and racial composition of the staff. A female housekeeper may complement a staff of male child care workers, a young cook complements older houseparents, and so on.

Support positions that are discussed below include relief workers, cook/housekeepers, clerical workers, maintenance personnel, and night caretakers.

Relief Workers

Almost all homes employing houseparents also hire relief workers to replace them during off-duty periods and to assist them during hours of peak activity. Relief workers provide a respite to help tired houseparents renew their vigor and enthusiasm. They can free houseparents from routine chores like shopping and chauffeuring. They lead recreational activities and keep an eye on the young people while the houseparent's attention is on other tasks. Reliefers free houseparents to attend training and counseling sessions and to participate in staff conferences.

For the residents the relief worker is a potential role model and a non-supervisory adult with whom they might develop an especially comfortable relationship.

Individuals who serve as relief workers are often college students with no special training prior to coming on the job. They assume a difficult role, in which their limited authority, confidence, and experience may be tested continually by the residents. On the positive side, competent, self-aware, and caring part-timers make major contributions to life in the facility. Their job is excellent training for full-time child care positions and, if supplemented by appropriate education, offers useful experience toward social work as a career.

Cooks/Housekeepers

Some homes employ full-time or part-time cooks or cook/housekeepers. By relieving child care workers of kitchen and other chores, such employees allow them more time to interact with residents and to recuperate from their fatiguing duties. A skilled cook can improve the quality and variety of food served in the home, which otherwise may include excessive servings of hamburgers, frankfurters, spaghetti, and packaged desserts. A cook also can reduce food costs by preparing meals from primary ingredients rather than serving more expensive TV dinners and canned items.

In research on New Jersey group homes several years ago, the author found that cook/housekeepers were much more common in homes employing houseparents than those employing shift workers. Houseparents have a special need for help with household chores because of their longer hours in the home and greater exposure to tension and fatigue. Another finding was that girls' homes rarely employed cooks or housekeepers, largely because their residents were required to do a larger share of the housework than boys were. In some boys' homes youths did not have to wash dishes or even launder their own clothes.

Experience strongly suggests that group homes that employ houseparents also should retain cook/housekeepers, at least on a part-time basis. Shift workers should be able to handle housekeeping tasks themselves if shifts are scheduled properly and workers have housekeeping skills.

Clerical Workers

Few directors and social workers have clerical assistance. They do their own typing, duplicating, and filing. They pick up the office telephone whenever it rings. Clerical chores consume time that could be spent on substantive work.

Homes affiliated with a parent agency often draw on it for clerical assistance. That is indeed a major advantage of affiliation. If independent homes cannot afford a secretary, they should try to recruit adult volunteers to help with clerical chores.

Maintenance Workers

Many homes occupy aging buildings that need continual patching and replacement of worn-out equipment. Living quarters and furnishings receive rough use that requires frequent painting, repair of laundry equipment, unclogging of drains, and regluing of tables and chairs. Such work is aggravating, expensive, and time-consuming. Often it falls to the lot of the treatment staff.

Most unaffiliated homes hire outside craftsmen at a high cost to make major repairs. A facility that is part of a larger parent agency, on the other hand, can share its maintenance staff. Some homes invite volunteers to help but must provide insurance against injury and tailor the tasks to their convenience and limited skills. Sometimes residents may volunteer for lawn-mowing, gardening, and painting, but such activities may bring objections from the placement agency and government wage and hour regulators.

Night Caretakers

Few homes employ a staff member to remain awake and to provide security and other services during the night. Probably only a minority of placement agencies require such caretakers. It is generally assumed that houseparents and live-in shift workers will provide adequate security, handle emergencies, check ill youngsters, and offer companionship to those who can't get to sleep.

In spite of its extra cost a good case can be made for the employment of night caretakers. By standing watch the caretakers relieve live-in workers of anxiety and help them get enough restful sleep in an otherwise tense and unpredictable environment. The youngsters also feel more secure and sleep more soundly with a night person on duty. They will not fear hazing, sexual molestation, nightmares, or the darkness. The likelihood of burglaries, theft by residents, runaways, and midnight escapades is reduced.

The night caretaker has a significant human relations role. He chats with youngsters who can't get to sleep, come downstairs for a glass of milk, or wake up to take medication. It is a good time for active listening and informal counseling. It is not necessary for the caretaker to have technical qualifications as long as he is a stable, sympathetic, and reliable person. A university student, a "moonlighting" teacher or nurse, or a retired neighbor may do a good job.

Chapter 5

BUILDING AND RETAINING
A COMPETENT STAFF

The supervision of up to a dozen or more troubled teenagers is a severe test of the character and competence of group home staff members. The combination of personal qualities and training they require is difficult to achieve. This chapter discusses the personal characteristics, education and experience that are most helpful to staff members. The causes of turnover and burnout among workers are also explored.

Personal Characteristics of Staff Members

Personality Traits

Many people think that the subjective personal qualities of group home workers are the most important of all. Some workers earn the trust and respect of young people right away, whereas others, equally dedicated and trained, can develop no more than a formal relationship with them. Worker A responds quickly and almost instinctively in a therapeutic manner to challenges from the residents, whereas Worker B, equally knowledgeable, cannot come up with the right response at the right time. The employer who is recruiting staff members must somehow evaluate such personality differences.

Staff members should have a deep interest in and concern for troubled youths. That interest and concern will have to compensate for the pressures, modest salary, and long hours encountered on the job. Workers must be dependable in meeting their responsibilities. They must be able to make reasonable decisions quickly and independently. In a small facility where employees are called on to make important decisions without consulting superiors beforehand, self-confidence, assertiveness, and willingness to assume responsibility are important traits.

Workers cannot act on impulse or permit their own ego needs to dictate the way they react to youths and adults on the job. Instead they must be able to participate in group home life in an objective manner consistent with therapeutic principles—even when they are angry, anxious, tired, or frustrated. The question always is "What effect will my response have on this youth?" rather than "How can I blow off steam, get revenge, make the kids love me, or show people who's boss around here?"

Emotionally stable workers do not manipulate others through tears, sulks, or tantrums, nor convert frustration into sustained resentment, self-pity, or plans for revenge. They acknowledge their negative feelings and go on to analyze what causes them and how the causes can be modified in a therapeutic way. Emotional stability also implies an absence of frequent mood swings—between depression and ebullience, despair and optimism, and love and hate for the same individual. A saving sense of humor and knowing when to relax are life-saving qualities in small residential facilities.

In a very small organization the ability to work cooperatively with colleagues is especially important. That includes a willingness to evaluate disagreements objectively, express viewpoints honestly, refrain from personalizing differences of opinion on technical matters, and accept compromises with good cheer.

If any single quality were to be identified as the most important for a staff member in a group home, it might be self-awareness. As defined here, a self-aware person is one who continuously evaluates his behavior, attitudes, motives, and feelings to recognize the patterned ways in which he responds to people and situations. Hirschbach (1976, p. 689) urges group home workers to "know thyself"; there is no better definition of self-awareness. The trait is the hallmark of true child care professionals.

Self-awareness helps staff members interact with residents and co-workers in a task-oriented, technical manner rather than in habitual ways that gratify their own unconscious feelings and needs. Here are examples of responses that do *not* reflect self-awareness:

> A worker responds to a child's disobedience as a test of his own manliness and creates a "win or lose" confrontation.

> A worker seeks love and admiration from the youngsters and is crushed by occasional hostility or noncooperation.

> A worker is afraid to make decisions because of unrecognized inadequacy feelings.

A worker is unable to recognize his fear of a burly, violence-prone resident and responds by unconsciously avoiding or yielding to the youth.

A worker resists advice from supervisors because of a generalized resentment toward all authority figures.

A worker is influenced by racial prejudice.

Charisma

Some home operators seek to employ charismatic directors or child care workers. They prefer dynamic, enthusiastic employees who are "natural leaders" and can elicit the adoration of residents. Not infrequently, such charismatic individuals have special accomplishments that earn the youngsters' respect; e.g., they may have been professional athletes, show business personalities, or members of the Green Berets. Disadvantaged inner-city youths may respond to a staff member who is "streetwise"; that is, who has successfully coped "by hook or crook" with the challenges of "making it" in a poverty-stricken environment.

On the face of it a charismatic personality would appear to be useful in managing troubled youths. Charismatic staff members encounter less disobedience and defiance. They are accepted eagerly as role models. In practice, however, serious problems can emerge from long-term reliance on a worker's magnetism, enthusiasm, and unique leadership qualities in a treatment program. Charismatic staff members tend to rely on exhortation, momentary enthusiasm, and the devotion of residents to modify behavior, rather than to encourage residents to develop their own judgment and problem-solving skills. They tend to become ego-involved; a youth who does not respond with admiration may be perceived as a competitor and ignored or held up to ridicule. Charismatic staff members are often unable to participate in counseling sessions, group discussions, and staff meetings in a nondirective manner. One may conclude that even the best-intentioned charismatic staff member can exert a countertherapeutic influence unless the trait is restrained by self-awareness and professionalism.

Realistic Expectations

To work effectively in a group home, staff members must have realistic expectations about the effectiveness of services for troubled youth and about the way disturbed youths respond in a treatment facility. Workers who expect to harvest love, gratitude, and admiration open themselves to disappointment. The child care specialist usually must be content with the knowledge that he is doing a worthy job in a technically proficient, caring way.

Single-minded persons who are convinced in advance that "what these kids need is more discipline"—or more love, hard work, religion, isolation from bad friends, adventure, exposure to nature, or what not—are unlikely to last long in group homes. Experience has taught group homes humility, flexibility, and the need to adapt their services to individual needs.

Age

The age of staff members often affects the way in which colleagues and residents relate to them. Some home operators prefer to employ middle-age and older individuals. They usually bring maturity, reliability, and experience to the job. Perhaps they have lower turnover rates than young workers.

On the other hand, youthful child care workers may view the life-styles, values, and policies of older directors and social workers as old-fashioned. The latter may be accused of inflexibility and failure to understand the changing world in which residents must live. There is the possibility too that residents might transfer hostility they feel toward their parents to an older staff member while perceiving a worker closer to their own age as a friend and role model.

Some homes make a deliberate effort to have a range of ages represented on the staff so that residents of varying needs can find at least one adult with whom to form a comfortable relationship. Facilities that employ child care workers on a shift basis may try hiring a mix of younger and older individuals. Those that employ houseparents try sometimes to balance their staff by hiring relief workers and housekeepers who are older or younger than the houseparents. In all facilities age differences and the feelings they arouse should be discussed at staff meetings and group counseling sessions.

Sex

Should group home staff members be of the same sex as the residents? Although the sex of group home directors and social workers probably does not make much difference, there remains a considerable difference of opinion with respect to the sex of child care workers. Group homes feel free to employ married couples as live-in houseparents, but there is reluctance to employ adults of the opposite sex as shift workers or as "reliefers" for houseparents. Many directors feel that shift workers of the same sex as the residents may understand the youths better and can serve as realistic role models. In the confined space of a small facility disturbed youths may tend to test workers of the opposite sex and to act out emotional problems related to sexuality in a disruptive way. Other directors argue that troubled youths benefit from close association with caring and trustworthy adults of the opposite sex.

Race and Ethnic Background

Another issue facing group homes is whether to employ staff members of the same race and ethnic origin as the majority of residents. One can maintain that disturbed youngsters who are facing the difficult adjustment to group living should not have to grapple with the additional tensions of learning to relate to staff of unfamiliar backgrounds and styles of life. Someone from their own group, who has shared their culture and youthful experiences, may be more empathetic and comforting. He also can serve as a more realistic model than a person of different background.

There are strong arguments on the other side of the issue too. The mere fact that a staff member is of the same group as the resident does not ensure a therapeutic relationship. Middle-class black and Hispanic employees, for example, may have as much difficulty empathizing with inner-city minority youths as white workers do. Workers who share a poverty background with residents sometimes bring to child care a certain inflexibility and punitive discipline that characterized family practices in their own cultural milieu.

Homes employing staff members of a single racial/ethnic group run the risk that placement agency caseworkers will come to regard them as appropriate only for youths of the same group. As the caseworkers refrain from referring youths of other races and ethnic origin to such a facility, their stereotype becomes a self-fulfilling prophecy.

It seems best to employ an integrated staff if possible. That helps all residents—white, black, Hispanic, Asian, or others—to feel secure and to find at least one staff member with whom they can achieve a special rapport. A mixed staff alleviates the anxiety of parents of those youths who represent a minority racial/ethnic group in the home. It encourages residents to evaluate and shed their prejudices against other groups. And it reduces the likelihood that caseworkers will stereotype the facility as one suitable only for a particular race or ethnic population.

Religious Background

Many residential care facilities have a religious affiliation. They may prefer to employ staff members who share their views on educating and rehabilitating youth. There are also financial considerations—the monetary compensation of nuns, priests, and others who view their work as a religious vocation is often lower than that of comparable employees, and they may put in longer hours on the job.

Catholic, Protestant, and Jewish groups have proved their ability to work with troubled youths in residential programs regardless of the religious affiliation of the residents. Problems have emerged only rarely, when a particular facility has pursued inappropriate policies based on fringe sectarian doctrines.

Health

Child care workers must be in excellent health and have a high energy level to handle their arduous job. They run up and down stairs, jump in and out of vehicles, accompany the youngsters on vigorous outings, and perform manual chores. Above all, during a hard day of work they must be capable of observing, listening, counseling, and interacting therapeutically with their difficult charges.

For Houseparents—Good Family Relations

Relations between houseparents and their spouses endure extra strains in a group home setting. To work effectively, therefore, couples must have a strong relationship capable of surviving under stressful conditions. Both husband and wife must be in agreement when accepting an offer of employment in the facility. If they have children, they should be in good health so that they do not absorb an abnormal amount of their parents' emotional and physical capacity. Conflicting commitments, such as a heavy load of college courses, the care of an aged parent, or a part-time job, should be reviewed to make sure that they will not impose excessive stress.

QUALIFYING EDUCATION AND EXPERIENCE

Training and experience for group home positions are difficult to acquire and once acquired may well command a salary higher than a group home can afford. To a large extent, therefore, group homes must hire inadequately trained persons who learn their trade on the job, aided perhaps by classroom training arranged by the group home itself. Education and training for the director, social worker, and child care workers are discussed below.

The Group Home Director

Group home directors require a knowledge of child care concepts and skills to plan and manage their programs. They must have sufficient professional training to supervise subordinates in credible fashion and to represent the home effectively in relations with the placement agency, other child care professionals, and the community.

Although a good education contributes to the effectiveness of group home directors, it is no substitute for practical work experience. It is only in working directly with troubled youths, staff members, and outside agencies that prospective directors can learn the dynamics of residential programs and test their professional skills.

The most relevant experience for new directors is employment as a supervisor or social worker in residential care facilities for youths. Other useful experience is employment in residential programs for the retarded, the mentally ill, and drug abusers; administrative work in nonresidential human service programs; counseling, therapy, and casework for troubled young people; and service as a special education teacher or supervisory juvenile probation officer.

Social Workers

Some placement agencies specify the qualifications that social workers must have to work in group homes, but most allow wide latitude. As a result, the backgrounds of persons employed as social workers vary considerably.

The degree of master of social work (M.S.W.) is the official credential for social workers. In recent years, however, universities have tended to separate their M.S.W. programs into several fields of specialization, such as psychiatric social work, group work, community organization, agency administration, and social research. It is advisable, therefore, to scan the courses and practicum experiences of job applicants to ensure that they have adequate preparation.

Recently many undergraduate colleges have developed programs leading to the degree of bachelor of social work (B.S.W.). Generally, the courses and practice available in such programs are not full preparation for social work in group homes. However, B.S.W. programs provide very good educational qualifications for child care workers and are an important source of recruits for that occupation.

Other university degrees that are relevant to social work in group homes are degrees in counseling, psychology, and special education.

Relatively few social workers have had previous experience in a residential care facility before they are hired by group homes. Typically, the worker is just beginning his professional career, reentering the labor market after a long period of absence, or shifting into social work from a related occupation. Group homes are unable to offer sufficient salaries, fringe benefits, and job security to lure highly experienced personnel from competing employers.

If possible, social workers hired by group homes should have experience in evaluating treatment needs, planning and arranging treatment services, and serving as counselor and/or therapist in a residential facility for troubled youth. In the absence of such experience, time spent as a social worker in residential care programs for adults and in nonresidential youth services (such as day care for disturbed youngsters, youth employment programs, drug abuse programs, and family guidance centers) helps to qualify a social worker. Experience as a caseworker in government child welfare, mental health, and probation offices is also helpful.

If the group home's social worker is expected to serve as a psychotherapist, it is particularly important to employ an individual with demonstrated competence in that specialized field.

Child Care Workers

Some people think that child care workers do not need formal educational qualifications. In their view college courses are too theoretical and tend to arouse idealized expectations about the job that lead to disappointment and early burnout. It is also alleged that college-educated child care workers tend to resist direction by professional staff members and that their rate of turnover is comparatively high. Those who deprecate formal education claim sometimes that the most important qualifications are warmth, concern, a cool head, and common sense. Everything else can be learned on the job.

Clearly, on-the-job training is essential for child care workers. However, that form of instruction alone is not adequate preparation. A worker learns the policies and routines of the home without understanding the principles and concepts on which they are based. It is difficult to learn how to lead group discussions, provide nondirective counseling, recognize the symptoms of psychological illness, combat racial prejudice, and manage peer group relations through on-the-job training alone. Essential parenting skills and self-awareness also require some classroom training.

One reason why on-the-job training is inadequate is that child care workers in group homes usually work alone. There are rarely co-workers nearby to provide advice or to set examples. The director and social worker are usually off duty or conducting business elsewhere during the worker's busiest hours.

In practice many child care workers are college graduates or students. For the most part, however, they have not specialized in child care, social work, or directly relevant subjects. A substantial proportion have majored in sociology, social psychology, and education. Others have specialized in unrelated subjects such as literature, music, and art.

Relatively few child care workers have had relevant work experience before coming to a group home. With few exceptions they must endure a stressful apprenticeship before they can expect to function effectively and confidently. With luck a group home may recruit workers who have had some experience in detention shelters, Job Corps centers, minimum security correctional facilities, residential treatment institutions, homes for the retarded or physically handicapped, and summer camps for disadvantaged youngsters. Also helpful is previous work in nonresidential programs such as day camps, day-care centers, and day-treatment facilities.

Volunteer work often provides skills that can be transferred to group homes. Examples are service as a foster parent, a Big Brother/Sister, scout master, tutor for problem children, and classroom aide.

Because most child care workers hired by group homes lack adequate experience and education, each facility must take steps to complete their training. It is strongly recommended that new child care workers spend at least 2 weeks observing and assisting experienced workers before assuming their responsibilities. During that period the professional staff should provide systematic instruction covering aspects of the new employee's job that do not lend themselves to on-the-job training. There also should be more structured in-service training for workers after they have been hired, which may include, for example, periodic staff discussions, talks by the home's psychologist, and arrangements to participate in workshops offered by outside agencies.

Group homes encounter serious difficulty in planning in-service training. Many cannot afford to pay for overtime work, so training must be conducted during normal duty hours. Sessions tend to be brief; as little as a half hour may be set aside each week for staff meetings. One or more shift workers or relief workers are likely to be absent because they are off duty when the meeting is held.

Moreover, group homes cannot readily afford to send employees through formal training programs now offered by a number of educational institutions. Small facilities even have difficulty paying for a qualified replacement while their houseparent attends a 3-day seminar; the houseparent represents virtually the entire child care staff!

The following are useful topics for structured in-service training:

1. Principles and concepts underlying the treatment of disturbed and maladjusted youth.
2. The symptoms of physical and mental illness.
3. Building a therapeutic social milieu.
4. Parenting skills.
5. The dynamics and management of peer group relations.
6. Techniques for informal counseling and group discussions.
7. Minority group cultures and relations.
8. Techniques for tutoring and other educational support.
9. Planning therapeutic recreational activities.
10. Nutrition and healthful food preparation.
11. Drug abuse and alcoholism.
12. Self-awareness.
13. Recognition and prevention of burnout.
14. Assertiveness training.
15. Managing anger and conflict.
16. Dealing with stress.

Because of the importance of "parenting" skills in influencing the development of the young people, they deserve special mention. Parenting skills are ways of relating to young people that minimize tensions and friction, foster emotional maturity and judgment, and respect the values and rights of both adults and children.

There are many similarities between the roles of parent and child care worker. As in normal parent-child relationships, the residents usually see the child care worker as an authority figure, protector, teacher, and role model. They seek affection, approval, assistance, and security from the worker and often develop deep emotional ties to him. The worker is the source of subsistence and the leader of family-type activities. Parenting is therefore a major aspect of the worker's job, and it strongly affects the way that youths respond to treatment. Instruction in that subject should be a component of every training program.

Of course, analogies between parents and child care workers must not obscure the major differences between those roles. Workers who try to behave exactly like parents may unintentionally encourage patterns of dependence, hostility, manipulation, peer rivalry, and other behavior carried over from the youths' preplacement settings. The workers expose themselves to emotional strain, disappointment, and burnout if personal feelings impede calculated professionalism. Staff members are, after all, technicians in a systematic treatment program.

In recent years, a variety of books and courses on parenting have become available. A recent article by Charlene Turner in *Child Welfare* (1980) is devoted entirely to an annotated list of sources of training and information on parenting skills. Local family guidance and mental health centers often provide courses in that area.

One of the earliest training programs—Parent Effectiveness Training (P.E.T.)—is still among the best. It is simple and practical, has a nationwide network of trainers offering week-long courses, and has developed stimulating training aids. A group home director or social worker who enrolls in one of those courses is qualified, in turn, to train the home's child care workers. Information on the P.E.T. program is available in Ms. Turner's article and in Gordon (1970).

REDUCING TURNOVER OF CHILD CARE WORKERS

High staff turnover is a problem in many, if not most, group homes. It affects all occupations but is probably most pronounced among child care workers. In New Jersey the author found an average duration of employment for "live-in" houseparents of 1 year in 1975. Shift workers averaged only 6 months on the job. In 1979 Connis et al. (p. 131) found an average employment of 11.7 months for live-in houseparents in 26 Kansas homes.

Turnover compels group homes to rely on inexperienced workers and to spend time and resources in continual training of new staff. It reduces the chance of developing stable relationships with neighbors and community. Worst of all, turnover affects the residents adversely by heightening their insecurity and shattering supportive relationships.

Four factors emerge as major causes of turnover among child care workers. They are (a) problems with child care as a career; (b) friction between child care workers and the professional staff; (c) burnout; (d) inadequate training.

These four factors are closely related; each affects the other. The need for better training has already been discussed above. In this section the three remaining factors will be explored, and some recommendations will be made to improve the situation.

Problems with Child Care as a Career

Most child care workers in group homes do not view their employment as a stage in a long-term career. Lacking opportunities for rising incomes and advancement, they often pursue outside objectives that lead them to change jobs in a short time.

The relatively low level of wages and fringe benefits, particularly in unaffiliated, privately operated homes, contributes to employee turnover. Working hours are inconvenient and vacations short. There are rarely opportunities to accumulate sick leave, severance pay, and pension rights—incentives offered by employers in other industries.

Opportunities for advancement are extremely limited. If a home is affiliated with a parent agency, there exists a possibility of promotion in some other facility operated by the agency. In a small unaffiliated home promotions are virtually impossible unless a paraprofessional can meet the educational requirements for directors and social workers.

A high proportion of child care workers view their jobs as only temporary from the outset. Liberal arts majors accept child care positions while they hunt for openings in their own fields. Workers may be waiting their turns for civil service jobs or be committed to a teaching position next fall. Typically, live-in houseparent couples, who can bank most of their earnings because living expenses are paid by their group home, plan to stay only until they save enough money to start a business, go back to school, or achieve some other objective.

As a high proportion of child care workers are relatively young, they share the mobility of young adults in today's society. They leave to marry, to accompany their husbands to another area, to raise a family, to return to school, or to venture on a year abroad. Workers who attend school during their employment are likely to leave promptly after graduation.

Despite such difficulties much can be done to develop paraprofessional child care work as a career. Establishment of degree programs in community and 4-year colleges for students specializing in residential child care would be helpful. To encourage enrollment by persons currently employed in child care, course credit should be allowed for experience gained on the job. Better salaries, fringe benefits, and employment of support staff to relieve child care workers of the most onerous, physically taxing aspects of their job are recommended. Development of a career ladder for child care workers by parent agencies of group homes would be another positive step. Realistically, there is not much that unaffiliated homes can do on their own in this area.

Friction between Child Care Workers and the Professional Staff

In group homes there is a potential for friction and misunderstanding among the child care workers, director, and social worker. In extreme cases supervisory tensions lead to smoldering resentment, surreptitious resistance to instructions, and deterioration of the social milieu of the home. Such friction can be a factor in the turnover of both paraprofessional and professional staff members. For a classic example of conflict between professionals and child care workers in larger residential treatment facilities, see Piliavin (1970); see also Shostack (1978).

Friction between child care workers and professionals reflects in large part the way their roles are structured. In many facilities the directors, social workers, and other professionals design the home's policies and individual treatment plans without full consultation with child care workers. Yet it is the child care worker—the person in continuous interaction with the youngsters—who is held accountable for implementing the policies and plans. Examples of interpersonal friction that may result include:

a.   Professionals blaming child care workers, rather than their own policies, for the failure of residents to make progress;

b.   Some directors and social workers, insulated from close interaction with the residents, accusing workers of responding to behavior impulsively, emotionally, or arbitrarily;

c.   Workers concluding that policies and treatment plans are impractical, too permissive, and based on an overidealized image of the residents;

d.   Child care workers, believing that they know the residents better than the professionals do, pursuing their own approaches to each youth's needs;

e.   Child care workers coming to feel that they are considered inferior and untrustworthy and are being left to grope and improvise on the job;

f.   Resentment experienced by long-service child care workers as each new director or social worker tries to direct their activities.

Inadequate communication further breeds suspicion and insecurity. The child care worker asks, "What is the social worker saying about me in those private counseling sessions with the youngsters?" "What are the director, social worker, and psychologist saying about me in their confidential meetings?" "Are residents complaining about me in group therapy sessions while I am not present to defend myself?"

Similarly, the social worker may wonder whether the child care worker is undermining his credibility with the residents, concealing behavior problems that might reflect adversely on the worker's competence, or criticizing the social worker in private talks with members of the board of directors.

Group home youths are not long unaware of friction and poor communication between professionals and child care workers. It is not uncommon for the young people to take sides. They may exacerbate the problem mischievously by carrying distorted tales, making up incidents, playing off one adult against the other, and trying to get them to make inconsistent decisions. Cases in which the residents have generated sufficient discomfort to cause the resignation of affected employees are not rare.

Some suggestions for strengthening staff relations are presented below:

1. Staff conferences, conducted at least once each week, are a must for all homes. In addition, the wise director and social worker make time for frequent informal exchanges with the paraprofessional staff.

2. Periodic written evaluations of all employees contribute to honesty in staff relations and help to bring problems into the open where they can be analyzed objectively.

3. As members of the "treatment team," child care workers should be consulted in planning the home's policies, admitting and terminating residents, developing individual treatment plans, and evaluating the progress of residents.

4. Group home directors should review periodically the authority and responsibilities assigned to staff members to ensure that they are clearly delineated and understood by all parties.

5. The director and social worker should spend a substantial amount of time in the home, including some evening and weekend hours.

6. To earn the respect and confidence of the paraprofessional staff, social workers must demonstrate their specialized skills. Those who conduct individual, group, and parent counseling and, better still, individual and/or group psychotherapy are more likely to receive acceptance than those who concentrate on office work and outside contacts.

7. Interpersonal conflicts should be the subject of staff counseling sessions.

8. Supervisors should express support for staff members. A word of praise, a commendation witnessed by the residents, and a special Christmas present cement good relations.

Burnout

The problem of burnout among workers in the human services has received growing attention in recent years. Experts believe it is a major factor in employee dissatisfaction and turnover (Bramhall & Ezell, 1981; Edelwich, 1980; Freudenberger, 1977; Mattingly, 1977; Pines & Aronson, 1981). In group homes burnout is a particular threat to the morale and efficiency of child care workers whose intensive interaction with troubled youngsters under difficult circumstances contributes to fatigue, stress, and upheaval in personal life.

The term *burnout* means the gradual extinction of a worker's motivation, drive, and energy to perform his job. Burnout is marked by some or all of the following symptoms (drawn in part from Zischka, 1981):

1. Feelings of frustration, cynicism, and hopelessness about achieving worthwhile goals.
2. Feelings of stress and pressure.
3. A growing indifference or resignation concerning the needs of residents, often accompanied by mindless concentration on routines and paperwork.
4. Increasing boredom.
5. Gradual reduction of effort on the job. Employees may begin to spend excessive time phoning outside friends, daydreaming, or "going through the motions" until retirement.
6. Psychosomatic symptoms such as excess fatigue, headaches, frequent colds, and proneness to accidents.
7. Mounting resentment toward supervisors and co-workers and aggrieved feelings concerning petty or vague staff incidents.
8. Depression; a feeling of being trapped in a meaningless routine.

Specific sources of burnout in group homes are not difficult to locate. Child care workers are under continuous stress. They deal with troubled youths who are often unpredictable and hostile toward authority. Workers must weigh each word, each action, for their effects on the residents. They are expected to keep their own feelings and spontaneous reactions under tight control while responding to the youngsters in a professional therapeutic manner.

Workers must be ready for emergencies such as fights, runaways, and illness at any time. A ringing telephone may herald the arrest of a resident for shoplifting, a youth's failure to show up at school, or the hospitalization of an accident victim. Even minor irritations may assume emergency proportions; for example, a breakdown of the plumbing, the van, or the television set.

Child care workers in group homes work in isolation from other staff members most of the time. They cannot walk across the hall to "unwind" with a colleague or consult a more experienced co-worker. Physical fatigue contributes to burnout. There is hard manual labor: cooking, chauffeuring, cleaning, maintenance, running up and down the stairs, accompanying mischievous residents on recreational trips. Live-in houseparents work particularly long hours. If they have small children of their own to care for, they bear an additional work burden.

The personal lives of child care workers tend to be affected adversely by their job. Working late hours and weekends, workers find that they lose touch with friends because they are not available at times when adult cultural, recreational, and social events are customarily scheduled. Shift schedules limit normal contacts with spouses, children, and other relatives.

Many new workers start with overidealized expectations about life and work in a group home, making them particularly subject to burnout. Unrealistic expectations are described in a thoughtful article by Vander Ven (1979), which is drawn on in part for the following list:

1. Young workers may treat residents as equals in the expectation that that will lead to cooperative relationships.

2. Workers expect to evoke love by relaxing discipline and yielding to inappropriate requests. For example, they may permit unauthorized smoking or "look the other way" when the curfew is violated.

3. Workers may enjoy a "rescue fantasy," expecting to solve the youngsters' problems through a quick insight, affection, or a showing of trust.

4. New workers may perceive the youths as helpless victims rather than as individuals who must assume some responsibility for their own behavior.

5. Workers may have what Vander Ven refers to as an "affective orientation"—the conviction that spontaneity and warm personal relationships are the most important ingredient of child care. Record keeping, neatness, routines in everyday life, and structured treatment services are seen as irrelevant and artificial.

6. Workers may be committed in advance to a particular psychological theory or treatment approach as a cure-all for youths with different needs.

It does not take long for workers with overidealized expectations to find that some troubled youngsters have difficulty relating to adults in authority—no matter how supportive—and that group homes cannot meet the needs of all residents. Such workers are bound to feel frustrated when inevitably a favorite youth is withdrawn from the home, a resident gets into trouble with the law, and turnover among residents prevents the application of a preferred treatment method. The realities of placement agency reporting requirements, restrictions imposed by parent agencies, budgetary limitations, and burdensome housekeeping chores also shatter overidealized expectations.

Workers who start with an authoritarian approach are also candidates for early burnout. In a group home they feel uncomfortable with gradual, nondirective ways of modifying behavior and are frustrated by limitations placed on the punishments and incentives they are authorized to use. Eventually some come to feel that their supervisors are too "soft" on the residents and are failing to support their efforts to maintain discipline.

Houseparent couples, who live in the group home around the clock, are subject to special strains that contribute to burnout. Those strains affect not only their job performance but their most intimate family relationships as well (Jewett, 1973; Shostack, 1978). The exceptionally long working hours of houseparents are a source of stress. Most are expected to be available in the home for 5 or 6 days each week—around the clock. In homes that require the houseparent's spouse to help around the facility, free time that the spouse may wish to share with his own family or to use for personal affairs and recuperation is drained by the demands of the residents and by odd jobs around the facility.

There is inadequate insulation from the tensions of the group home during periods intended for relaxation. The great majority of houseparents are not provided with quarters outside the home where they can recuperate while off duty. Most simply remain in their rooms within the facility, subject to intrusions by relief workers and residents. Lacking a private kitchen, the off-duty houseparent couple continues to mingle with the residents at meal and snack times.

A lack of privacy required to nurture marital relationships contributes to the burnout of houseparents. Most have no separate parlors where they can relax, share each other's company, or entertain personal friends. A few share their bedrooms with their own children. Those who are fortunate enough to have separate quarters outside the group home for off-duty periods often find that relief workers are expected to take over their room, beds, closets, and bath during their absence.

Always the houseparents are surrounded by the natural curiosity of the residents. Their intimate conversations, the contents of their drawers—even their sex lives—are the focus of the youngsters' attention.

Putting in long work days and work weeks, living in cramped quarters, unable to escape the pressures of everyday life even during their "free time," and lacking personal privacy, houseparents are exposed to marital tensions. A significant number of couples leave their jobs because they tend to disrupt their marital relations. Some couples separate while employed or soon after.[1]

Some suggestions for minimizing burnout among child care workers are offered below:

1. Workers should receive adequate training to cope with their stressful and complex tasks.

2. Professional staff members should meet frequently with child care workers to learn their needs and provide support.

3. Homes should help workers enroll in relevant courses and workshops that provide needed breaks in routine and permit participants to draw reassurance from others in the same occupation.

[1]In the author's study of 18 New Jersey homes most directors employing houseparents reported that the latter were encountering problems in their marriages.

4. Counseling should be available for all child care workers on a confidential basis. The counselor, who might be the home's psychological consultant or other neutral figure, should encourage the workers to explore their feelings about their jobs, their fellow staff members, and the residents. The counselor also should help workers with their family and other personal problems.

5. It is suggested that group home operators encourage child care workers to join with peers in nearby group homes and related treatment facilities to form support groups. Such groups meet regularly to share concerns and experiences, to help members clarify their feelings and evaluate their behavior, and to provide feedback in matters on which members seek the group's assistance. Opportunities for reassurance, increased self-awareness, the exchange of information and advice, and the pleasant companionship of people in similar circumstances make support groups a valuable resource.[2]

6. Houseparent couples and live-in shift workers must be furnished with quarters that provide comfort, dignity, and privacy.

7. Where necessary, separate quarters outside the home should be provided for the use of houseparents on off-duty days.

8. Group homes should experiment with flexible shift schedules that allow child care workers adequate time for family responsibilities, continuing education, relaxation, and personal interests.

9. Houseparents and live-in shift workers should enjoy adequate paid vacations and a minimum of 2 days off each week.

10. In homes serving disturbed and maladjusted youths, it is a good idea to employ a night care person to permit the live-in staff to get a full night's sound sleep.

11. If only one member of a houseparent couple is designated as a paid employee, the other should not be expected to perform work for the home.

12. A cook/housekeeper should be employed, at least part-time, to free houseparents from energy-consuming household chores.

[2]Formation of support groups to combat burnout also has been suggested in the American Public Welfare Association's Newsletter, *Washington Report*, 17 (December 1982).

Chapter 6

THE ADMISSIONS PROCESS

The process by which youths are admitted to group homes is complex and time-consuming. It depends on the timely referral of an adequate number of potential residents by the placement agency, the home's skill in evaluating and selecting residents, and the responses of parents and youngsters to offers of admission. In some cases judges and other court personnel also are involved. The proof of success is the home's long-term ability to build and retain a therapeutically balanced population.

Each of the participants has its own special perspective. The placement agency (represented by its caseworkers) tries to choose a residential program geared to each youth's needs. The group home tries to select youths who will adapt readily to its program. Parents influence the choice of a facility for their children because most group home placements require parental consent. The preferences of the youngster are taken into account because to do otherwise is to risk the admission of a resentful, vengeful trouble-maker and potential runaway. And courts become involved when placements are made pursuant to court orders or are reviewed by court personnel.

In the following pages the first section focuses on the placement agency caseworkers who are responsible for selecting a home for each youth. The second section discusses admissions from the viewpoint of group homes, and the third section considers the influence of parents and children on placement decisions.

THE ROLE OF PLACEMENT AGENCY CASEWORKERS

The day-to-day work of evaluating, placing, and following the progress of youngsters supervised by child welfare agencies is conducted by caseworkers, each of whom serves a case load of youths and families. Caseworkers identify appropriate placement sites, arrange necessary approvals and paperwork, plan services for the young people and their families, and monitor the treatment process. They are also key figures in the termination of placements.

Some placement agencies assign a single worker to each youth or family, who remain in that worker's case load from intake through termination. Others prefer more specialization, perhaps with different caseworkers handling intake, placement, monitoring, termination, and aftercare for each youth.

Responsibilities of caseworkers usually include the following:

1. Collection of background information on the legal status of the youth, the family's composition, history, and financial status, the youth's social and psychological history, the youth's educational status, and his physical health. The worker may be required to classify each youngster on the basis of his social/psychological characteristics and need for services.

2. Recommending whether the placement agency should assume supervision of the youth, whether the youth should be removed from the family setting, and what type of placement might be the most suitable. Support services for the parents and other family members also are proposed.

3. Explaining the proposed services to the parents and youth to enlist their cooperation. Otherwise the parents may refuse to consent to a placement, fail to participate in recommended services, and/or trigger administrative or court actions likely to delay the provision of services. They may even leave the local area or state.

4. Selecting appropriate residential facilities for youths. That process is simple if the local placement office assigns youths to only one or two facilities. If the office has a choice of numerous group homes, the process is more complex. Caseworkers must have reliable knowledge about the kinds of youths served in each facility, the services each provides, the qualifications of their staff members, and current vacancy rates.

As a basis for choosing a group home, workers can review the agency's list of approved facilities and evaluations of each facility prepared periodically by agency monitors. In addition, they exchange experience and impressions about the competence of various homes and their ability to care for residents of different kinds. The office grapevine exerts an important influence on the selection of the right group home. Facilities are well-advised, therefore, to keep in close touch with the caseworkers, particularly those in distant offices, to solicit visits and suggestions, to keep them abreast of program changes, and to notify them about the availability of vacant beds.

5. Referring youths to a facility. After identifying one or more group

homes that are appropriate for a youth, the worker must determine whether those homes are willing to consider the youth for possible admission. The great majority of group homes are permitted to reject youngsters referred for consideration.

Homes that express a preliminary interest are provided with information on the youth's background and characteristics. Where several facilities are interested, it is a common practice to send copies to all of them simultaneously, to expedite the placement process. If more than one home expresses interest in a youth, the caseworker may be in a position to offer the youth and parents a choice of locations.

6. Arranging preplacement visits. Unless there are compelling reasons to the contrary, caseworkers arrange visits to the potential placement sites. A visit permits the group home staff to interview the prospective resident and the parents. It also gives the youth and parents an opportunity to get a first-hand impression of the staff, services, physical facilities, and surroundings of the home.

7. Implementing placements. After the caseworker, parents, youth, and group home reach agreement on a placement, the caseworker completes the paperwork; e.g., agency approvals, parent consent forms, notices to courts and placement review bodies, forms to authorize reimbursement of the group home, and correspondence to fill gaps in the youth's file. Transfer of the youth to a new public school also may involve substantial documentation and negotiation. Finally, a mutually acceptable date is set for the new resident's entry into the home.

The placement process rarely works as smoothly and predictably as its official description would indicate. Caseworkers operate within a variety of frustrating constraints that group homes must take into account when planning their admissions policies.

Heavy case loads are a problem. The typical caseworker may be responsible for 40, 50, or more children being evaluated, placed, supervised, and/or readied for termination. Each case requires conferences with parents, residential facilities, service agencies, and co-workers; forms and reports; long telephone calls; travel to placement sites; attendance at court and placement review sessions; and other time-intensive activities. When one deducts time for vacations, sick leave, in-service training, and other auxiliary activities, caseworkers are lucky to find even a few minutes to devote to each youth and facility during their work week.

Because of their limited time, workers must give the bulk of their attention to new cases, emergencies, and families facing the most serious crises. Counseling sessions with parents may be perfunctory and infrequent, with little follow-up or coordination with other agencies serving the family. The workers may rely on written progress reports from group homes, rather than on visits to the facilities. Shortcuts and informal methods may be employed. Parents who are not assertive, youths who do not engage in dangerous behavior, placements that are not challenged, and group homes that are not the subject of complaints—those may receive only the permissible minimum of attention.

Another chronic problem is the long period of time required to place some youths. The collection of information, evaluation of youths, identification of a suitable residential facility, preplacement visits and trial periods, preparation of official documents, and negotiations on an admission date can easily drag on for weeks or months. Meanwhile some youngsters may have to be detained for long periods in shelters for status offenders. Others, left with their own families until a placement can be arranged, drive parents and siblings to despair. Residential facilities may suffer a loss of revenue while holding a vacant bed for a prospective resident.

Budgetary constraints are a third difficulty. In some localities, a lack of funds makes it difficult to place troubled youngsters at the most appropriate time. For example, if the placement agency's budget for residential services has been consumed in the first three-quarters of the year, placements proposed in the last quarter may have to be postponed. A shortage of funds for residential facilities may require caseworkers to assign children to less expensive alternatives, such as foster families. Placements may hang on the size of next year's appropriation, local office quotas, and freezes on expenditures.

Even if funds are available, there may be a scarcity of group homes in the state or area for certain types of youth; e.g., for girls or older boys. There may be no time to seek the best facility for a youth who must be removed immediately from a dangerous family environment. The demands of parents for a placement in a prestigious or distant facility may have to be accommodated. Inevitably, such "practical" considerations influence the matching of homes and residents.

All of those problems are exacerbated by the relatively high rate of turnover among caseworkers. Many are frustrated by their heavy work load, paperwork, bureaucratic bottlenecks, and arguments with collaborating agencies. They are rarely in a position to witness a quick success story or to follow a youngster's progress over a long period. Burnout is a common phenomenon.

Often caseworkers are mobile young people who leave readily to follow a spouse to another area, raise a family, return to school, or change careers. Promotions, transfers, leaves, and extended training programs shift them to other offices. It is not uncommon for a youth or family to be assigned a succession of caseworkers over a short period. The result can be discontinuity and inconsistency in the supervision of both group homes and their residents.

THE GROUP HOME'S PERSPECTIVE

From the viewpoint of the group home, the placement process is successful if placement agencies refer the kind of youths who can benefit from the home's program and if referrals are sufficient in number to keep the home's beds filled. A dwindling of the flow of potential residents or pressure to admit youths whose problems are beyond the capability of the home's program can lead to disaster.

Securing an Adequate Number of Referrals

Some homes receive more referrals than they can accommodate; others receive too few to fill their beds. Among factors that influence the number of referrals are the home's reputation among placement agency caseworkers, the area served by the home—e.g., a single community versus the entire state—the size of the home's target population, and the number of placement agencies served. Shortages or surpluses of group home openings and seasonal placement patterns also affect referrals.

Group homes receiving many referrals can afford to be selective in choosing new residents. A facility with a bad reputation, on the other hand, faces special hardships. Caseworkers may simply boycott it without warning or explanation, even if it remains on the placement agency's list of facilities authorized to receive children.

To reduce chronically high vacancy rates, homes sometimes take desperate action. They may lay off a shift worker or housekeeper, adding to the burdens of the remaining staff. They may pay substandard salaries, resulting in loss of their best employees. They may stint on maintenance work, giving the facility a rundown appearance. Cultural and recreational activities may be cut back. There are even worse consequences if such homes lower their admissions standards. A home with high vacancy rates may attempt to outrace its competitors by offering to admit a youth after only a superficial evaluation. The home may offer extra incentives to persuade him to choose it over other facilities; e.g., agreeing to help the youth pursue an expensive hobby, agreeing in advance to the youth's choice of a roommate, or permitting the youth to bring a pet.

The result of extraordinary efforts to fill vacant beds is usually disappointment. Homes find themselves with disruptive residents, a high proportion of runaways and expulsions, and complaints by neighbors and school authorities. Special privileges promised to a few residents stir jealousy among the others. Promises that the home is unable to keep stir additional resentment. As the home's difficulties mount, it is likely to receive still fewer referrals, to be offered only residents rejected by other facilities, and to be forced to accept the highest-risk youngsters. A vicious circle may emerge, in which desperate steps result in a higher vacancy rate than before.

What can an underutilized group home do to achieve full occupancy in a positive manner? The following are some steps worth trying:

1. The home operator and staff should review their program for needed changes of services, staffing pattern, and physical/social milieu. Sometimes a qualified consultant can suggest new approaches.

2. A frank discussion of the home's difficulties with the placement agency may lead to a mutually acceptable plan to improve services and increase referrals.

3. Group homes serving more than one placement office should develop a systematic way of keeping them informed about the kind of youths sought by the home, the services provided, recent program changes, and the availability of vacant beds. Periodic reports on vacancies, periodic conferences with placement caseworkers, and the preparation of a descriptive brochure are examples of good communication.

4. Homes with high vacancy rates should explore the possibility of serving additional placement agencies, a larger geographic area, and/or a broader target group.

5. To avoid being stereotyped as serving a particular racial/ethnic group, homes should seek to maintain a racially balanced population and staff.

6. All homes, and particularly new ones, must have a reserve of capital that can tide them over periods of high vacancy rates.

Placement agencies should provide group homes with periodic written evaluations of their programs, offer facilities an opportunity to respond to negative findings, and inform placement caseworkers promptly when deficiencies have been corrected. No group home should be barred from receiving placements without due notice and the right to appeal to a higher administrative authority. Placement agencies also should limit the number of licensed group homes to avoid excess capacity.

Evaluating Potential Residents

To identify youths who are suitable for admission, the home's staff must predict whether they will benefit from its services, relate positively to staff members and fellow residents, and adapt to the relative independence of life in an open, community-based program. A youth's ability to function in the local public school also must be considered. There is no guarantee of certainty in that evaluation, and there are many misses and near-misses.

Group homes depend on background information furnished for each youth by the placement agency and interviews with the youngster and the parents. In addition, some homes require youths to spend a short trial period in the facility before they are admitted officially. Such sources usually are sufficient for experienced staffs to piece together a good picture of the youth's background, personality, and treatment needs. However, the information often has significant limitations. There may have been insufficient time to complete the file on an abused child in need of immediate placement. School districts, doctors, psychologists, and parents may be dilatory in forwarding necessary records. A youth's criminal record may be withheld to protect its confidentiality. Standard psychological and educational classifications are often too broad to predict a youth's responses in the facility. Without adequate information, admissions can be risky for both the home and the prospective resident.

The interview with the potential resident and, if available, the parents fills in some of the blanks in the youth's file. The youth's history, relationships with family members, attitudes, and character become somewhat clearer. Of course, a couple of hours of talk and observation can hardly be expected to reveal all characteristics. The interviewee is likely to be tense, guarded, and on his good behavior. The parents also are likely to feel uncomfortable. Even the home's staff members may, unconsciously, behave in a manner that differs from their everyday style.

Some directors and social workers prefer to meet parents and youths outside the facility in order to preserve confidentiality and avoid upsetting current residents. Others conduct interviews at the group home but only at hours when the residents are away at school. Still others do not hesitate to conduct interviews in the group home while the residents and paraprofessional staff are present.

If the interview goes well, parents and child are allowed to tour the facility and often are introduced to other staff members and residents. Some directors feel free to invite interviewees to share a meal and other activities with the current residents.

It is a good idea to spend some time talking separately to the youth and parents so that they will not be inhibited in their responses. That can be achieved informally by having one staff member take the potential resident aside for some activity while another worker remains with the parent(s).

Group homes that require youngsters to spend a trial period in the facility before a placement is consummated view such a period as an opportunity to evaluate prospective residents under realistic conditions of group life. Typically, a visit lasts from 3 to 5 days. Prior to that period child care workers must be briefed on the youngster's background so that they can observe and report his behavior in a meaningful way. Both weekends and weekdays should be included in the period, to give the youth a balanced picture of life in the home.

It is not a good idea to extend the trial period beyond several days. Superficially, it seems easy enough to say to an individual, "Try our program for a month. If you don't like it, you can return to your family or transfer to a different group home." In practice, however, there are usually administrative barriers and aggravating delays in transferring a resident. The process can be a sad or bitter experience for a youngster and can disrupt his schooling. The individual may exert a disruptive influence in the facility until a new placement can be arranged.

Trial periods have limitations. Conditions during the visit rarely duplicate normal life in the home. The visitor cannot attend school with the residents nor experience treatment services, such as psychotherapy, offered by the facility. Knowing that the visit is temporary, workers have no incentive to resolve serious communication and behavior problems.

The most difficult aspect of trial periods is the reaction of current residents. They may cooperate to make the period a positive experience or they may seize opportunities for hazing the visitor. Making up horror stories about the home's staff, giving misleading information about the program, and making outright threats are always possibilities if the young people are determined to dissuade a visitor from enrolling in the facility.

To gain the residents' cooperation the staff should discuss the objectives of trial periods with them and invite their suggestions on how to structure the visits, which room to assign to visitors, which recreation and work activities to demonstrate, and so on. Trustworthy youths may be asked to serve as a "buddy" or guide for a visitor. It is also helpful to arrange at least one group counseling session in which current residents and the visitor can share frankly their placement experiences and impressions.[1]

THE PERSPECTIVE OF PARENTS AND YOUTHS

Participation by Parents

Not only can parents demand a voice in the selection of a group home for their children, but their influence continues after a placement has been made. If dissatisfied with their child's progress or with conditions in the facility, the parents may demand the return of their child. There may be legal limits to the right of parents to revoke their consent, but in practice most child welfare agencies are reluctant to retain a youth in a group home against their will unless acting under an order of the court.

The cooperation of parents is helpful even in placements made pursuant to a court order. Suspicious and angry parents can express their dissatisfaction with a residential facility by lodging complaints about its services and by filing appeals with higher administrative and judicial authorities.

The attitudes of parents affect their child's adaptation in the home. Cooperative parents provide support and reassurance, visit and write at appropriate intervals, and participate in family counseling and other supportive services. Others exert a negative influence by feeding their child's anxieties, stimulating racial prejudice against fellow residents and staff, and refusing family services.

The parents' criteria for evaluating homes may be quite different from those of the caseworker. Although most are legitimately concerned about the

---

[1]The report of the Citizens Committee for Children of New York (1976, p. xiv) recommends that residents be permitted to meet with a prospective entrant and "discuss with him and with staff their daily program and his potential relationship to the group."

adequacy of the home's services, their child's safety, and their ability to keep in touch with the youngster, it is not uncommon for parents to apply other standards that are not in the child's interest. They may insist on a particular facility because it is more prestigious than others, refuse to have their child sent to an agency identified with mentally ill or retarded youths, or demand that their child be placed in a nearby or distant facility. Prejudiced parents may reject a group home on the basis of the racial/ethnic composition of its staff, residents, and neighborhood. Others are reluctant to see their child assigned to a home that requires their participation in family counseling because of indifference, fear of being labeled as abnormal or inadequate, anxiety about upsetting delicately balanced family relations, and a desire to maintain secrecy concerning extramarital relationships, illegal activities, and sources of income.

As human service professionals, group home staffs must deal with recalcitrant parents in a sympathetic, therapeutic way. For many parents the placement of a child is a traumatic experience, involving feelings of shame, guilt, and failure. A large proportion are single parents who have experienced considerable conflict and emotional upheaval in their own lives. Some are confused by the complex procedures required for a placement and lack the verbal skills needed to get answers to their questions. Low income makes it difficult to hire an attorney to protect their rights.

To gain the parents' cooperation the home's services and rules should be explained simply and honestly. Parents should receive a tour of the facility —no hidden dungeons here! They should be introduced to child care workers and the support staff. Sometimes worried parents may find a nonprofessional worker, such as the housekeeper, more reassuring than the professionals. Parents also appreciate periodic written reports about their child's activities and progress.

If parents will be required to participate in individual or group counseling, monthly meetings, or other treatment-related activities, those should be described. Where lack of transportation is a barrier to family visits and participation, the placement agency may be able to provide bus fare, with group home staff members picking the parents up at a transportation terminal or dropping them off on their way home.

The Youth's Perspective

Naturally, the youths who are the subjects of all of this activity have strong feelings and preferences in the choice of a placement site. A youngster who is adamantly opposed to a particular group home may complain continuously to the parents and caseworker, resist treatment services, and engage in disruptive behavior. He can make life difficult for staff members and other residents, or simply run away. Hirschbach (1973, p. 25) shares the view that the success of group home programs depends on involvement by youngsters who are "willing and conscious participants."

The young people have some very real concerns that deserve straightforward answers. They want to know: What kind of young people live here? What is the staff like? Will I be safe here? Will I find friends? Will I be separated from brothers and sisters who are also scheduled for placement? Who will my roommate be? Can I bring some special things from home? Can family members and friends visit me? Can I go home to visit them? How often? Is the program strict, difficult, scary? What will my new school be like? Can I continue guitar lessons? Keep my stamp collection?

Potential residents should be informed about all aspects of the home's program so that they will know what to expect and will not come to feel that they were persuaded to enter the home under false pretenses. At the initial interview they should receive a handbook summarizing the program, a copy of the weekly schedule, a list of the home's rules, and other descriptive material. If the parents have been well informed, they can also help to advise their child constructively.

There is always the possibility that youths may use inappropriate standards in evaluating a group home. Their consent may hinge on a wish to remain near old friends who are a negative influence, inaccurate rumors about the home's policies, prejudice against houseparents who are older or of another race, an instant "crush" on a staff member or resident, conflict with a current resident during the trial period, rejection of reasonable rules, and the availability of a special recreation activity such as horseback riding or bicycling. If such criteria are important to a youth, they should be discussed during the initial interview and trial period, if any.

DECIDING WHOM TO ADMIT

Since the director of a group home is ultimately responsible for the program, he should have the final word on whom to admit. The decision is usually made in consultation with the social worker. It is recommended that child care workers also participate in the decision process.

Should the residents of a home help decide which applicants should be admitted? Although it is not common, some reasonable arguments can be made for that practice. Current residents can make a visiting or newly admitted youth feel at home, safe, and accepted. Alternatively, they can inspire fear and resentment in someone they dislike. If the residents are consulted, it is possible that they will be supportive of new entrants. At least their attitudes can be exposed in group counseling sessions that contribute to their judgment and self-understanding.

The majority of home operators take a different view. They argue that many residents are too disturbed to make reasonable judgments. They may employ irrelevant criteria; e.g., whether the new youth is good at sports, owns popular records, or has an unpleasant body odor. An older resident may reject a potential competitor for leadership in the peer group; a young resident may favor the admission of someone younger and weaker than himself. Young people living in the home are unlikely to take a long-range view; they fail to perceive that interpersonal friction and symptoms of maladjustment might be eased gradually through therapy, counseling, and other services. For those reasons the opinion of residents is rarely solicited, and they are generally given only minimal information about youngsters referred to homes.

One objective of the home's admission policy is to achieve a balanced population that is conducive to good group work and maintenance of a therapeutic social milieu—two basic tools of a group home's program. The population must include a sufficient number of long-term and relatively well adjusted residents to exert a positive influence on newcomers and on seriously disturbed youths. Positively oriented youths should be sufficient in number to prevent the dominance of negative leaders in the peer group. The number of youths with difficult problems must not exceed the capabilities of the peer group and the staff to keep them under observation and control. Differences in age, size, intelligence, and experience must not be so great as to fragment the population and interfere with the therapeutic group process.

Within such limits, however, there is room in a balanced population for some higher-risk youths. A home may be able to care adequately for one youngster with a history of running away but not for larger numbers. Perhaps the home may be able to accept a youngster with a history of sexual deviation, one given to self-endangering actions, or one with a physical handicap.[2]

The nurturing of community support also must influence a home's admission policies. Because group homes are open facilities, usually located in residential neighborhoods, the behavior of their residents is of concern to the local population. Youths exhibiting bizarre or threatening behavior, incidents that bring the police frequently to the home, and racial prejudice may lead to the ostracism of residents by neighbors and schoolmates, and to community clamor to close the facility. Careful selection of residents and the maintenance of a racially integrated population and staff help a group home reconcile its need for community support with its human service objectives.

The home's decision to admit a youth may reflect a variety of other considerations, depending on its treatment concepts and administrative constraints. To cite just a few examples:

1. Some facilities automatically reject girls who are pregnant, have given birth to a child in the past, have had an abortion, or are in sexual relationships with boys. Other homes evaluate girls in such categories individually and admit them under appropriate circumstances.

2. Some homes accept only youths whose families own automobiles or

[2]The objective of a balanced population is suggested by Hirschbach, 1973, p. 27; and by Schwartz and Kaplan, 1961, p. 10.

can be reached by public transportation. That facilitates visits to and by the family and relieves the staff of the need to chauffeur the young people to and from their homes.

3. Some facilities exclude youths who have spent time in correctional facilities. They fear that such individuals might introduce the "reform school" culture to the home's residents, encouraging manipulation of the staff, evasion of rules, inappropriate relations in the peer group, and resistance to treatment services.

4. Homes serving several placement agencies may try to maintain a balance of residents from each to avoid overdependence on a single referral source.

5. The availability of special education classes in the local public school and the school's attitude toward problem youngsters may influence the number of learning-handicapped youths that a home can admit.

A final word: In trying to present a realistic description of the admissions process there is a danger that the problems have received undue emphasis, that the reader will be left with the impression that the system is random and ineffectual. Such an impression would be far from the mark. For all of their problems, child welfare agencies are able to arrange reasonably adequate residential care for thousands of troubled youths each year. Most of the young people are assigned to facilities that are appropriate for their needs. The interplay of the participants in each placement, coupled in many states with oversight by the courts or other independent authorities, provides checks and balances to minimize unwise decisions. And the cumbersome bureaucratic routines are lubricated by large numbers of conscientious and dedicated individuals who try to humanize the placement process.

Chapter 7

EVERYDAY LIFE IN A GROUP HOME

Six to 12 disturbed or maladjusted youngsters of disparate backgrounds living together in a community-based residence—neither institution nor family—under the care of several adults: How can everyday life in such circumstances be managed so as to exert a positive influence on their character, capabilities, and adaptation in society? That question preoccupies all operators of group homes.

The structure of everyday life is a crucial component of a home's treatment program. It can determine whether the social milieu is marked by cooperation or conflict; whether an air of order, comfort, and safety prevails; whether creativity and spontaneity are evoked or dampened; and whether the young people can concentrate on schoolwork and wholesome recreation activities. It strongly influences the attitudes, values, and coping skills that residents will acquire. Because of its importance, the structure of everyday life cannot be left to chance or ad hoc decision but must be included in planning each home's program.

This chapter discusses objectives, problems, and alternatives in managing everyday life. Five facets of everyday life will be covered: (a) the routines of a group home; (b) free time in group homes; (c) free time outside the home; (d) common issues in the supervision of everyday life; (e) dating.

The Routines of a Group Home

Daily routines in a group home serve a number of useful functions:

1. At the simplest level, routines make sure that necessary work gets done: getting off to school on time; doing homework; meeting appointments with the doctor, social worker, and psychologist; housecleaning; and the like.
2. Routines let residents know clearly, in advance, what the staff and fellow residents expect of them. That improves cooperation and reduces friction in the facility.
3. Routines structure daily activities in a way that affords reassurance and security to anxious youths.
4. By implementing a sharing of responsibilities around the home, routines contribute to the cohesion of the group.
5. The planning and management of routines provide opportunities for residents to participate in decision-making and to develop cooperative work habits.
6. Some routine tasks, such as housekeeping and cooking, offer opportunities for young people to acquire skills that are useful in adult life.

Despite such useful functions the routinization of everyday life can have negative effects if carried too far. Care must be taken to avoid the introduction of routines that serve no therapeutic purpose, stifle individuality, and contribute to unnecessary confrontations between staff and residents.

An example of a daily routine that invites frequent confrontation is the making up of beds in the morning. Some youths grumble about that chore, saying: "It's my room and I like it this way. An unmade bed is no health hazard. It doesn't hurt anybody. I never made my bed at home. It's a waste of time." There is some validity to those arguments. Staff members must decide whether the routine really serves a useful purpose that outweighs the accompanying irritation and confrontations.

In homes that limit routines to a necessary minimum they may arise spontaneously through the interaction of residents. The youths may fall into the habit of taking a walk together after dinner, viewing a specific television program at the same hour each evening, or baking cookies every Sunday night. The staff need not feel that it must structure every minute of daily living; the residents themselves may fill the gaps in a natural, comfortable way.

Essential routines of a group home are discussed below.

Morning: Waking Up, Taking Breakfast

The way the young people wake up in the morning affects their mood for the rest of the day. It is best to respect the residents' privacy and take account of their individual differences. Banging on doors, pulling off the covers, and ringing a loud bell are best left to the military. Instead, residents can depend on their alarm clocks to wake up on time, or the child care worker can turn on some quiet music or the news.

Like adults, youths vary in the amount of time they need to get ready in the morning. If they are permitted to wake up at their own best times, they can prepare for the day at their own pace, without scolding and arguing. With such flexibility there will not be a simultaneous rush to use the bathrooms. The only rule necessary is that all residents must be awake soon enough to prepare for the day properly and to get to school on time.

On days when there is no school and no early scheduled activities, sleeping to a later hour should be acceptable.

Many youths and adults get by habitually with minimal breakfasts, and efforts to compel them to eat more rarely succeed. The best the staff can do is to make available nutritious and tasty food every morning and ensure that the residents learn about good nutrition so that they can make intelligent choices in their diet.

Breakfasts are generally served informally, and the youngsters do not necessarily eat at the same time. Hot or dry cereal, scrambled eggs, rolls, juice, milk, fruit, and other simple items may be dished out cafeteria-style, or residents can simply put together their own breakfasts whenever they are ready.

Reference already has been made to the irritation that accompanies the making up of beds and straightening of rooms in the morning. As with other routines, indirect incentives are more effective than punishment in getting that chore done. If the bedrooms are attractively furnished and attractive bedspreads are issued, residents are likely to take pride in their rooms and keep them neat willingly. Posting the occupants' names outside their rooms also encourages neatness.

After School: The Afternoons

After the routines, confinement, and frustrations of the school day, teenagers need a period of relaxation and freedom. On return from school, residents should find a pleasant welcome from the staff and a tasty nourishing snack waiting for them. Some may wish to relate the day's events to the child care worker or simply to chat or ask advice. Others may prefer to go off on their own. This is no time for chores, scolding, lectures, or treatment services.

Generally, the afternoon is a good time to "unwind" in nonscheduled activities. Youngsters may prefer to play ball, go shopping, join neighborhood friends, jog, read, or listen to records. Some may have part-time jobs, such as delivering newspapers, at this time. Staff members should not try to structure activities but be available to any resident who seeks them out for information or conversation. They should be particularly alert to the need for companionship of isolated youngsters and newcomers.

Some important routine activities do intrude into the afternoon from time to time. Appointments for medical and dental care, psychotherapy, and individual counseling often fall unavoidably into the afternoon hours. If group meetings and discussions conducted by the home's staff are scheduled for the afternoon, they should be convened just before dinner; say, between 5:00 p.m. and 6:00 p.m., after the youths have had time to relax and "blow off steam." Indeed, a group discussion before dinner, if it does not evoke strong emotions, may help to cool active youngsters down for mealtime after strenuous afternoon play. However, intensive group counseling and group therapy are best left for after-dinner hours.

Dinner

Dinnertime provides opportunities to influence residents in ways that support the treatment program. Eating together helps build cohesion among the young people. This is a good time to observe their relationships and to provide unobtrusive "curbstone" counseling. There is an opportunity for staff members to model good manners and thoughtful conversation.

Dinners are usually prepared by the home's houseparent, cook (if one is employed), or by a child care shift worker. It is normally served around 6:00 p.m. In most group homes dinners are served family-style; i.e., the youngsters sit around one or two tables and either help themselves from bowls of food set out in advance or are doled out individual servings.

To build good relations a child care worker should always eat with the residents. The director and social worker also should share their dinner at frequent intervals.

Dinner need not be a drab, boring episode to which residents are dragged reluctantly and from which they rush off as quickly as possible. Meals should be varied, tasty, and marked by elements of graciousness. Tables should be set in an attractive manner. Occasional flowers and candles help to make this a special event. Youths might take turns at reading a poem of their choice, describe something good that happened that day, or share a moment of meditation before the meal begins.

Participation of the youths in planning, preparing, and serving dinner increases its therapeutic influence. The residents should be consulted in advance about the week's menu. Individuals should be encouraged to prepare dishes of which they are especially fond and to share them with the group. All of the residents might be assigned turns as "Assistant Cook of the Day," helping the adult cook while learning culinary skills. Setting and clearing the table, sweeping up, washing the dishes, and taking out the trash are also chores to be shared by everyone.

Despite the staff's best efforts, hamburgers and pizza from the local fast food establishment will probably be regarded as special treats by the young people on the cook's day off!

The Evening Hours

The hours between dinner and bedtime offer additional opportunities for constructive routines. However, time also should be reserved for individual activities and relaxation The home should be an inviting place to stay in the evening, rather than a place to escape from as soon as possible.

It is suggested that on weekdays the interval following dinner be designated as a study period. Depending on the ages and needs of the residents, the period might last for an hour or so, say between 6:30 p.m. and 7:30 p.m. During the study period residents can do their homework, read, and receive tutoring. That simple routine is likely to have a significant effect on how well the young people do at school and indirectly on their adaptation in the home's program.

Group counseling or psychotherapy sessions, usually conducted once or twice a week, may best fit into the daily schedule at the completion of the evening study period. At that point the youths have digested their dinners and are in a relatively quiet mood. At the end of the group session, around 8:30 p.m. or 9:00 p.m., there will still be time for recreation and relaxation before it is time to go to bed.

On most evenings the study period is simply followed by free time. For a couple of hours the youngsters are on their own—playing ball outdoors, shopping, visiting or hosting friends, watching television, playing indoor games, using the telephone, working on a school project, reading, and just chatting on the porch. It is also a time for personal chores: doing the laundry, ironing, mending, washing one's hair. Young people with special interests can use the time to practice their musical instruments, bake a cake, take sewing lessons, participate in choir practice, or engage in other projects.

Some group homes add variety to weekday routines by scheduling a group recreational outing in midweek. Such excursions, however, cut into sleeping and study hours, and leave youngsters worn out and overexcited at bedtime. Midweek outings play a more valuable role in the summer months, when the residents are out of school and the constructive use of leisure time presents special challenges.

Bedtime

There is a need for flexibility in bedtime routines. Everybody doesn't necessarily get sleepy at the same time. Youths of different ages differ in sleep requirements. Rules that are applicable to school days may be inappropriate for weekends and for the summer months. Some well-meant rules may simply be unenforceable; e.g., a taboo on whispering after the lights are turned out. A flexible approach avoids confrontations and makes this a relaxed, pleasant time in the home.

The following suggestions are worth considering in planning bedtime routines:

1. Routines should help the youngsters quiet down gradually from earlier vigorous activities. For example, residents should be required to be back in the home an hour before bedtime, to allow time to relax and prepare for bed. A pre-bedtime snack also helps residents slow down.

2. Residents should be in their bedrooms by a specific hour. However, they should be permitted to keep the lights on for perhaps a half hour longer while they continue to "unwind." Finally, a time is set for "lights out."

3. In homes whose residents vary widely in age, older residents may require a later bedtime than younger ones.

4. It is usually advisable to set a later bedtime for weekends and other periods when schools are closed.

5. A flexible policy minimizes irritation. In fact, some homes that have no scheduled bedtime or "lights out" rules report that their residents drift up to their rooms spontaneously around 10:00 p.m. and go quietly to bed. The best prescription for a good night's sleep is an active and interesting day, comfortable beds and rooms, and a sense of security in the facility.

6. Residents should participate in making rules for bedtime.

7. Some behavior problems at bedtime that seem like simple mischief may actually reflect underlying psychological disturbances. Such cases require understanding and treatment, rather than merely disciplinary action. For example, residents who are ashamed to admit that they are afraid of the dark or of recurring nightmares may misbehave to postpone bedtime. New residents may have trouble adjusting to shared bedrooms and new surroundings. Youngsters who wet their beds can be so ashamed that they may dread and resist bedtime. A youth may have trouble getting to sleep because he is afraid of hazing or practical jokes by other residents. Recent arrivals, younger and weaker residents, members of whatever racial group is in a minority in the home, and those who are regarded as deviants by the peer group experience the greatest risk of losing sleep.

8. It is helpful to assign a friendly, reliable roommate to a new or fearful resident. The troubled youth might be assigned the bedroom nearest the houseparent's own quarters. Night lights in the room and hallway are also helpful.

9. Employment of a night caretaker facilitates sound sleep for residents and live-in staff.

Weekends

The staff's objective is to make weekends relaxing and enjoyable while encouraging residents to engage in constructive activities and to meet obligations to their families, school, and the group home itself. Some routines are necessary to meet that objective.

Saturday morning is time for general housecleaning in many homes. Cleanup chores at that time do not interfere with schoolwork and other competing demands. The youngsters not only can get the job done quickly but they often have fun and develop a sense of "togetherness" as they work.

Assignment of cleanup tasks must be done in a manner that is perceived as fair by the residents. Cooperation is improved if residents participate in alloting chores and tasks are rotated. Generally, the cleanup should not take more than an hour; otherwise, flagging interest and mounting resentment may lead to discipline problems. Mayer (1958, p. 95) suggested that chores never exceed one half-hour for youths under fourteen years.

As always, positive incentives are more effective than compulsion in getting the work done. An effective incentive is the scheduling of a group treat at the end of the cleanup—something to look forward to but that can be postponed until all the young people have met their obligations. For example, the treat might be a special snack, followed by the weekly recreational outing. If the residents are motivated to complete the chores by the prospect of the snack and outing, they may apply peer pressure to "slackers" and lend a hand to those who fall behind in their assigned tasks.

Motivation also is heightened if the child care worker participates in the cleanup. After the cleanup is completed, praise and expressions of appreciation contribute to the group's readiness for next week's chores.

After the cleanup Saturday afternoons lend themselves to an enjoyable group outing. Having completed a week at school and other obligations, the young people look forward to an exciting change. Recreational outings are discussed in detail in Chapter 11.

In most group homes religion plays a minimal role in daily life. Few youths choose to attend church services. Involuntary participation and the propagation of religious beliefs are prohibited by placement agencies.

Religion can have therapeutic benefits for some troubled individuals. It can be a source of solace and support and can reinforce positive values and life-styles. Participation in a church helps a youth to make friends and in some cases to keep in touch with members of his own ethnic group. Church-sponsored social gatherings are a wholesome place to socialize with members of the opposite sex. Often churches conduct educational and recreational programs for young people.

It is suggested that group homes facilitate church participation by providing information about local churches, providing transportation, and leaving a place for attendance in the Sunday schedule. For residents who do not choose to attend church services the staff may wish to experiment with group discussions on Sunday mornings. Such sessions might encourage the youths to share their beliefs, goals, and philosophies. They can cover issues in ethics, values, human relations, or current events raised by the young people. Staff members or qualified adult volunteers serve as discussion leaders. Such discussions not only contribute to the development of the young people but they help to make Sunday a special day that breaks up the sameness of everyday life.

It is not advisable to structure the youngsters' weekend activities further unless there are compelling reasons to do so. They need free time to complete homework, participate in athletics, pursue a hobby, read, and watch their favorite television programs. They have personal chores to do. They need to spend some time with their friends or to take in a movie on a rainy afternoon. Weekends are also the best time for visits to and by the youngsters' families.

Some weekend routines may arise spontaneously within the group, however. For example, residents may tend to gather in the recreation room every Sunday afternoon to watch the football game. If the cook has Sunday off, canned soup and grilled cheese sandwiches fixed by the residents may become a group home tradition. Such spontaneous routines strengthen group cohesion and add an extra spark to everyday life.

FREE TIME IN GROUP HOMES

Staff members would like the youngsters to spend their free time doing constructive things and associating with good people. They would like free time to be enjoyable but safe and "respectable." However, the preferences of the staff are not necessarily the priorities of the residents. Young people seek adventure, freedom to experiment, and opportunities to test and assert their independence. Some have a need to get away from the daily give-and-take of the home from time to time. A home's policies on free time must take such a mixture of objectives into account.

Free-time activities are difficult to control. It is impossible to follow the youngsters about to learn their whereabouts. Prohibitions and exhortations have only limited effects. The use of free time must in large part be influenced nondirectively—a task that demands sensitivity and patience from the staff.

Free-time activities in the group home are covered in this section. Those that occur outside the facility are discussed in the following section.

Building a Milieu for Free Time

The extent to which the residents stay around the home during their free time depends on their age, their ability to find friends in the neighborhood, their feelings about the group home and fellow residents, recreational opportunities in the area, transportation facilities, and other factors. There are seasonal differences as well. Too much time spent in the facility may reflect underlying problems that require staff attention. The young people may be rejected in the neighborhood as mentally disturbed, delinquent, or as members of a racial minority. In high-income residential neighborhoods social and economic class differences may impair the residents' ability to make friends with youngsters living nearby.

Some things can be done to make the group home an inviting place in which to spend free time. Adequate space and materials should be made available for indoor and outdoor recreational activities. Staff members should not take advantage of youths spending free time in the facility by assigning them unscheduled chores. Nor should they nag them with unasked advice and criticism during that period. Mayer (1958, pp. 23–24) pointed out that adolescents often seek privacy, seclusion, and time for introspection. That need should be respected by the staff.

Television

Television sets are never absent from residential youth facilities, and they are put to heavy use. If a set is removed for repairs, panic ensues over how to fill the vacuum. Group homes cannot be blamed; the young people bring their addiction to television with them from the outside world. However, busy staff members must beware the temptation to use television as a pacifier, sedative, or substitute for therapeutic interaction with and among the young people.

There are television shows that contribute to the knowledge and maturity of young viewers. Many others are fun to watch and do nobody any harm. The concern of the group home is with programs that give a distorted picture of the justice system and paint a positive picture of immorality, violence, and other bad behavior. There are also practical problems that concern the staff: television may interfere with schoolwork and scheduled services or lead to disputes over which program to watch.

Simple rules, made in consultation with the residents, can keep television watching within bounds. It is a good idea, for example, to turn the television set off during study hours, mealtimes, and other scheduled activities. A fair system for deciding which programs to watch should be established with the residents' help. Residents should not be allowed to keep individual television sets in the facility, as they may lead to jealousy, theft, and excessive television watching.

Enriching Free Time in the Home

The residents' free time is their own, and the staff should not impose its own interests on them. However, no home can rest easily with a population that spends all of its free time watching silly television shows, bickering, and hanging around in listless idleness. It is reasonable for group homes to plan ways of enriching free periods.

One step that can be taken is to celebrate major holidays. Tree trimming and the exchange of gifts at Christmas, parties on Halloween and New Year's

Eve, and picnics on the Fourth of July add variety to everyday life and build group cohesion. Important occasions in the life of residents and staff members, such as birthdays, anniversaries, graduations, and departures also should be celebrated.

Youths who wish to pursue special interests should be encouraged and furnished with necessary materials. One may enjoy baking bread; another may enjoy gardening; a third, redecorating his room. From a therapeutic viewpoint, such activities are well worth the risk of messing up the kitchen, tracking mud on the porch, and spattering paint on the floor.

Child care workers who are good at arts or crafts should share their skills and serve as role models in the constructive use of free time. If they are lucky, they can stimulate some group projects, such as making a patchwork quilt or painting a mural on the garage wall.

Staff members can provide some discreet guidance at strategic times. Sensing a mood of depression and restlessness, for example, the skillful worker tries to get up a ball game or challenge some youths to a game of cards. Occasional surprises, like a picnic in lieu of a conventional dinner on a fine summer's evening, also brighten group life.

Visits by Friends

Visits from neighborhood and school friends should be encouraged unless there is reason to believe they are countertherapeutic for particular youths. Visiting helps residents make and keep friends who live in noninstitutionalized settings. The right to invite friends makes them feel that the facility is really their home. Youngsters who can entertain friends are likely to spend more time in the facility.

There are, of course, potential problems. Unless controlled, visitors may interfere with scheduled activities, study periods, or preparations for bedtime. If the home is in a bad neighborhood, the staff may find all kinds of disreputable people hanging around the house. Youths who have no visitors may feel isolated and rejected. Visitors of the opposite sex may become the subject of conflict. Thefts, licentious behavior, and the sharing of illegal drugs are possibilities. Rather than curtailing visits by friends, however, group homes should try to develop policies that make them a positive part of the home's social milieu.

The extent of visiting varies from home to home. The fewest visitors are probably found in facilities that are located in nonresidential neighborhoods, admit youths for only short periods, and draw residents from distant communities. If residents are bussed to distant schools, visits by school friends are curtailed by transportation problems. Homes for girls will probably be visited by both boy and girl friends; those serving boys seem mainly to have male visitors.

If the ages of the youngsters span a wide range, they cannot share their friends. In fact, older youths may be embarrassed to let their friends know that they live in a facility that also accommodates much younger children.

Neighborhood attitudes also affect visiting patterns. There are fewer visitors if local people are suspicious and prejudiced concerning the home's population.

Some suggestions can be offered for a constructive visiting policy:

1. All homes should include recreation areas where residents can entertain visiting friends.

2. To make them feel welcome and to establish a noninstitutional atmosphere, visitors may be invited to share snacks or a meal with the residents.

3. Ways to make visits by friends both enjoyable and constructive are a good topic for group discussions and group counseling.

4. The staff should be sensitive to the feelings of residents who receive few or no visitors. In a facility for girls, for example, a popular resident might be asked to invite extra boys so that a lonely resident can have companionship during visiting periods. One or two neighborhood youths who are well behaved and trustworthy may be allowed to drop in at the facility without requiring a specific invitation so that they might interact informally with residents who have no invited visitors.

5. If possible, residents should participate in making rules for visiting.

6. Permission to invite a visitor should be obtained in advance. First-time visitors should be introduced to the staff member on duty.

7. Disruptive visitors should be banned by the staff.

8. Normally, individual residents should not have more than one or two guests at a time. There should be no more than a reasonable number of visitors in the building at any time.

9. Visitors must remain in designated areas of the facility where they can be under staff observation. They might, for example, be restricted to the first floor. It is a good idea to declare the bedrooms off limits to visitors in order to protect the residents' property and avoid unacceptable behavior.

10. Visitors do not belong in the home during the study period, scheduled program activities, and the interval before bedtime.

11. It is not usually helpful to punish a resident by prohibiting visits from friends for more than several days. Because residents can associate with anyone they please when they are outside the facility, it is wise to allow their pals to visit in the home, where they can at least be observed and supervised.

Visits by Parents

Visits by parents play a positive role in the treatment of many residents. They reinforce ties with the family—to which most residents expect ultimately to return. They give the staff an opportunity to observe family relationships. The staff must be alert, however, to visits that impede a youth's progress.

In many group homes, parental visits are infrequent. There may have been intense friction between parents and children, exacerbated by child abuse and neglect. Poverty, lack of transportation, baby-sitting problems, and parental indifference keep visits to a minimum. If the facility serves local youths, they may prefer to visit their parents in their own nearby homes. Quite often, youngsters do not invite parents because they are embarrassed by their eccentric behavior or poor appearance.

The staff also may face the problem of a parent who wants to visit too often. Overprotective parents stir the anxieties of a youngster or make the child an object of ridicule by the peer group. The parents' concern should be the subject of sympathetic counseling.

It is necessary for group homes to maintain reasonable controls so that parental visits will not disrupt treatment plans. The following suggestions are likely to be helpful:

1. Parents should be required to give advance notice of their visits.

2. Visits should be made only during days and hours when they will not interfere with program activities.

3. If indicated by a youth's treatment plan, parents may be requested to refrain from visiting during the youth's first week or two of residence. Thereafter, if parent-child relations are tense, visits should be limited to short periods until the problem is alleviated.

4. If visits leave a youth depressed, frustrated, enraged, or confused, the parents should be asked to suspend them temporarily. This action requires consultation with the placement agency caseworker because it raises questions about the rights of children and parents.

5. The home's staff should counsel parents concerning their plans and expectations for each visit to ensure that they are realistic and supportive. The staff can suggest ways for the family to spend its time; e.g., playing cards, taking a walk, or having a snack together rather than sitting passively in a movie or watching television.

6. Parents should be asked not to give "junk" food or money as gifts to their children. Books, games, and records are good gifts. Only inexpensive items are permissible.

7. Residents also should be encouraged to develop realistic plans and expectations for parental visits.

8. It is important for the staff to know how parents and children interact. After each visit, therefore, a staff member should solicit the impressions of both parents and child.

FREE TIME OUTSIDE THE HOME

When not engaged in scheduled activities, residents can leave the facility to take a stroll, play ball, shop, and visit friends. They frequent local parks, the Y, movie theaters, and other recreation facilities. They go out on dates with young people of the opposite sex, are invited to parties, join clubs, and participate in extracurricular activities at school.

Contacts with the outside world help youngsters learn how to get along with peers of both sexes in normal life encounters. They teach self-reliance that will be needed for noninstitutionalized living. In addition, access to community resources provides opportunities to develop new interests and talents.

Activities outside the home also can create problems. Physical safety is a major concern—the possibility of injuries from traffic accidents, crime, and dangerous horseplay. Another potential problem is experimentation with illegal drugs and, for some disturbed youths, delinquent activities like shoplifting and fighting. Youths may spend too much money on trinkets and junk foods, and associate with "bad" people in disreputable places. Some youngsters may engage in promiscuous or other self-harming sexual relationships.

In a group home the staff is left with only nondirective methods of influencing residents when they are away from the facility. It tries to foster self-awareness, good judgment, wholesome interests, positive values, and inner controls that will cause the young people themselves to prefer to behave in a positive way. Some suggestions to achieve that objective are made below.

Leaving the Premises

Because the group home is responsible for its residents, it is reasonable to require them to report where they are going when leaving the premises, with whom they will be associating, and when they expect to return. In particular, residents who wish to leave the home's immediate neighborhood and those who expect to return later than usual from school or other activities should notify the staff in advance. Some facilities keep a sign-out book at the door.

Generally, the young people will not object to such rules. They are similar to rules found in most ordinary families. The youths appreciate staff concern, and some find that rules help them resist peer pressure to spend time in unpleasant activities. They are particularly likely to cooperate if they are consulted in making the rules; for example, in delineating the areas to which they can go without special permission and in setting the hours during which they may be absent from the home.

Rules about leaving the home should be applied in a flexible commonsense way. Youths would not normally need permission to go to a nearby store or ball field or to stroll around the block. Requirements should take account of the time of day, the age of the youngsters, and the length of time they expect to be absent. Homes in safe neighborhoods might take a more relaxed view than those in areas with a potential for danger.

Curfews

Virtually all group homes impose curfews—rules requiring the residents to be home by a specified night hour. The typical deadline is 9:00 p.m. or 10:00 p.m. on weekdays. A later hour is often set for weekends and the summer months. In general, residents should be in the facility about an hour before bedtime.

A reasonable amount of flexibility helps to gain acceptance for the curfew. For example, the curfew should take into account differences in the ages of the residents. If possible, it should be consistent with the hours observed by neighborhood friends. Later deadlines may be set by homes in "safe" neighborhoods than by those in questionable ones. To achieve safety in numbers, residents who go out during the evening in groups of two or more may be permitted to return later than those who go off on their own. The curfew also should be adjusted on nights when residents attend recreational events.

If the curfew is reasonable, there is usually no problem in securing compliance. The youths are generally glad to return home after an active day. The hour before bedtime can be turned into an experience they look forward to, when snacks are served and child care workers are available to talk about the day's activities.

Occasional violations of the curfew are, of course, bound to occur. Fortunately, the curfew is one of the few rules that are relatively simple to enforce. Violations are easily observed and penalties can be discussed in advance with the residents so that they will not be viewed as arbitrary or excessive.

Socializing with Friends

Residents do not always socialize with each other during their free time. Those who originated in the local area may prefer to spend their time with old neighborhood friends or siblings. Older residents often spend most of their free time with friends of the opposite sex. Schoolmates may become friends.

Some relationships exert a negative influence. Residents may cling to old companions who are likely to get them into trouble. They may develop ties to outsiders who are much older and more sophisticated than they are, who are sexually promiscuous or deviant, who belong to gangs or cults, or who are otherwise inappropriate. In such cases the staff must consider remedial action.

A simple prohibition on associating with a particular companion is unenforceable and arouses stubborn resistance. It rarely helps to exclaim: "If I ever catch you with Harry again, you'll lose your allowance." The youth will see to it that he will not be caught. Better to try a nondirective approach— facilitating constructive free time activities, providing opportunities to meet appropriate new friends, and exploring the functions and consequences of questionable relationships in counseling sessions.

A group home can influence the kind of people its residents will encounter by locating itself in a stable residential area. It can evaluate and monitor outside relationships by encouraging residents to invite friends to the group home. The staff also can arrange recreation activities in positive settings to enable residents to meet appropriate new friends. For example, YMCA/ YWCA and swim club memberships might be purchased for the young people. They might be enrolled in a day camp during the summer months. They can be encouraged to participate in volunteer programs, evening courses, and extracurricular activities at school. For young people whose outside contacts are seriously self-harming, psychotherapy may be indicated.

Visiting the Family

Many residents rarely visit their families. They harbor strong negative memories of parents and siblings. In some cases parents actively discourage visits. They may have remarried or have acquired a new extramarital partner. They may dread emotional scenes and doubt their ability to control their youngster.

Home visits should be encouraged when they strengthen family relationships and prepare the youth for eventual return to the family. However, the staff must be alert to potential harmful effects that might impede a youth's treatment. Conditions to watch for include the resident's return from a visit in an angry or dejected mood, evidence of beatings or physical injury, resumption of a relationship with former associates who exert a bad influence, and evidence of drug abuse, alcohol consumption, and inadequate sleep.

Following are a number of suggestions to help group homes formulate a home visit policy:

1. The frequency and duration of home visits should be an element in each resident's individual treatment plan.

2. A visit to the family during the first couple of weeks in residence is countertherapeutic if it is likely to increase homesickness, renew parental abuse, expose the youth to bad influences, or reduce the youth's commitment to the program. Later, the frequency of visits can be increased as the resident demonstrates a capacity to handle family experiences in a positive way. As the resident's termination date approaches, still more frequent visits ease the transition to the family setting.

3. The duration of home visits should reflect individual needs. Some youngsters do well on weekend and overnight visits; for others, a couple of hours is the indicated maximum.

4. Limits on visits to the family should be discussed in advance with the placement agency caseworker if possible. Agreement on a visiting policy will help the caseworker counsel the parents and respond to any complaints.

5. It is almost essential that parents receive some counseling from the home's staff to manage the visit in a way that minimizes tension, strengthens family relationships, and provides essential supervision of the visiting youngster. Counseling also dispels unrealistic apprehensions and expectations. In the absence of counseling, some parents plan a frenzy of continuous activity and large outlays of money. Others insist that their child accompany them to unloved relatives or boring activities. The counselor can suggest shared activities that are enjoyed by both parents and child while giving them opportunities to communicate in relaxed settings.

6. If the home's social worker is familiar with a family, he can offer more specific advice on relations during a visit. The worker might, for example, suggest that a parent refrain from belittling, threatening, or nagging the youth; praise a new hobby or progress at school; or take notice of the youth's smart new shoes and haircut. There may be advice on ways to ease tensions between the youth and step-parents or paramours. The role of grandparents, aunts, and other close relatives can be reviewed to eliminate negative influences. Parents who have been contributing to sibling rivalry can be shown ways of reducing friction between their children.

7. The question of discipline comes up often in parent counseling. Parents need advice about rules they can reasonably enforce during the visit, how to respond to challenging behavior, and what to do if their youngster insists on visiting old "hangouts" and contacting "bad" friends. Otherwise, they may revert to previous patterned responses such as physical punishment, giving up in despair, or breaking off communication. The counselor can suggest nonconfrontational ways of resolving family differences.

8. The residents, too, need to be counseled. "Visiting home" is a good topic for group counseling: what to expect, how to behave, how to plan satisfying use of the time, and how to cope with disappointment.

9. The staff should be in touch with both the parents and their child after each visit to learn what happened, how the participants felt and what improvements might be helpful.[1]

SOME COMMON ISSUES IN EVERYDAY LIFE

Not only major activities but the small events of everyday life present issues for group homes. Five secondary areas of everyday life that require pol-

[1]Useful approaches in managing visits are found in Adessa and Laatsch (1965, pp. 245–251).

icy decisions are discussed in this section: use of the telephone, smoking, pets, spending money, and the purchase of clothing.

Telephones

Residents need access to telephones for calls to and from parents, friends, caseworkers, shops, recreation facilities, and other outside contacts. Such open communication with the outside world sets group homes apart from intensive treatment facilities.

Ironically, that commonplace instrument is a major source of friction in group homes—as it often is in a normal family setting. Residents accuse each other of monopolizing the phone. They run up bills for nonessential long distance calls. Occasionally, a youth may be accused of improperly charging long-distance calls to an outside number or of making prank calls. A resident's friends may think it is fun to call their buddy at very late hours. Such problems indicate a need to regulate use of the telephone. Some suggestions are offered below:

1. To enlist their cooperation, residents should participate in making rules governing telephone use.

2. Except in unusual circumstances, the staff should not screen incoming personal calls to weed out those that it believes to be countertherapeutic. Nor does it do much good to forbid a resident to telephone a particular individual. Aside from the potential violation of the residents' rights implied by such measures, the ban can easily be evaded by walking to the nearest public phone.

3. If undesirable telephone contacts must be curtailed, it is advisable to consult the placement agency caseworker. He may be able to influence family members or other disruptive callers.

4. It is helpful to install both a coin-operated phone and a residential-type phone in the home. The pay phone is to be used for outgoing personal calls for which residents pay from their personal funds. The residential-type telephone can be used for incoming calls, thus reducing competition for time at the pay phone. In addition, the residential instrument can be used by the youths to make program-related calls, free of charge. Such free calls include contacts with placement agency caseworkers, parents (once or twice a week), doctors, schools, therapists, and so on.

5. The duration of calls should be limited to give all residents a chance at the phone. For example, residents might agree that a maximum of 10 minutes at the phone is reasonable if others are waiting to use it.

6. Reasonable hours for phone use should be set. Calls should not be made or accepted during dinner, the study period, or group counseling sessions. Nor should calls be accepted after bedtime.

7. Authorization to make or receive calls should not be suspended as a punishment. Residents have a right to receive and send communications.

8. There are several nondirective ways to influence use of the phone. Individual counseling makes residents aware of inconsiderate and unwise practices. Reasonable limits on the amount of the regular weekly allowance paid to residents give them a financial incentive to cut down outgoing calls. The peer group can be guided to consider the harmful or unfair use of the telephone, and to influence offending youths in positive directions.

Smoking

Smoking is very common among group home residents. Naturally, staff members are concerned about the health of the smokers and the money spent to buy cigarettes. They are concerned about complaints from parents and community people.

Group homes have tried a variety of ways to control smoking, from outright prohibition to material incentives. None is fully effective. Many homes do not try to control smoking directly. They accept the idea that it is a common practice among teenagers and that it may even relieve tensions a bit. In the light of the more pressing psychological problems of the residents, staff members in some facilities do not believe that smoking is a sufficiently urgent issue to justify the friction that would emerge if the practice were restricted. It is therapeutic to minimize conflict over peripheral issues while concentrating on more serious adjustment problems.

Approaches for coping with the smoking problem vary with the age of the residents and placement agency requirements. However, there are several guidelines that can be helpful in most situations..

1. An outright ban on smoking or a limit on the number of cigarettes per day is not enforceable and merely contributes to friction between staff and residents.

2. Residents should be provided with factual information on the harmful effects of smoking.

3. Staff members should try to serve as role models by abstaining from tobacco. Easier said than done!

4. Parents should be advised not to nag or threaten their children about smoking but to let the staff work on the problem nondirectively and gradually. Parents should be urged to refrain from giving cigarettes as gifts to their children. Nor should they give their children extra money that might be used to purchase cigarettes.

5. A group home should not provide cigarettes for residents. Smokers should buy them with their personal funds to compel them to make a choice between smoking and spending their money on other activities. Furthermore, money allowances given to residents by the home should not be so large as to make the choice an easy one.

6. The staff should not use cigarettes as a reward, nor a prohibition on smoking as a punishment. The former practice encourages smoking, and the latter is easily evaded—often with the help of fellow residents.

7. Residents should participate in making reasonable rules governing smoking. Examples of such rules are restriction of smoking to areas of the home where it is not a fire hazard nor a source of discomfort to others, and a prohibition on smoking in bedrooms after "lights out."

8. Establishing more restrictive smoking rules for younger than for older youths is not recommended. Apart from being nonenforceable, the practice confirms younger residents in the impression that heavier smoking is a grown-up and sophisticated activity—something worthwhile to look forward to.

9. Some facilities prohibit the borrowing or lending of cigarettes. That is done to reduce bickering, to prevent bullies from extorting cigarettes from weaker youngsters, and to prevent the peer group from furnishing cigarettes to youths whose allowances have been docked as punishment for some infraction. Probably such prohibitions are nonenforceable in a group home setting. About all the staff can do is to advise residents not to lend cigarettes, to bring up the problem in counseling, and to warn the youths that the staff will not help them recover cigarettes from delinquent borrowers.

Pets

Generally, residents should not be allowed to have their own cats or dogs in the home. Disturbed youngsters cannot be depended on to give the animals proper care. The animals may trigger phobias among some residents and be subjected to abuse by others. In a goodly number of homes live-in child care workers have dogs or cats that may serve a positive function as mascots, but even they can distress individual youngsters.

Personal Funds of Residents

All group homes make available to residents a reasonable amount of money that they can spend on their own. The availability of personal funds challenges the youths to manage financial resources in a responsible way, rather than relying passively on adults to meet their needs. They have an opportunity to test their values as they weigh alternative expenditures, and to develop good judgment and self-discipline.

Residents use their personal funds to buy extra clothing, cosmetics, records, snacks, cigarettes, gifts, and decorations. They spend money on movies, bowling, magazines, and video games. In some cases substantial sums are available to them because allowances paid by the home may be supplemented by job earnings and gifts from family members.

Allowances should cover unavoidable expenses, such as school lunches and carfare, and leave a surplus to be spent at the youth's own discretion. The surplus should be large enough to encourage saving for long-term objectives and to enable a youth to fit into neighborhood and school peer groups. The amount of the allowance varies with the age of the residents, their expenses, and their opportunities to earn extra money from part-time employment.

Group homes that pay bonuses or impose fines as a means of influencing the behavior of residents also must take those into account in determining allowances.

Like ordinary parents, staff members are concerned about how personal funds are spent. Some youths tend to squander money on useless trinkets, trashy magazines, or pinball machines. An overweight youth may spend all of his money on junk food. Another resident may become involved in gambling, from pitching pennies to shooting craps with unsavory acquaintances. In extreme cases personal funds may be used to buy illegal or dangerous items such as drugs, alcohol, or even weapons.

Money can become a self-harming means of gaining affection or acceptance from other people. A resident may buy expensive gifts to gain the favor of a girl or boy friend. Another may give all of his money to an exploitative family member. A third may waste money on long-distance phone calls to unresponsive relatives.

The availability of personal funds leads sometimes to conflict between residents. There are spats about borrowing or lending money. Large amounts of money lying about and costly purchases coveted by other residents invite thefts in a facility.

Prohibitions and warnings are not likely to be effective in controlling expenditures outside the home. There are, however, nondirective ways to influence use of personal funds. It is most important to set the amount of the allowance at a level that compels the young people to weigh alternative expenditures with great care. To sustain that pressure, parents should be asked to refrain from giving their children money or expensive gifts. To encourage saving, residents should be helped to start individual bank accounts. Those with earnings from outside employment should be required to bank a reasonable proportion of their wages. Money management should be a topic for group discussions and counseling sessions. Finally, staff members should serve as role models. The worker who turns up in $200 cowboy boots or flashy jewelry may be admired by the residents, but he is not setting a good example.

Buying Clothing

The staff must ensure that money allocated for clothing by placement agencies is used efficiently and can be accounted for. As a result, a home is tempted to insist that all clothing be purchased at a particular store because it offers discounts, credit, and return privileges. The same type of jacket or blue jeans may be purchased for all residents because it happens to be on sale one day. Residents may be shepherded simultaneously to a store because it is inconvenient to accompany them to scattered stores of their choice at different times.

Excessive restrictions on the individual selection of clothing, however, is not consistent with treatment objectives. They deprive the young people of opportunities to learn how to manage their money. Differences in the tastes of staff and teenagers breed unnecessary confrontations. Uniformity in the clothing purchased for residents creates an institutional atmosphere and enables neighborhood people to identify them as group home youths. Therefore, it is best to allow residents reasonable leeway in selecting their own clothing. Some practical suggestions for implementing that policy follow:

1. "Intelligent shopping" should be a topic for group discussions and group counseling.

2. Rules for the use of group home funds to purchase clothing should be made in consultation with the residents.

3. Where possible, staff members should serve as consultants, rather than as decision-makers, in selecting clothing. They can furnish information on quality, materials, style, comparative costs, and serviceability—without forcing their opinion on the youngsters.

4. Staff members should serve as role models by wearing appropriate clothing.

5. The home may wish to designate specific stores where older residents can draw on their clothing allowance to buy clothing on their own, subject to later approval by staff members. By prearrangement, such stores should agree to charge the sales to the home's account and to permit the return and/or exchange of purchases that are found to be inappropriate.

6. Youths who dress in a bizarre or indecent fashion may be expressing, through their choice of apparel, underlying feelings such as resentment of adult authority, a desperate need to gain status in the peer group, a wish to be transferred from the group home, sexual deviation, or a drift from situational realities. The home's staff should be alert to such signals, which may respond to counseling or psychotherapy.

DATING

Dating is a common free-time activity of teenagers in group homes, as it is among other teenagers. Relationships vary in intimacy, from an occasional walk around the block to long-term commitments. Sexual activity is not uncommon. Dating reflects the normal emergence of strong sexual feelings in adolescence and is an essential stage in the transition to adulthood.

Frequently, dating is a source of anxiety to staff members. They are concerned about the home's reputation in the community and about complaints from the parents of residents involved in sexual or interracial liaisons. They fear harmful effects on the morals and character of the young people. Prostitution, homosexuality, promiscuity, venereal disease, pregnancies, and secret abortions are potential problems.

Life in a residential care setting can be a negative factor. Youths who have spent time in unisex institutions before coming to a group home have had only limited opportunities for normal relations with young people of the opposite sex. Once in a group home, the chances of making outside friends are reduced by prejudice among school and neighborhood peers. Peer group pressures in residential facilities can be countertherapeutic: residents may accord high status to youths who are sexually promiscuous or exploitative. In a home for girls, residents may gain prestige if they date older men or if they have had an aborted pregnancy.

Group homes have a responsibility for strengthening the capacity of their teenage residents to form positive relationships with the opposite sex. Accepting pubescence, sexual experimentation, and the drive to form sexual relationships as a normal stage of growing up, staff members can influence those developments by providing reliable information, fostering constructive attitudes, and facilitating wholesome social contacts. Some specific suggestions follow:

1. Staff members should become well informed about adolescent sexuality and develop awareness about their own sexual feelings and attitudes to feel comfortable about discussing boy-girl relations with the residents.

2. The staff must accept the youngster's dating and sexual exploration as normal adolescent behavior. Taboos on the subject or efforts to make residents feel ashamed will simply keep them from discussing their feelings and activities frankly and from asking for reliable information and advice.

3. Human sexuality and dating should be a subject for both group and individual counseling. Residents should be encouraged to discuss their attitudes, feelings, expectations, and dating experiences. To be avoided are lectures that simply condemn or threaten the youngsters or that do not take into account the considerable "street knowledge" about sex that many of them have accumulated.

4. Group homes should facilitate activities through which residents can meet members of the opposite sex under wholesome and safe conditions. For example, attendance at school dances can be encouraged by financing the purchase of proper "party clothes," providing transportation to and from the dance, and arranging dancing lessons for youths who lack that important social skill. The staff may be able to identify similar social events sponsored by the Y, churches, and community recreation departments.

5. Friends of the opposite sex should be welcome in the group home at appropriate hours under staff supervision. Under some circumstances it is helpful to allow the residents to plan parties to which boy and girl friends may be invited.

6. A few simple rules are necessary. Outsiders should be introduced to an adult caretaker when they first call for their date or visit the facility. Residents leaving on dates must tell a child care worker where they plan to go and whether they have arranged safe return transportation. Reasonable curfews are necessary to make sure the young people are home at a safe hour.

Such rules are generally accepted by residents, especially if they are consulted in formulating them and feel that the rules have been issued for their own benefit rather than for the convenience of the staff. Excessively rigid rules, however, can be counterproductive. In an open community-based facility they can be evaded as soon as a youth turns the corner, and they give rise to resentment and confrontations.

7. In some cases it is necessary to provide counseling for parents who are exerting a negative influence.

8. If the dating activity of a resident continues to follow self-harming patterns, the staff must take stronger corrective action, including steps to transfer the resident to a more structured institutional setting. Left unchecked, promiscuity, prostitution, association with persons of bad character, victimization, exploitation, and potential health problems can lead to serious psychological and physical harm.

Chapter 8

THERAPEUTIC HUMAN RELATIONS IN A GROUP HOME

Psychotherapy, counseling, and education are essential components of a group home's program, but it is mainly through the everyday interaction of staff and youngsters that homes exert their greatest influence on the character of their residents. Ordinary day-to-day relations form the social milieu in which the young people must find acceptance, security, relaxation, stimulation, and support for self-enhancing behavior. A therapeutic social milieu is the goal of all group homes. It does not occur by accident but requires careful planning and continuous nurturing.

Since child care workers share the most intimate and continuous contact with the youngsters, this chapter focuses mainly on ways in which they can influence the social milieu. The professional staff, however, must also be fully aware of human relations in the facility if they are to evaluate the residents and guide the child care workers.

This chapter suggests some principles for managing human relations in group homes. It discusses the interaction of staff members and residents and, equally important, relations among the residents themselves.

Everyday Interaction between Staff and Residents

There can be no rigid formula for staff-resident relations. Flexibility is essential to take account of the wide differences in "styles" found among competent workers. All child care workers must be pleasant, stable, and caring people. But whether they bustle about, talking, laughing, singing, and touching everybody in sight, or work quietly, communicating with no more than a well-chosen word, a twinkle of the eye, or an arching of an eyebrow must reflect each worker's individual personality.

Some general guidelines for staff members can be suggested, however, subject to their adaptation to conditions in each home.

Physical Security

Physical security is a prerequisite of a therapeutic social milieu. Both staff and residents must feel safe from physical harm if good human relations are to emerge. Staff members should be alert to prevent the entry of unauthorized persons. Within the home the staff must try to control bullying and hazing, even when victims do not report incidents. The assignment of compatible youths as roommates contributes to a sense of physical security. So does employment of a night caretaker.

Psychological Security for New Residents

It is sometimes hard to remember that even a big, tough-talking youth who arrives at a residential facility can really feel anxious, insecure, and rejected by family and society. Staff members should devote time to welcoming newcomers and to creating a good first impression of the home. Paperwork and chores can wait. Reassuring introductions and a cup of hot chocolate with some of the other inhabitants are more timely at this point.

The room assigned to the new resident should be clean and inviting. It is all right to allow him to put up a poster or two and to do some minor redecorating to emphasize that "This room is mine. I belong here."

During the first couple of weeks, lighter chores, rather than the most onerous, should be assigned to new residents. Imposition of unpleasant chores as a kind of initiation may stir resentment, homesickness, and even thoughts of running away.

Some youths fear that they will not be allowed to remain very long. That fear is not unrealistic; they may have been shuffled about on short notice by parents, guardians, and placement agencies in the past. It is possible that an anxious youth may behave in a manner that invites ejection in anticipation of an early transfer from the group home. The staff can reduce anxiety by counseling new residents and making clear their status and rights while in residential care.

New residents should be informed about their obligations in the program—what the staff expects of them and the kinds of activities they will encounter. Particular care is needed in informing youngsters who have language difficulties, including foreign-born youths who do not speak or understand English well and individuals who have impaired hearing or speech.

For examples of how cultural differences may affect a child's perceptions of foster care, see Adler (1985) and Baker (1982).

"Primary Group" Relations

Residents must regard child care workers as deeply significant figures in their lives if they are to exert a strong influence on the way the youths feel, think, and behave. Only if there is a "primary group" relationship with a substantial degree of personalized and emotion-supported contact is the resident likely to seek the worker's approval and accept him as a role model. Remarks like "Who cares what you think?" or "What makes you such a big shot?" imply that the resident does not consider the child care worker to be a deeply significant figure in his life.

There are some simple things that help child care workers build a primary group relationship with each resident:

1. Workers should spend time with individual youngsters and demonstrate their interest in what each is doing at school and during free time. Joining a game of cards or basketball, inviting a shy youth for a walk around the block, and chatting on the porch help to penetrate the barriers to a personal relationship. It is particularly important to spend extra time with newcomers and "isolates."

2. Workers can show their personal interest by small helpful actions: shortening a girl's skirt, preparing a youth's favorite dish, sewing a costume for a Halloween party, sharing an avocational skill, or providing materials for a school project.

3. It helps to show each youngster that he is liked and valued. Workers should find opportunities to praise something about each resident. A good idea is a periodic awards ceremony at which *every* resident receives a token gift for progress in at least one area—even if it is only for holding one's voice down or combing one's hair every morning.

4. Staff members should make themselves available if sought out by youngsters looking for reassurance, consolation, and other support. Responses like "I'm busy. See me tomorrow" or "You are always complaining" do not present a caring image. An "arm around the shoulder" is still potent psychological medicine.

5. Shift workers, who come on and off duty on a rotating schedule, have greater difficulty in developing intimate ties with residents than do round-the-clock houseparents. To build primary relationships, it may be helpful to designate each shift worker as a "counselor" for specific youngsters, in addition to their overall responsibilities.

"Curbstone" Counseling

Although child care workers are not expected to be professional counselors, they provide informal counseling in the course of everyday interaction. Such "curbstone" counseling exerts a substantial influence.

Workers should learn to be good listeners. Persons who do most of the talking or are too ready with opinions, advice, and exhortation are not providing sensitive counseling. Instead, the objective is to serve as a supportive presence in which young persons can feel comfortable about describing their experiences, needs, and feelings; "thinking out loud" about their responses to people and situations; and considering ways to resolve their problems.

It is recommended that staff members try "active listening." In that technique one neither listens idly nor rushes to advise, persuade, or preach. Instead the worker tries to identify the feelings that underlie the content of the youngster's conversation. At appropriate points the worker offers his impression of what those feelings are. The worker might say, for example, "You seem to be very angry about that incident," or "I gather that you are worried about your new teacher," or "You really are crazy about your new girl friend, aren't you?" The youth may affirm or correct the worker's impression and is likely to continue the conversation with additional information about the situation.

This simple process of "feeding back" interpretations of what the youngster seems to be feeling provides evidence of the worker's concern and desire to understand. It helps the youth clarify and evaluate his feelings. It seems to divert the counselee from nonproductive mulling over anxieties and grievances to consideration of realistic solutions. With a little practice, active listening can be a potent "curbstone" counseling tool. The technique of active listening is described thoroughly in Gordon (1970).

Open Lines of Communication

It is not uncommon to observe youths responding to adult caretakers in a guarded, secretive manner. "Where have you been?" "Just around." "What have you been doing?" "Oh, nothing." For child care workers to play a therapeutic role, residents must trust them sufficiently to permit open, two-way communication.

Workers should be honest with the young people. Justifying a prohibition on smoking "pot," it is better to refer to legal requirements and potential damage to the home's reputation than to overstress the drug's unproven effects on health. If self-incriminating information offered by a youth cannot be kept confidential, the worker should inform the youth in advance, if possible.

Communication can be blocked or distorted by anger, anxiety, fatigue, and other emotional distress. It is best, therefore, to choose a time for communication when the participants are not in the grip of their emotions.

When oral communication is blocked by anger or anxiety, a youngster can sometimes express his grievances and feelings by writing a letter to a staff member. The process of writing almost compels the youth to evaluate the situation in a more objective manner, to take account of the viewpoints of other participants, and to suggest a solution. Staff members, too, can use written communications to present their views to residents who shut out verbal communication.

Group counseling enhances communication by enlisting the support of the peer group in helping its members express and evaluate their feelings and needs.

Respect for Individuality

Youngsters respond positively to staff members who respect their individuality and allow them a reasonable degree of autonomy. The young people will not accuse such workers of being "picky" and they will not be preoccupied with evading their supervision.

Staff members should listen to differences of opinion and avoid authoritarian decisions where possible. Compromise solutions in which no one is the "winner" or "loser" contribute to good relations and teach a positive social skill to the youngsters.

In recognition of differences in tastes, living habits, and interests, a measure of choice should be built into everyday activities. For example, the young people may be permitted to select some of their own clothes, visit with friends or stay home instead of attending a concert with the group, and add personal touches to their own rooms. There usually is no reason to create a confrontation if a resident prefers to spend the evening alone, skip a meal, or choose a distinctive hairstyle.

The youngsters' privacy should be respected. Unless there are compelling reasons, one should never read their private correspondence nor go through their lockers and drawers. Room searches should be made only in emergencies and only with the knowledge of the residents. Occupants of an open community-based facility can easily conceal contraband off the premises if they feel that the staff may secretly invade their privacy at any time.

Respect for individuality poses difficult dilemmas when residents demand the right to pursue their own values and tastes even though those are defined as self-harming by the staff. A youth may insist on smoking heavily or sporting a bizarre hairstyle. Another may associate with much older friends. Still another may be sexually active at the age of fifteen. In such situations efforts to force a change result in rage, resentment, and evasion. Probably the youth's parents had encountered the same response.

Where questionable values and tastes pose no immediate threat of irremediable damage to a youth and do not adversely affect other people, it seems best to rely on nondirective methods of inducing change over a period of time. That approach will test the staff's patience and professionalism, but it can lead to permanent improvement in the long run as a youth responds to counseling, psychotherapy, peer pressure, positive incentives, new role models, and new opportunities to achieve status and self-realization. Nor is that an example of permissiveness but a realistic recognition of the limits surrounding discipline in an open, community-based program.

Consistency

Consistency in everyday interaction with the residents contributes to their feelings of security and improves relations with staff members. Several aspects can be distinguished. Consistency in relations with a single youth provides him with a clear picture of what the staff expects and how it will respond. There are no mixed signals that might create anxiety or tempt the youth to test the staff. Consistency in dealing with the residents as a group prevents jealousy and charges of favoritism among the youths. There also must be consistency among staff members in implementing treatment plans. Otherwise, differences of opinion between professional and paraprofessional workers and among child care workers employed on a shift basis cause residents to lose respect for the staff and to take advantage of staff differences in a manipulative way. Finally, there should be consistency between the behavior of staff members and the advice they give to residents. Staff members who do not "practice what they preach" cannot influence the young people in positive directions.

Need for Controls

Because the preceding pages have focused on nonauthoritarian ways of relating to group home residents, it is important to stress that the success of such methods depends on an underpinning of structured controls. Sensible limits on their behavior are therapeutic for troubled young people, even though they often rail against them. Certain controls are required by placement agencies, schools, and probation departments that share child care responsibilities with the home.

Nondirective techniques by themselves are not appropriate for coping with behavior that is illegal, dangerous, or a persistent violation of the rights of others. In such cases clear regulations and sanctions are necessary safeguards. Repeated violations of the curfew, repeated use of dangerous and illegal drugs in the home, bullying or stealing from fellow residents, refusal to cooperate in the program, violence against staff members, criminal activities outside the facility—these require a firm reaction by the staff.

ENCOURAGING SUPPORTIVE PEER GROUP RELATIONS

The peer group exerts a major influence on the behavior of all teenagers. It is particularly powerful in residential care facilities. The group can exert a positive therapeutic force or, under negative conditions, can actually undermine a home's program.

As residents interact in the home over a period of time, the expectations and evaluations of other members of the group deeply influence their behavior and attitudes. Individuals assume distinctive statuses and roles in the group. Informal leaders emerge—youths who set standards and initiate activities for other residents and are accorded prestige by them. Folkways—informal rules on how to dress, talk, and behave—appear spontaneously. Within the peer group, individuals select each other for special relationships, friendly or hostile, and form pairs, cliques, and other subgroups. Inevitably, the group takes on a life of its own that bears only an uneasy relation to the planned program of the home.

To be a positive force the standards of behavior approved by the peer group must be consistent with the objectives of the home. The group must value conscientious schoolwork, wholesome leisure-time activities, cooperation in everyday commitments, and efforts to progress in the home's program. It must accept as legitimate the authority of the staff. Newcomers and deviants must be accepted and supported. Group leaders must not derogate the staff, program services, and incentives offered for positive behavior.

At the opposite extreme, a peer group or its subdivisions exert a counter-therapeutic influence when they disparage the work ethic, conscientious schoolwork, and conformity to the rules of the home. The group may delight in provoking and testing staff members, particularly inexperienced or rigid individuals. New residents may be isolated and hazed. Group leaders may derive prestige from harmful behavior, risk taking, and sabotage.

Harmful peer relations have been particularly damaging in larger, closed institutions for troubled young people. For example, in his classic study, *Cottage Six*, Polsky (1962) describes the emergence of a "deviant sub-culture" that rejected the institution's standards for positive behavior. Instead, the group valued toughness, cunning, excitement, and nonconformity with the rules. It accorded prestige to aggressive youths and tried to undermine the authority of child care workers.

Group homes are more fortunate. It is one of their major advantages that peer relations are generally much more positive than in larger, closed facilities. In New Jersey homes surveyed by the writer, for example, serious fights among residents were rare. The peer group was likely to withhold support from youths engaging in persistent truancy, drug abuse, hazing, and other harmful activities. Most newcomers developed supportive relations with at least a few residents in a short time. Relations between racial/ethnic groups were relatively smooth. Informal leaders within the peer group usually had a positive orientation. Even the common taboos against tattling to the staff seemed to be less stringent than in larger institutions. And there were few reports of concerted efforts to wear down or compel the resignation of staff members.[1]

Some reasons that peer groups in group homes tend to have a relatively positive orientation can be suggested. To begin with, most homes screen and reject unsuitable candidates for admission. Disruptive residents, including

---

[1]In one such incident, a live-in child care worker was assailed by a shower of shoes hurled at her bedroom door in the middle of the night. An identical incident in a closed institution is reported in Henry (1972, p. 126).

those occupying positions of leadership in the peer group, can be expelled. The small size of group homes enables the staff to provide close supervision and security, and intensive group work offers opportunities for the youths to express their feelings and to influence the home's activities in an open, direct manner.

In group homes the peer group cannot achieve the all-pervasive influence over the thought and behavior of its members that is found in closed institutions. Residents are not totally dependent for support and companionship on fellow inhabitants of the home. They interact with outside friends in school and neighborhood. They belong to clubs, marching bands, and other organizations, hold part-time jobs, and "hang around" local recreational sites. Living in an open setting, they are free to go off on their own—to take a course at night school, to date a member of the opposite sex, to visit their families and friends in their home areas, or just to wander alone. For considerable spans of time, individuals cannot be observed by the other inhabitants of the home. As a result, evaluation and acceptance by fellow residents are not a totally dominating force, and the emergence of a distinctive peer group subculture in the home is almost impossible.

To understand and guide group relations the staff must be aware of differences in the status and relationships that emerge among group members. Those may include leaders who surface spontaneously in the group, aspirants to leadership, aggressive youths who are feared but not regarded voluntarily as leaders, and followers. There are voluntary isolates who spend most of their leisure time alone or with nongroup members. Such youths may be busy with an outside job or avocation, have a steady girl/boy friend, or pursue special interests because they are older or younger than the other residents. There are also involuntary isolates who are ostracized because of their eccentricity, aggressiveness, oversensitivity, repellent appearance, or other traits. Young people who are very withdrawn as a symptom of a deeper psychological disturbance also may be considered involuntary isolates. Common are scapegoats—youths who are persecuted and held in contempt by the others. Their status may reflect small size, timidity, oversensitivity, or toadying to curry favor. Sometimes a near-retarded youngster is "picked on."

Within the group may be found dyads—pairs of youngsters who spend time together and have developed very close bonds. Sometimes they are siblings. In a self-harming variation of paired relations, one partner may have an emotional "crush" on the other, which may or may not be reciprocated. There are also larger subgroups of youths with a special affinity for each other. Such cliques may be based on racial or ethnic identity, similar ages, previous acquaintance, or common interests. Youths who are popular or sexually sophisticated may form separate cliques. So may young people who come from the same hometown, who attend the same public school, or who have shared the experience of a detention shelter.[2]

[2]Various authorities have identified typical roles played by youths in residential facilities. Their observations have, however, generally been based on large closed institu-

Such statuses and relationships undergo continuous change. New young-sters arrive and others leave. The positions of individuals are altered as they age or develop under the influence of counseling or therapy. New leaders emerge and old ones fade. A scapegoat may be replaced by a younger resi-dent or rise in status after his tormenters leave the home. A disruptive resi-dent becomes an isolate after accepting a part-time job outside the home. Pairs of "best friends" separate and request new roommates after a while. Alertness to fluctuations in peer relations helps the staff encourage positive relationships and maintain a therapeutic balance in the facility's population.

Peer relations can be influenced by direct measures, such as the expul-sion of a disruptive youth or the separation of mismatched roommates. Much more important, however, are indirect measures, which are likely to have more subtle but longer-lasting effects. Some measures for influencing rela-tions among residents are suggested below.

Coordination

Coordination among staff members is necessary to gather a full picture of peer relations and to prevent the peer group from manipulating individual workers. It is necessary to conceal staff disputes from the youngsters; other-wise they may try to play one worker off against the other. It is also essential for the staff to support workers who are under attack by the group, a sub-group, or negatively oriented leaders.

When the staff collaborates on policies and treatment plans, child care workers feel secure enough to discuss honestly the behavior problems they have encountered, the ways they are dealing with them, and their successes and failures. Workers can respond confidently and firmly to the youngsters' behavior without extraneous concerns that complaints from the residents may threaten their job security or efficiency rating. If residents gang up on a child care worker, he can cope with the situation with the support of all co-workers.

Physical Security

It is essential that residents feel safe from physical violence. Stronger, older, or more aggressive youths must not be in a position to intimidate or ex-ploit others. Group members must feel that it is safe to disagree with group leaders and factions and to assume a leadership role on issues of concern to them. They also must feel safe to report threats and violations of the rules to the staff.

---

tions rather than group homes. Empey and Lubeck (1971, p. 156) refer to four "socio-metric types": isolates, "beggars," "loved ones," and "aloofs." Morris Mayer (1958, pp. 39–50) identified "isolates," the withdrawn, "scapegoats," and leaders. He discerned three kinds of isolates: newcomers, withdrawn children, and those who are group-rejected. Polsky (1962, chapter 5) identified "toughs," "con artists," quiet youths, "bush boys," and "scapegoats."

Selection of Residents

Selection of an appropriate mix of residents is a key step in building a supportive peer group. There should be a sufficient number of positively oriented youths to enable the group to influence disruptive members in constructive directions. If possible, the home should limit the proportion of residents who have had experience in correctional facilities, where peer group influences are often countertherapeutic. Efforts should be made to maintain a reasonable racial and ethnic balance in the group.

Age of Residents

The range of ages admitted to a group home affects peer group relations, but it is difficult to predict its precise effect. In a home serving a wide age range, there is always the possibility that older youths will dominate and exploit younger ones and set bad examples. On the other hand, some homes that serve a wide age group find that older youths develop a sense of responsibility and protective concern for the welfare of younger residents.

Group Counseling

Group counseling is the home's most powerful tool for influencing peer relations. Under skilled nondirective guidance the group can air and help resolve interpersonal problems, influence group leaders in positive directions, evaluate the behavior of subgroups, provide opportunities for recessive members to express their views safely, and support youths who cooperate in the program.

Encouraging Acceptance by Peers

The staff should try to foster supportive relations among residents. A useful step is the assignment of compatible roommates and "buddies" to help residents adapt in the home. Even a particularly hard-to-accept youngster might find some support from pairing up with another isolated individual. Opportunities should be provided for out-group youths to show their more attractive qualities; e.g., a good singing voice, prowess in weight-lifting, skill at cooking, and so on. Isolates may be encouraged to volunteer for tasks that increase their contacts with other residents, such as serving as receptionist at the front desk, collecting money to buy a get-well card for a hospitalized resident, and soliciting suggestions for next week's menu.

It is important to counsel youths concerning positive ways to relate to peers. Counseling may modify the behavior of individuals who are trying to buy the favor of others with loans, gifts, or submissiveness—and are becoming scapegoats in the process. Youngsters with body oder or "bad breath" can be guided to bathe, launder their clothes, and take other corrective steps.

Gradually, out-group youngsters may improve their relations with peers as they benefit from the home's treatment program. Increasing seniority and turnover in the home's population also may improve their status.

Building Group Cohesion

In a therapeutic social milieu, youths come to identify themselves as members of the group rather than as unrelated individuals thrown together for a required period of residential care. That sense of affiliation with the group and the group home, which may be termed group cohesion, can yield therapeutic benefits. It increases the influence of the group on its members, encourages residents to accept some responsibility for each other's welfare, and stimulates their concern for the effectiveness and reputation of the facility.

Under appropriate circumstances, cohesion develops spontaneously. The staff may learn that older residents are protecting younger ones at school, describing the facility to outsiders with pride, or trying to make it look attractive to visitors. Residents may work hard to assist each other in group counseling sessions. The group may, of its own accord, exert pressure on disruptive members or bring their negative behavior to the staff's attention.

Generally, however, group homes cannot depend on cohesion to develop of its own accord. Many residents stay for too short a time to develop strong ties to peers and staff. The formation of cliques and strongly attached dyads weakens ties to the group as a whole. Age and race differences splinter the home's population. And instead of a sense of pride and identification with the home, some youths are likely to regard its services as an imposition to be evaded and undermined.

Shared routines, such as family-style meals and the weekly cleanup, build group cohesion. Homes should experiment with additional shared routines that might be acceptable to the residents; e.g., morning calisthenics or a weekly hour of aerobic dancing. A group might enjoy working together on a large mural, patchwork quilt, or a very large jigsaw puzzle. Parties to celebrate birthdays and other special occasions give residents a "we-group" feeling. So do shared adventures such as camping and canoe trips.

Cohesion increases if residents feel that they share some responsibility for the home's program. That feeling can be stimulated by providing them with information on the history of the facility, conducting frank discussions of its financial and community relations problems, and encouraging participation in decision-making.

Residents should be provided with opportunities to help each other. Reference was made previously to the appointment of buddies for newcomers. Youths doing good work at school might be asked to tutor slower learners. Popular boys or girls can be asked to introduce withdrawn residents to some of their outside friends. Youngsters should be encouraged to visit fellow residents who have been hospitalized and to send them get-well cards.

Participation in group counseling stimulates cohesion as residents share that confidential experience from which outsiders are excluded and as they work together to provide mutual support.

In an effort to encourage group cohesion, some residential facilities employ methods that can be counterproductive. For example, they punish the entire group for offenses committed by one of its members or by unidentifiable culprits. They may issue uniform jackets, pins, or ties to their residents —adding to "we-group" feeling but effectively labeling them in school and neighborhood as troubled youths in residential care. Homes may compel all residents to attend the same cultural or recreational events, even though some are not interested in a particular activity. Pressing cohesion on youths in those ways creates resentment and resistance.

Encouraging Outside Relationships

To prevent total dependence on the in-home peer group for approval, leadership, and support, residents should be encouraged to form positive relationships with outside youths. Helpful steps include: facilitating extracurricular activities at school, facilitating participation in youth programs sponsored by community groups, and arranging opportunities for wholesome contacts with the opposite sex.

Expulsion of Disruptive Residents

To maintain a balanced group that contributes to a therapeutic social milieu, youths who continuously exert a disruptive influence on peer relations should be expelled as a last resort.

Influencing Peer Group Leaders

Child care workers are sometimes ambivalent about youths who emerge spontaneously as leaders of the group. Although workers want to encourage youths with leadership potential, they may feel threatened by their competition and charismatic qualities. That may be true even if the leader tends to influence the other youths in a positive direction.

The concerns of child care workers are understandable. Negative leaders can undermine their authority, counteract the influence of program services, and even embark on a ruthless campaign to force their resignation. To help them deal therapeutically with leaders, child care workers should be encouraged to discuss their problems and anxieties freely with supervisors, and they should receive the support of fellow staff members. Working together, the staff should analyze the roles played by informal leaders and plan ways of guiding them into positive channels.

Bickering with peer group leaders, humiliating them publicly, or competing with them are not helpful measures. They may arouse even greater group support and earn reprisal in kind. The staff should try instead to identify legitimate means for leaders to achieve recognition and gratification; e.g., through participation in athletics, part-time employment, serving as chairman of a committee, or tutoring slow learners. However, leaders should never be given any functions that are normally reserved to the staff, such as supervising chores, taking up collections, distributing the weekly allowance, or enforcing rules. Such a delegation of responsibility provides opportunities for abuse.

To limit the influence of negative leaders, all residents should be encouraged to express their views in group discussions and to participate in decision making. Group sessions should not be monopolized by the angriest, loudest, or most articulate participant. With staff encouragement, followers and even isolated youths may be able to take the lead occasionally in subjects that are their specialty, such as the bowling team, cooking a special meal, or typing official notices.

Individual and group counseling may help to reorient negative leaders and to improve the contributions of positive ones. Once they understand their role and its consequences for both themselves and the group, some of the intelligent and articulate young people will make an effort to utilize their potential for personal growth and the general welfare. For a discussion of the relations of informal group leaders and child care workers, see Mayer (1958, pp. 29ff).

Chapter 9

MODIFYING NEGATIVE BEHAVIOR

We expect adolescents to question custom and authority, to seek forbidden adventures, and to reject adult values for those favored by their peers. Such responses are even more marked among the disturbed and maladjusted teenagers placed in group homes.

The simplest negative behavior in group homes consists of mischief, discourtesy, and infractions of minor rules. There are always youngsters who engage in horseplay, use foul language, "goof off" on chores, tease a new resident, or sneak a cigarette after "lights out." Such deviations are the least difficult to deal with because they are comparatively superficial, easy to identify, and not necessarily symptomatic of serious psychological disturbance.

Violations of major rules are a more serious matter. They may endanger the welfare of the resident and others and may involve conflict with the law. Examples include curfew violations, frequenting off-limits places, truancy, drug abuse, theft, and assaults on residents and staff members.

Most difficult to deal with is disruptive or self-harming behavior that reflects a long-term character disorder. For the offending youth such behavior may have become a habitual way of relating to people and of responding to the demands of everyday life. The behavior may have been reinforced over a long period by its success in helping the individual manipulate others and attain some of his objectives. For example, threats of violence may have helped a youth intimidate parents and siblings, earn prestige in the peer group, or compensate for some physical or mental deficiency. Reinforced over the youth's lifetime, such behavior becomes a facet of the youth's character.

Other examples of behavior that may reflect character disorders are (a) continual bullying of weaker residents; (b) reflexive rejection of adult authority; (c) persistent involvement in physically dangerous activities; (d) recourse to temper tantrums or sullen withdrawal; (e) lying as a habitual way of relating to others; (f) behaving and dressing in bizarre, frightening, or indecent ways.

Lacking the intensive supervision and ability to control the social environment that are found in closed institutions, the staff of a group home must rely heavily on indirect means of modifying behavior. The process is often slow and frustrating. Too often a youth is transferred or terminated before the results of patient staff work have had time to surface. This chapter suggests some practical guidelines for staff use.

SOME NONDIRECTIVE STEPS FOR BEHAVIOR MANAGEMENT

Long-range versus Short-range Goals

From the viewpoint of the child care worker, the immediate goal in responding to negative behavior is to ensure that residents conform to the home's rules, meet daily commitments, and cooperate in group life. This short-range objective is essential for a safe and orderly residential facility. However, child care workers also must keep in mind the long-range goal of the treatment program; i.e., the development of positive attitudes, values, and patterns of behavior representing lasting character change.

Sometimes a worker's responses, although effective in changing behavior in the short run, can actually influence a youth's character in the wrong direction. For example, threats, angry outbursts, bribes, and reprisals may get the chores done and everyone to school on time, but such measures are counter-therapeutic if the youngsters accept them as appropriate ways of relating to people in their daily lives.

The aim of the staff member is to respond to negative behavior in a way that meets short-range requirements while simultaneously supporting long-range treatment objectives.

Avoiding Impulsive Responses

To the extent possible, staff members should try to respond to negative behavior in a reasoned, technical manner, rather than acting on impulse or under emotional duress. That is, of course, easier said than done. It is hard for a tired and frustrated worker to keep from becoming upset, snapping at offending youngsters, and reaching for the first punishment that comes to mind. Frustration and anger lead easily into confrontation. In that way, minor behavior problems can balloon into serious disruptions.

It is often helpful to allow time to cool off before discussing a negative incident with an offending youngster. The worker might say, "I feel very upset and angry, and so do you. We'll talk about this later when we've both cooled down." It serves no therapeutic purpose to interrogate and inflict punishment on a runaway who has just returned. Better to give the youngster a welcoming cup of soup, say, "We're glad you are safe and are back with us," and defer intensive communication until all concerned have had some rest and time to think things over.

In serious cases, workers can benefit from discussing an offender's behavior with a colleague before taking corrective action. A co-worker may have a fresh and neutral perspective and some good suggestions.

Prevention—The Best Response

Prevention is the best remedy for negative behavior. When such behavior occurs, a competent staff will try to identify the conditions that have evoked it and to take action to control them. Useful preventive measures include the following:

1. Rules should be kept to the minimum required for the safety and welfare of residents. They should be no stricter than necessary. For example, it is hard to justify a fancy dress code that requires boys to wear ties or girls to wear dresses at dinner. A curfew hour that is so early that the youngsters must come home while their neighborhood friends are still free to play outdoors may well be too strict.

Demands that overweight youths adhere to a drastic diet, that heavy smokers quit "cold turkey" while under the stress of residential care, and that a hyperactive youth sit without fidgeting during a 1-hour counseling session are likely to be self-defeating. It is better to discuss the problem and agree on short-term, feasible goals for improvement.

2. Constructive and enjoyable activities reduce negative behavior. The staff should encourage the young people to pursue their special interests in their spare time and should plan ways of eliminating long periods of idleness.

3. When residents participate in making rules and decisions, the inclination to violate the rules is reduced and infractions are easier to deal with when they do occur.

4. Stealing, a common behavior problem in residential facilities, can be reduced by providing locked closets or lockers for all residents and warning them not to flaunt or leave untended their money and other valuables. (To avoid an institutional atmosphere, locks on bedroom doors are not recommended for most homes.)

5. To reduce bickering, rules for sharing the television, telephone, and bathrooms fairly should be developed with the residents. Quarters and furnishings should provide adequate space so that individuals are not forced into irritating contact or competition. Air conditioning keeps tempers cool in warm weather. Steps to combat racial prejudice reduce friction.

6. Staff members should learn effective ways of physically restraining participants if fights should occur. It is important to terminate fights promptly before someone gets hurt, others join the fray, and neighbors or police get involved.

7. Truancy is common among youths placed in group homes. Preventive measures—attacking the causes of truancy—are more effective than punishment in that area.

Access to a good public school is a basic requirement. For residents who are not doing well at school, diagnostic tests, assignment to special education classes, and tutoring may lead to improvement. Youths who are persecuted or bullied by students during the school day may benefit from counseling and the support of fellow residents. Individuals who reject conventional schools may be willing to attend an alternative school or a work–study program. The aim is to foster positive feelings about school rather than to compel reluctant youths to attend.

8. Problems in getting the chores done can be forestalled by consulting the residents on fair ways of assigning tasks, limiting chores to no more than a half hour in length (perhaps an hour on weekends), and trying to make the weekly cleanup a zestful group project.

9. Youngsters who "get their kicks" from playing on the railroad tracks, climbing the framework of bridges, or other dangerous behavior might be diverted from such self-harming activities by opportunities for approved adventures under the home's control. Examples are weekend camping trips, horseback riding, skiing, canoeing, or bicycling. Homes should provide facilities for intense physical activity such as basketball games, weightlifting, and bicycling to help young people work off their boundless energy.

10. The likelihood of residents slipping out after "lights out" can be reduced by such security measures as locating bedrooms on an upper story and attaching a buzzer to the upstairs fire door. Employment of a night caretaker is another good preventive measure.

11. Mischievous and grumpy behavior while the group is traveling can be reduced by bringing along extra staff members or adult volunteers, stopping for refreshments at appropriate intervals, breaking out books and puzzles, involving everybody in games ("Twenty Questions"), distributing song sheets for a sing-along, and other distractions.

Positive Incentives

An effective way to reduce negative behavior is to reward constructive behavior. The objective is to provide incentives that can outweigh the real or imagined benefits that youths gain from harmful activities.

Positive incentives available to the staff are numerous and powerful. They include the prospect of an increased allowance, more privileges, verbal recognition, and enjoyable outings. A monthly awards ceremony at which certificates are distributed for progress in self-discipline, schoolwork, holding one's temper, keeping one's room clean, athletic achievement, or other positive behavior encourages improvement.

Small gifts such as an imprinted T-shirt or a little stuffed animal may be distributed for extra work or effort. However, any implication of bribing or favoritism should be avoided, and the use of material incentives should have the approval of the group in advance.

Homes that have available single rooms may wish to assign them as rewards to youths demonstrating positive behavior over a period of time. However, not all young people view this as an incentive; some prefer to live with roommates.

Role Models

Staff members can exert a powerful influence by modeling good lifestyles and interpersonal relations. Distinguished guest speakers and other volunteers also can serve that function.

Corrective Action Tailored to Individual Needs

In responding to negative behavior, staff members should take account of individual differences and the circumstances surrounding each episode. For example, different responses are required to address truancy caused by boredom at school, inability to keep up with the class, fear of a hostile schoolmate, or embarrassment over nudity in the locker room. Persistent truancy requires a different response from a first-time offense.

A second example: violation of a rule by a new resident may be due to ignorance, malice, peer group pressure, or other reasons. In responding, the staff member can choose from such varied alternatives as punishment of the offender, punishment of troublemakers in the peer group, individual counseling, a group counseling session, or clarification of the facility's rules.

A youth who does not make up his bed because he wet it last night requires a different response from that made to one who is lazy or is testing the child care worker's authority. A resident who violates the curfew because he had to baby-sit with a sibling is in a different category from one who has been joyriding or drinking with bad companions. The age of the offender is still another factor to consider. Even the response to theft can vary, depending on whether it reflected mischief, malice, dire financial need, or an uncontrollable psychological compulsion.

Resolving Differences Constructively

Professionalism in child care implies that a worker must not react to a resident's negative behavior as if it were a personal challenge. Such a reaction might be termed the "High Noon" syndrome: "It's either him or me; we'll see who's boss around here!" Instead of going on an "ego trip," a skilled worker focuses on the question, "What is the most therapeutic response to this resident at this time?"

It is wise to avoid "either-or" demands like "Either you apologize or I'll make you sorry you ever opened your mouth!" Or "You'll stay in your room till Jane gets her watch back!" Even if the apology is made and the watch returned, the residue of resentment and humiliation is hardly a therapeutic outcome. It is often better to leave the offending youth an honorable line of retreat in which negative behavior is corrected without total domination or submission.

It is particularly unwise to back a youth into a win-or-lose situation in the presence of peers. Here the individual's status in the peer group is at stake. A humiliating defeat may lead to merciless teasing and a loss in prestige, whereas a refusal to submit to staff requirements may be perceived as courageous and exemplary behavior. For that reason it is best to discuss disciplinary matters in private, where the offender does not have to play a role imposed by the peer group and the staff member is not concerned about projecting an authoritative image in the presence of the group.

A nonconfrontational way of responding to disagreement between a youth and a staff member is to seek a compromise solution. The aim is to reconcile the needs of the youth with the objectives of the staff in a way that leaves nobody totally victorious or vanquished but leads to improvement and cooperation.

Compromise solutions are limited only by the imagination of the participants. A simple example: a seventeen-year-old refuses to accompany the group on outings. It appears that he is ashamed to be seen in a group with the other residents, who are much younger, and he does not share their interests. As a compromise, the youth might agree to go along on outings, but in the role of "assistant leader" of the group. Or an adult volunteer might be found who is willing to take the youth periodically on separate outings more in line with his age and interests. Still another possible solution: The youth may be permitted to invite a neighborhood friend of equal age to come along on some trips. As a result of the compromise process, sullen insubordination is converted into positive behavior, and the resident may have acquired new problem-solving and human relations skills (see Gordon, 1970).

Preserving Staff-Resident Relationships

Despite the irritation created by negative behavior, staff members must avoid responding in a way that severs their working relationship with offending youngsters. Workers who shout in a fit of anger, "From now on, stay out of my sight!" or "If you have anything to say to me, put it in writing or tell it to your caseworker!" cannot build a sense of trust and acceptance required for extended treatment.

The staff member's objective is to correct negative behavior without rejecting the youth himself. Talking to a youth who has refused to do chores, the worker may make clear the possible consequences, discuss possible solutions, and penalize the behavior. But a child care technician may not withhold the caring and acceptance that are parts of a treatment program.

A nonrejecting way of responding to negative behavior is to send "I-messages," rather than "You-messages" when discussing the matter with an offender. Instead of *"You* are a very bad boy because you refused to wash the dishes," the worker expresses, in the first person, his own feelings about the negative behavior; e.g., *"I* feel concerned about your refusal because it isn't fair for others to do your work for you." Responding to a curfew violation, the worker might say: *"I* was very worried when you came home late because of the possibility that you were in trouble."

Such "I" messages show continued acceptance of the youngster, rejecting only his unsuitable behavior. In some cases residents will respond by discussing the reasons for their behavior and ways to improve it (Gordon, 1970).

To affirm the caring relationship while correcting inappropriate behavior, it often helps to use the "sandwich technique." In that approach, a necessary reprimand or criticism is preceded and followed by recognition of some positive characteristic or action of the young person. "I think you've really decorated your room in good taste. However, I'm concerned that you haven't been making up your bed in the morning. That only spoils the nice room you've created."

PUNISHMENT

Despite the stress on nondirective methods of influencing young people in a community-based group home, punishment remains an indispensable therapeutic tool. Its objective is to make the costs of negative behavior sufficiently high to outweigh its rewards for an offending youth. At the same time, workers require skill and sensitivity to ensure that punishment does not leave a harmful residue of rage, rejection, anxiety, and humiliation. Punishment is most effective when offenders understand its reasons, accept it as just, and feel that it does not permanently scar their acceptance by peers and staff.

Workers will find the following guidelines helpful in applying penalties in a therapeutic way.[1]

Punishment Is a Last Resort

The long-run effects of punishment can rarely be predicted with certainty. Therefore, that tool should be used only after considering alternative ways of responding to the problem.

[1]Mayer (1958, pp. 135–40) offered some thoughtful suggestions on dealing with negative behavior, although geared to an institutional rather than a group home setting. Those suggestions were particularly helpful in formulating some of the approaches described in this chapter.

The correction of foul language furnishes an example. A 25-cent fine for each improper word is likely to control the offense—at least in the presence of a staff member. However, there may be alternative responses that are less likely to challenge the youth to find other opportunities to display his street words. To cite the simplest response: a respected staff member can sometimes stem the flow of epithets with a raised eyebrow or a quizzical grin. Simply asking the youth to repeat his comments in plain English is a humorous, noncombative, corrective measure. Over a longer period of time, role modeling by the staff, recording and playing back a youth's conversation, and group counseling can be helpful.

Foul language may have been customary in a resident's former milieu. As such, its use may simply be habitual and unrelated to underlying negative attitudes and feelings. For other youths foul language may reflect distorted feelings about family, sexuality, and self. Its use may be a means of proving one's manliness and toughness and of gaining acceptance by the peer group. For such offenders individual and group counseling may be more therapeutic over the long run than punishment.

That is not to say that punishment is never the appropriate response for foul language. It is appropriate when, for example, a youth uses foul language to convey threats, to intimidate, to dominate decision-making, or to challenge staff authority.

Participation by Residents

Some residential facilities have experimented with resident courts, resident juries, and other ways of allowing youths to determine the guilt and/or punishment of their peers. That does not, however, seem an appropriate function for the youths. Judging the guilt or innocence of fellow residents and determining their punishment create friction in the peer group and impair its ability to exert a therapeutic influence. Moreover, one is never certain whether maladjusted youths will use good judgment or will be inhibited by peer group pressure from acting fairly. It seems best to encourage residents to participate in making the rules (the "legislative function") but to leave it up to the staff to enforce them (the "judicial function") (Mayer, 1972).

Group Punishment

Some residential facilities inflict group punishment; i.e., they penalize the entire group for offenses committed by one or several of its members. The intention is to compel the group to identify offenders and to control their behavior by peer pressure. Although widespread, the practice is not recommended for group homes.

Group punishment can take various forms. For example, to ferret out the identity of a youth who has stolen a fellow resident's property, the staff may compel all residents to share the cost of replacing the property unless the thief comes forward. Or the entire group may be kept in a marathon counseling session until a confession is obtained or the property reappears.

Other examples: residents may be restricted to the grounds if they do not report the unauthorized midnight absences of their roommates. The entire group may go without home-cooked food until a recalcitrant member takes his turn washing the dishes. The television may be shut off because two youngsters had a violent dispute over which program to watch.

Although group punishment may resolve a specific negative incident, its long-term effects are questionable. It is, in the first place, unfair to punish residents who have committed no violations. Their punishment is likely to evoke justified resentment. Second, group punishment stimulates hostility among peer group members, weakening the group's ability to support and influence individual residents. Even worse is an alternative scenario: the peer group may respond by sticking together, protecting the offender, and resisting staff authority. Third, in extreme cases the group may employ physical violence, threats, or ostracism to force a confession from a suspected offender. That endangers the safety of individual residents, violates their rights, and is hardly likely to exert a therapeutic influence.

Offsetting the Rewards of Negative Behavior

Young people may derive substantial rewards from negative behavior in terms of both their conscious values and their unconscious needs. From smoking a marijuana cigarette or getting high on alcohol a youth may gain not only some immediate physical gratification but increased prestige among fellow residents. A temper trantrum may well help a youth dominate the people around him. Staying out overnight at his girl friend's house makes a teenager an important person around the group home and is likely to be great fun, to boot!

To be effective the pain of punishment must outweigh the rewards of negative behavior. Restriction to the grounds for a day or two after school hardly discourages a youth from enjoying a night out on the town with friends. Nor will a 50-cent fine deter a youth who refused to help with weekend chores. More stringent penalties might prove that negative behavior does not pay and encourage a youth to seek better ways of gaining satisfaction.

Negative behavior that raises a youth's standing in the peer group is particularly difficult to deal with. The acclaim of fellow residents is a powerful incentive for mischief. In addition, fellow residents are often able to offset minor penalties imposed on an offender. They may lend money to make up for a canceled allowance, slip banned materials to him, and provide supportive companionship if the youth has been restricted to the facility.

Penalties that reduce the offender's prestige in the group are effective deterrents against even hardened violators. A youth who is required to stay home while everyone else goes off to the ball park is diminished in stature. He has missed a treat that fellow residents enjoyed; the consequences of his negative behavior, therefore, will not seem glamorous to them. Moreover, there is no way in which the peer group can counteract the penalty because it can make available no equivalent activities for the offender.

No Cruel or Excessive Penalties

Although punishment must outweigh the real or imagined benefits of negative behavior, it must never be cruel or excessive. Those are difficult terms to apply in specific cases. For one youth a mild rebuke may sting for weeks and spell rejection or worthlessness. Another may barely notice a rebuke or simply attribute it to the unfairness of the staff member. A worker's sensitivity to such individual differences counts here.

Physical punishments are tabooed by placement agencies. Beatings, withdrawal of food, or locking a resident in a room are impermissible. Washing a youth's mouth with soapy water is no longer an acceptable response to foul or impertinent language. These days, even grabbing a resident's arm may bring charges of child abuse from youth, family, or caseworker.

Withdrawal of smoking privileges is not a recommended punishment. It represents a particularly severe hardship on heavy smokers. It is difficult to enforce because cigarettes can be slipped to the youth by fellow residents, and there are plenty of opportunities to smoke unobserved at school and neighborhood play areas. In addition, using the smoking privilege as an incentive implies that smoking is valuable and desirable—a message that will not be lost on the youngsters.

Punishments must not violate the legal rights of parents and youths. Family visits, use of the telephone, and the sending or receiving of letters must not be prohibited.

Duration of Punishment

Punishment must not exceed a short period of time. After the interval the youth should be able to feel that he is starting with a clean slate, is accepted by the staff in the same way as other residents, and can rely on staff support in the future. If punishment persists more than 2 or 3 days, a youth may come to feel that there is no point in doing better because the staff has rejected him and will view future behavior with a biased eye. Punishments imposed for subsequent violations will have a steadily diminishing influence.

Depriving residents of television, recreational outings, outside visitors, or opportunities to leave the home over long periods can have some special ill effects. Such restrictions may exacerbate depression, withdrawal, and alienation. In extreme cases they may motivate affected residents to run away.

Fines

As a form of punishment, the fining of residents has advantages. The offenses that occasion fines and the amount of fines can be discussed in advance with the group, so that penalties are not perceived as arbitrary when they are imposed. Fines can be scaled to the severity and frequency of each offense and to the resources of the offender. They also may be linked to restitution —a concept of justice that is understood by most young people.

If fines are levied, it is important to leave the offender with sufficient funds to meet all legitimate needs. Otherwise, a youth may be tempted to borrow money from fellow residents and outsiders or even to turn to shoplifting or thefts in the home. Moreover, fining away a youth's entire allowance leaves him indifferent to further financial penalties.

The effectiveness of fines is limited if the resident has a substantial income from outside sources such as a part-time job or gifts from family members. That is one of the reasons why residents with outside jobs should be required to bank part of their earnings and why parents should be asked to refrain from giving money to children in placement.

Chores as Punishment

It is not a good idea to assign a chore, like cleaning the bathrooms, as a punishment. Work for the common good should not be perceived as something onerous to be avoided but as part of cooperative group living shared by all residents.

Appropriate Punishments

What forms of punishment remain at the disposal of group homes? They have available a broad range of measures. For everyday offenses there are the following, listed roughly in order of increasing severity..

1. A reprimand.
2. Sent to own room to cool off for an hour or two.
3. No television for a day or two.
4. Fine deducted from allowance or loss of points or tokens if such are in use.
5. Restitution for minor damage.
6. No outside friends allowed to visit in the home for a day or two.
7. Missing a recreational or cultural outing.
8. Earlier curfew for one or several days.

Serious offenses, such as assault and theft, require a firmer response. The staff may have to file complaints with the police, notify the placement agency, and/or arrange the temporary transfer of a youth to the local shelter for status offenders or mental health crisis facility. Sometimes workers are reluctant to involve law enforcement and other outside officials. Yet if an assault victim's nose turns out to be broken, a runaway does not return in a day or two, or an irate parent complains to the placement agency, the group home is in a difficult position if it has not reported the incident to appropriate authorities.

There is room for flexibility, taking into account the characteristics of the offender and the circumstances surrounding the offense. Depending on the individual, it might be more therapeutic to respond to initial experimentation with marijuana by issuing a stern warning than to hale the youngster into court. If the staff feels that it is countertherapeutic to bring a case of shoplifting to the attention of the police, it may be possible to persuade the shopkeeper to refrain from pressing charges in return for full restitution. An assault on a fellow resident that does not cause significant injury, had strong provocation, and does not reflect a habitual pattern of violence might best be handled by in-house punishment, coupled with counseling and measures to prevent a recurrence.

When a youth's negative behavior is persistent and may lead to expulsion, a formal letter of warning from the director is an effective therapeutic measure. In the warning letter, the director should express his concern in a firm but caring way. The youth's negative behavior and its probable consequences should be reviewed. The letter should make specific suggestions about what the resident can do to avoid termination, ending on a hopeful note with expressions of support.

A written warning is a significant event in the youth's life. It compels the recipient to evaluate his behavior seriously, ponder alternatives, and consider the future. That kind of confidential communication may still be found under the youngster's pillow or pasted inside his locker weeks later. Letter in hand, the youth may appear at the door of a staff member, ready to talk honestly about his feelings, needs, and status.

BEHAVIOR MODIFICATION "SYSTEMS"

Many residential facilities have adopted structured behavior modification "systems" as a technique for encouraging positive behavior. Such systems do not rely on the on-the-spot judgment of staff members to choose the right response to the good and bad behavior of residents. Instead, staff and residents receive a manual that lists the home's rules and specifies the rewards and penalties for observing and violating each rule. The manual may list, for example, the fines and restrictions that are to be imposed for violations of the curfew, for truancy, and for refusing to straighten one's bedroom in the morning. Points, tokens, prizes, and privileges may be awarded for positive behavior such as completion of homework assignments and cooperation in group chores. The intention is to let the young people know what is expected of them and to apply consistent rewards and penalties to reinforce positive behavior.

In addition to requirements that apply to all residents, some behavior modification systems set behavior goals and standards for individual residents. For example, a youth with a hot temper may be given the special task of controlling it in encounters with fellow residents. A reward for each tantrum-free week and a punishment for each lapse would be set in advance, in consultation with the youngster.

Numerous variations and degrees of intricacy are encountered.

1. Some facilities issue very detailed lists of banned behavior and their corresponding punishments, covering everything from sulking to carrying a concealed weapon. Others include only a handful of rules, covering only key areas of group home life.

2. In facilities that award points to encourage good behavior, youngsters may start at zero each week and earn their weekly quota of points by doing satisfactory work. Alternatively, residents may start the week with the maximum number of points, from which points are subtracted for bad behavior as the week progresses.

3. Some homes encourage youngsters to accumulate points, tokens, or cash rewards over a long period in order to earn a bicycle, camera, or other expensive reward. Other facilities believe that incentives lose their influence if residents are not required to exchange points or tokens for gifts and privileges by the end of each week.

4. In some facilities youths are rewarded for meeting specified behavior standards by advancement through a system of "levels" or stages marked by increasing privileges and independence. Residents also can be moved back to a lower stage for negative behavior.

Proponents of the simplified behavior modification systems found in some group homes claim a number of advantages for this treatment tool. They point out that since prespecified rules and incentives can be developed in consultation with the residents, they are more likely to elicit their cooperation than ad hoc instructions and penalties. Staff members are not perceived as arbitrary, and they can be consistent in responding to negative behavior. A more controversial claim is that positive behavior induced by behavior modification systems gradually becomes habitual and an ingrained part of the residents' character.

There are also practitioners who question the usefulness of behavior modification systems in group homes. They maintain that staff responses require judgment, sensitivity, and flexibility; they cannot be dictated in advance for all youths and situations.

A ceaseless torrent of tasks and problems makes it very difficult for child care workers to respond to negative behavior in the precise way specified by a home's behavior modification system. They cannot stop to look up the number of points charged for filching an apple, switching television channels, slamming a book to the ground, teasing a fellow resident, or making a threatening gesture. Major offenses such as theft, assault, obscene phone calls, sexual promiscuity, and tormenting the group home dog do not fit into the system. Neither does such behavior as sexual deviance, passive withdrawal, compulsive stealing, or refusal to turn off the lights because of fear of the dark.

It is argued that a behavior modification system cannot make allowances for the varied causes of negative behavior, its frequency, the offender's objectives and state of mind, or his remorse. If the staff adheres to the system, it would respond to truancy caused by fear of hostile schoolmates in the same manner as to truancy caused by a desire to go fishing.

There are some practical problems in implementing a behavior modification system. After an offender's entire weekly allowance or quota of points has been fined away, additional fines have no further influence. If the excess of fines accumulated in one week is levied against a youth's allowance or quota of points in the following week, he may lose hope of ever catching up, and that further weakens the system's restraints on his behavior.

In homes where residents are advanced from lower to higher stages or levels if they meet prespecified standards of behavior over a period of time, youngsters may bounce erratically from level to level on the basis of short-term changes in behavior. They may attain level 4 today, be set back by some infraction to level 2 tomorrow, more up to level 3 in a few weeks, and be back at the starting post after a temper tantrum a few days later. Each change involves a revision of the resident's privileges and daily schedule; possibly a change in rooms and roommates.

If the residents view a home's system as unfair, they are able to neutralize some of its rewards and penalties. They may accord prestige and leadership status to youths who violate the rules. They may haze or accord low status to conformers. They may offset fines by lending money and cigarettes to the offender. Disgruntled residents will deride the certificates, awards, gifts, outings, and other prizes offered by the system. Of course, the peer group's attitudes and values affect the results of informal behavior management as well as those of behavior modification systems. However, the latter seem particularly vulnerable because of their relative inflexibility.

The most important questions raised by doubters concern the long-range effects of behavior modification systems on the character and personal growth of the residents. They wonder whether youths who conform to the rules in order to gain material rewards and to avoid punishment are really acquiring self-discipline, conscientiousness, independent judgment, and other good character traits to carry over into adult life. This is still an uncertain area for group homes, with good arguments but little data on both sides.

For homes that wish to utilize a formal behavior modification system, it is recommended that the system cover only a few areas of important behavior. Conformity to the rules in those areas should be easily verifiable, and the rules should lend themselves to enforcement by simple rewards and penalties.

Examples of behavior that lends itself to regulation by a simplified system are adherence to the curfew, performance of chores, school attendance, and keeping appointments for treatment services. They represent only a fraction of the vivid and tumultuous activity found in a group home. However, fixed rules and sanctions in those areas serve as a framework for everyday life, leaving more complex and elusive behavior to be guided by the staff in a flexible, individualized way. A description of behavior modification concepts is given in Pizzatt (1973). Descriptions of intricate behavior modification systems in larger institutions are presented in Meyer et al. (1973) in an issue of *Child Welfare* devoted to behavior modification and in McInnis and Marholin (1977). A pioneering behavior modification system in a small residential setting is described in Phillips et al. (1973), and a realistic appraisal of a formal system appears in Scallon et al. (1976).

Chapter 10

STRUCTURED TREATMENT SERVICES

With the development of a therapeutic social milieu and a supportive physical environment, a group home has achieved two essential objectives of its program. This chapter discusses a third essential program component—the provision of structured treatment services.

As used here, the term *structured treatment services* covers the professionally designed and administered psychological, educational, social, and health services that group homes are required to make available. Such services are usually scheduled for specific times and places, and participation is a requirement for designated residents of the home. Structured services found in typical group homes for disturbed or maladjusted youths include development of treatment plans for each resident, individual counseling, individual psychotherapy, group counseling, group therapy, and counseling of parents.

Those services will be discussed in turn in this chapter. Also available to group home residents are education, recreation, and health services, which will be taken up in the following chapter.

INDIVIDUAL TREATMENT PLANS

Once a new resident's needs have been evaluated, the next step is to prepare an individual treatment plan, which identifies the group home's goals for the resident, the services that will be provided, and ways in which the staff should deal with the youth in everyday life. The plan need not be lengthy or complex, but it should be in writing to ensure that it is understood by all concerned and that it covers necessary subjects in sufficient detail.

Usually, individual treatment plans are prepared by the home's director or social worker, in consultation with the child care workers. Often the home's psychologist and the placement agency caseworker are involved.

It is also advantageous to consult the residents concerning their treatment plans. That gives them new insights into their problems and a chance to take stock of who they are, where they are going, and what they must do to progress in the program. Often they have useful suggestions. Participation may motivate them to become partners, rather than sullen antagonists in the home's activities.

Individual treatment plans should contain at least the following elements.

1. The period covered by the plan and the date at which the plan will be reviewed and updated in the future.

2. Background data such as the resident's admission date, age, place of residence, legal status, educational status, and health.

3. An abbreviated social history—perhaps a paragraph or two—indicating why the youth has come under the supervision of the placement agency, previous placements and services, family background, contacts with the juvenile justice system, and other social factors that might influence the youth's treatment.

4. A brief description of the youth's psychological characteristics, including symptomatic behavior, psychological diagnoses, and official classification, if any. For a balanced view, it is a good idea to describe the youth's positive characteristics as well.

5. Treatment objectives for the youth, including long-term objectives such as reconciliation with the family, passing grades at school, relief from psychosomatic symptoms, and preparation for independent living after leaving the home.

Short-range objectives, covering periods of no more than 1 to 3 mcnths, also should be included. For example, a youth may be expected to desist from foul language, begin verbalizing his feelings in group counseling sessions, attend school regularly, control temper tantrums, and handle a family visit successfully by the date of the next scheduled review of the treatment plan.

6. Guidelines for staff relations with the resident. The staff may plan to give extra praise to an angry youngster, spend 15 minutes each day tutoring him, respond to a volatile temper in a specified way, or assign a sympathetic child care worker to serve as informal counselor to the youth. The plan may indicate ways to nurture a youth's relationship with another resident, help him find a part-time job, or develop his leadership qualities.

7. Guidelines for relations with the resident's family, covering such items as the timing and frequency of visits, parent counseling, referral of family members to other agencies for services, and ways of responding to hostility, indifference, overprotectiveness, authoritarian rigidity, and other counter-therapeutic attitudes.

8. Required contacts with the public school, health facilities, probation officers, and other outside agencies.

9. Structured treatment services to be provided, such as individual psychotherapy, remedial education, or health care.

Individual treatment plans must be updated periodically to keep abreast of the residents' changing needs. A good way to involve residents in the periodic review is to invite them to submit written self-appraisals describing the progress they have made, the problems experienced, and the adequacy of services received. Such a document also can suggest objectives and services for the next planning period. To help residents who have difficulty in verbalizing their views, the home can make up a standard self-appraisal form that simply requires the resident to respond to written questions concerning previous and upcoming treatment plans.

In some group homes short-term "contracts" between the staff and each resident supplement individual treatment plans. In that approach the social worker or director meets with residents periodically to review their progress and to agree on a set of goals for the next few weeks. For example, a resident might agree to attend school regularly, spend an extra half hour at homework, and accept tutoring by a child care worker each day. The group home, in turn, might offer specified incentives such as transportation to basketball practice or advancement to a higher level in the behavior modification system.

Typically, the contract is a written agreement, signed by the youth and a staff member. That attaches to it an aura of authority, indicates that residents are partners in their own treatment, and motivates them to keep their part of the bargain.

At the end of each contract period the director or social worker and the youth review the progress that has been made and prepare a new agreement. Successive contracts are intended to move the resident in small, attainable steps toward the long-term objectives of his treatment plan.

This treatment tool must be used with caution and adapted to individual characteristics in a flexible way. Used simplistically, contracts cover only overt behavior without addressing the underlying causes of behavior problems. They do not lend themselves to the treatment of negative behavior that is beyond the conscious control of individuals, such as phobias, compulsions, obsessions, and psychosomatic symptoms like enuresis. Furthermore, there is a possibility that disturbed youths who fail to meet rigid contractual targets will experience depression, anxiety, and lowered self-esteem that hamper further improvement.

INDIVIDUAL COUNSELING

Individual counseling of residents permeates everyday life in group homes and is a major tool in their treatment program. Much of the counseling is informal, or "curbstone" counseling, provided on an ad hoc basis by all staff members whenever and wherever a need or opportunity presents itself. Equally important is individual counseling provided as a structured treatment service, which is almost always conducted by the home's social worker or director at scheduled times in a private setting.

As a structured service, individual counseling probes more deeply into feelings, needs, and causes than does "curbstone" counseling. With sessions scheduled over a period of time, the counselor is able to introduce subjects of deep concern to the youngster and to work systematically toward long-term change. The counseling process can concern itself with the gradual development of self-awareness and judgment; adoption of positive attitudes and values; management of anxiety, anger, and frustration; acquisition of problem-solving and human relations skills; and other lasting character change. Routine program requirements or minor irritations in everyday life are of only secondary interest, perhaps as paths that may lead to the counselee's more fundamental concerns.

Individual counseling should be scheduled at regular intervals for all group home youngsters. Typically, counseling is provided weekly but can be offered more or less frequently as required. The frequency depends on the needs of each resident and on the types of related services he is receiving. For example, a resident who is receiving psychotherapy may require fewer counseling sessions than one who is not and may have trouble fitting individual counseling sessions into a busy treatment schedule. Residents may require frequent counseling when they first enter the group home but fewer sessions as they adapt to group living and respond to the home's program.

Activities that require the staff to meet with residents for evaluation and planning purposes provide opportunities for individual counseling. Examples of such activities are the periodic review of individual treatment plans and contracts, periodic evaluations required by behavior modification systems, review of school report cards with residents, preparation for visits to or by the family, and "de-briefings" conducted after each visit.

Most counseling sessions last from a half to a full hour, depending on individual needs. Even a long-term resident who has adapted well can profit from a half-hour of give and take every couple of weeks.

Most suited to group homes is a nondirective approach to counseling. The counseling session becomes a time for listening, self-evaluation, and joint efforts to address the youth's needs—rather than a time for exhortation, blame, or rigid demands. Rather than a fixed agenda, counselees are encouraged to discuss any activities, feelings, problems, and experiences that are on their minds. Even if the subject is superficial, it may be a signal of more serious concerns that will emerge later as the youth develops self-confidence and trust in the counselor.

Written materials can be useful tools in nondirective counseling. Residents may benefit from writing self-appraisals, autobiographies, and not-to-be-delivered letters to parents, teachers, and other significant figures. Together counselor and youth can make lists of the latter's objectives, strengths, problems, needs, fears, grievances, areas of progress, and/or plans for improvement. A resident facing an important decision might be asked to list all alternative courses of action and the pros and cons of each. Examples of other written lists: In what ways can I improve my schoolwork? What are my career objectives? What steps should I take to attain them? What are the good and bad things that happen during my visits to my family? Such lists help some youths to clarify their feelings and thoughts and to become better aware of their behavior and its consequences.

On the basis of information gained in counseling sessions, the counselor is in a position to suggest corrective changes in the services and environment provided for the resident. He may wish to meet with a school official to discuss educational problems uncovered in counseling. Parents may be contacted to discuss a family problem revealed by their child. Counseling may lead to a change of roommates, arrangements to transport a youth to and from band practice, or measures to provide sex education. Child care workers may be advised to assign the youth additional responsibilities, help him check the help-wanted ads, or offer more positive feedback whenever the resident demonstrates improved behavior.

Honest and uninhibited expression can be achieved only if a counselee is sure that communications will be treated as confidential. If the counselor realizes that information emerging in a counseling sessions may have to be revealed to outsiders, it is best to tell the youth about that requirement in advance. Usually, however, the counselor is able to share information with staff members or others in a very general way, offering only enough information to justify necessary corrective action.

GROUP COUNSELING

Group counseling is exceptionally well suited to group home settings. Most homes employ or have access to a social worker who has had at least some training in group work. The normal population of a group home—from 6 to 12 residents—is about the right size for group counseling. The youngsters are not so severely disturbed that they cannot respond to group interaction, and they usually include a sufficient number of positively oriented individuals to exert a therapeutic influence on more maladjusted residents. Furthermore, the residents share common characteristics and experiences that can serve as a basis for meaningful discussion.

Despite the apparent suitability of group counseling, a substantial number of homes still do not utilize that technique. Some cannot distinguish it from group discussions and routine group meetings. In other homes staff members feel threatened by group counseling. They fear that residents will provide misleading information about them "behind their backs" or band together to resist authority. Such attitudes are unfortunate because they deprive the facility of its most effective therapeutic service.

In group counseling, participants discuss subjects of importance in their lives under the nondirective guidance of a qualified staff member. Reliance is placed on interaction within the group to influence the behavior, attitudes, and values of participants. The group exerts this influence by pointing out patterns of behavior and attitudes that handicap individual members, helping members evaluate the consequences of their ways of thinking and behaving for self and others, encouraging members to clarify their objectives and to explore positive ways of achieving them, lending support to members who make positive changes and pursue positive goals, and exchanging information, experience, and advice (Empey & Lubeck, 1971, pp. 16, 87–88).

The frequency of group counseling depends on, among other factors, the theoretical orientation and capabilities of the group home's staff, the age of the residents, how long they have been in the facility, and the severity of their problems. For the typical home, group counseling once or twice a week seems adequate. Extra sessions can be added on an ad hoc basis to resolve issues left over from an earlier session or to discuss unexpected events that have had a significant impact, such as a fight, accident, or runaway. There are homes, however, that place such emphasis on group counseling that the activity is conducted as frequently as every day.

Group counseling sessions normally do not exceed an hour in length, to remain within the attention span of restless teenagers. Occasionally, a session may be extended to resolve a pressing issue, follow up an emerging insight, or dissipate aroused emotions. Counseling should not occur just before mealtimes because hungry youngsters are not in a receptive frame of mind, and emotions stirred up during the sessions may spoil their meals.

Group counseling is usually conducted by the home's director or social worker because they are more likely than child care workers to have the required professional skills. In a few homes group counseling is provided by an outsider such as a professional employed by the parent agency, who visits the facility for only an hour or two and is not deeply involved in its everyday life and social milieu. That approach is likely to be much less effective.

Should child care workers participate in the group counseling session? If they attend, their intimate knowledge of the youths and their special perspective may enrich the counseling process. They will gain new information about how the young people think and feel, enabling them to adjust their practices in a therapeutic manner. They will not harbor suspicions that the counselor is undermining their authority. Workers who participate in group counseling are likely to take a positive view of the service and support it in their contacts with the youths.

There are arguments for excluding child care workers, as well. The youngsters may be inhibited by a worker's presence. Inadequately trained workers may be critical or directive. If participants complain about the worker's performance or request program changes, the worker may interpret that as a personal attack, and the counselor may be placed in the awkward position of arbiter, advocate, or judge of the participants' grievances. For those reasons child care workers are excluded from group counseling sessions in some homes.

After considering the pros and cons, it seems reasonable to include the houseparent or a shift worker in group counseling sessions. In a group home their influence is too pervasive to permit their exclusion from group activities. With good training, sensitive workers will learn that they must stay in the background, weigh their comments, and maintain objectivity. They will not hold grudges against critical youngsters. Workers who cannot participate in a supportive manner probably do not belong in a group home in the first place.

A wide variety of group counseling approaches has been described, from frank discussions to marathon encounters. Some lend themselves to group home settings; others do not. Group home social workers should be acquainted with all relevant methods.

Whatever approach is used, a basic element of group counseling is nondirective leadership. The counselor tries to serve as unobtrusive facilitator, encouraging the youngsters to bring up topics of concern to themselves and to share their ideas, experiences, and feelings. He makes sure that everyone has a chance to participate, protecting recessive youngsters and restraining those who might dominate the sessions. The counselor also serves as a source of factual information and makes participants aware of constraints and alternatives that must be taken into account.

That does not mean that the counselor is merely a passive observer, although observation of the responses and interaction of participants is an important function in group work. The counselor may guide the discussion to relevant topics, the needs of a particular individual, or an issue that has caused friction in the facility. The counselor calls attention to a convergence or difference of views, a shared concern, efforts by a youth to dominate the group, the anger of another youth, or failure to resolve an issue. There is direction in nondirective counseling, but it is subtle and adjusted to the group's own readiness and flow of thought.

Ideally, group counseling sessions are best left relatively unstructured, without a prearranged topic or assigned roles for participants. However, some counselors introduce a limited measure of structure to facilitate the group process. They may commence a session with 5 minutes of silence or allow each youth several minutes to talk about his recent activities and concerns before the general discussion. Role-playing, brief panel discussions, and the designation of recessive youngsters as timekeepers and summarizers are techniques for "breaking the ice" and encouraging interaction among participants.

In one controversial approach to group counseling the group is asked to concentrate on the problems and needs of a single youth during each session. The youth may volunteer to be the subject of discussion or may be selected because he has engaged in self-harming behavior, can benefit from recognition, is at odds with peers, is leaving the program shortly, or for other reasons. Such an approach should be used, if at all, only with caution. Care must be taken to protect the targeted individual from group-inflicted wounds that can lead to rifts in the peer group, depression, withdrawal, resentment, and even running away. Confidentiality concerning the youth's problems also must be protected. An example of this approach is "guided group interaction," described in McCorkle et al. (1958) and Harstad (1976).

What do participants talk about in group counseling? There are two basic techniques: the group may be invited to raise any subject it wants to discuss, or a specific topic may be designated in advance for each session. In the former approach participants simply bring up their current concerns and experiences. Under skilled leadership the discussion may turn spontaneously to matters of therapeutic significance, such as the evaluation of a youth's behavior, identification of problems, conflicts of value and attitudes, and constructive ways in which group members can relate to each other.

The preselection of topics provides reassuring structure for counselors who are uncomfortable with the nondirective approach. It ensures that each session will focus on a relevant subject, whereas a group that has no topic set in advance must expect some sessions that are, on the surface, unfocused and lacking in tangible short-term results.

If topics are preselected, they should touch the feelings and emotions of residents. Dental hygiene is best left to group discussions rather than counseling sessions. Examples of appropriate topics are self-harming behavior, race relations, relations with the opposite sex, recognizing and managing anger, relations with peers and family, assertive versus aggressive behavior, vocational plans, and preparation for leaving the group home.

For the average social worker who is not a counseling specialist the best approach is probably to mix preplanned sessions with those that are open forums. Even with a designated topic it is a good practice to allow the discussion to evolve in a spontaneous way and to follow up emerging subjects that seem important to participants.

At the end of each session a number of things can be done to ease tensions. The final minutes can be set aside for a summary of the information, opinions, and insights that the group has shared. The counselor may remind the group about any actions that members have agreed to take. Inviting the group to evaluate the session and to suggest topics for future meetings also fills an interval in which the group can "wind down." Group sessions that end with some positive outcome or decision are likely to be perceived as particularly satisfying by participants.

INDIVIDUAL PSYCHOTHERAPY

Although seriously mentally ill young people do not belong in community-based group homes, many homes do serve residents whose emotional disturbances and social maladjustment are sufficiently severe to require individual psychotherapy. The psychological distress of such youths cannot be relieved by providing customary incentives for positive behavior, counseling, education, and a supportive social milieu. Instead, it stems from deep-rooted unconscious forces that can be approached only through intensive professional treatment.

Some of the symptoms of mental illness encountered among group home residents that suggest a need for individual therapy are minor delusions, obsessions, phobias, paranoid tendencies, depression, passive withdrawal, sexual disturbance, debilitating anxiety, deep, diffuse rage, pathological lying, and various psychosomatic symptoms like chronic headaches, lethargy, and bed-wetting.

Rarer are youngsters who pose a serious danger to self and others through compulsive stealing, potentially self-destructive activities like hitchhiking, a tendency toward violence, alcoholism, drug abuse, and sadistic or masochistic ways of relating to other people.

It is possible that individual psychotherapy is overused in group homes. Because group home youths are not severely disturbed, often lack introspection and verbal skills, and may remain in a facility no more than a few months, most are unlikely to derive substantial benefit from that form of treatment.

Reliance on individual psychotherapy may reflect excessive expectations about its potential results in the short run and a lack of confidence in alternative services such as counseling and group therapy. The attitudes of the young people play a role: in one home known to the writer individual therapy was provided for all residents because seriously disturbed youths are more willing to accept treatment if other residents also are required to do so. Homes for girls in New Jersey seemed to make much greater use of therapy than boys' homes because boys are said to have stronger prejudices against that service.

But the greatest motivation to overuse individual psychotherapy is that it is free! Unlike the cost of counseling and group therapy, the cost of individual psychotherapy conducted by an authorized outside professional is usually reimbursable under the Medicaid program. For that reason it can be provided with excessive liberality, justified as the highest-quality care at the lowest cost to the home and the placement agency.

The professional qualifications of psychotherapists vary widely. Group homes can choose psychiatrists, clinical psychologists, or psychiatric social workers. Some individuals with degrees in psychiatric nursing and counseling also offer therapy. There is a choice of therapists in private practice, group practice, community mental health centers, family guidance centers, and other organizational settings. In some areas, therapists must meet high standards to be licensed; elsewhere, licensing may be pro forma or nonexistent.

If the group home's own social worker is not qualified to provide psychotherapy, the second best alternative is a therapist who has worked closely with the group home and is familiar with its policies and population. Homes that purchase psychological services from an organization employing several practitioners should insist that only a single psychotherapist be assigned to work with its residents. Otherwise, several therapists may try to divide the job between them. Such fragmentation makes it difficult for the therapists to grasp the dynamics of group home relationships and to form a total picture of the program.

Like their professional qualifications, the theoretical orientation of therapists varies widely. It ranges from the intensive probing of psychoanalysis to the physical release of tension in "scream therapy." Some methods involve in-depth analysis of the causes and unconscious functions of the patient's behavior and feelings over a long period of time. Others concentrate more narrowly on modifying specific behavior patterns without regard to underlying causes. Therapists also differ in their reliance on drugs to relieve the symptoms of psychological distress.

The following characteristics help to identify therapists with an orientation that is appropriate for group homes:

1. Extensive experience with youthful patients.

2. Willingness to forgo long-term intensive analysis and to address negative behavior patterns and distressing psychological symptoms over a short period.

3. Employment of techniques that are not so unconventional as to bring a negative reaction from parents, community, and the placement agency.

4. Willingness to spend time learning the home's program, sampling the social milieu, and meeting the staff.

5. Familiarity with human relations in residential programs; if possible, the therapist should have had experience in a residential setting to understand fully the influence of the peer group, relations between staff and residents, and a therapeutic social milieu.

6. Familiarity with the cultural background of the home's population and the subcultures of detention facilities that may have touched the lives of some youths.

7. Assignment of a high value to group work, family counseling, and preventive educational programs.

8. While observing confidentiality in the treatment of patients, a willingness to provide the home with periodic evaluations of each

youth's needs and with suggestions for adjusting services and staff–resident relations.

9. Holding use of psychotropic drugs to a judicious minimum.

Psychopharmaceuticals play a useful role in the treatment of some group home youngsters. The drugs are not expected to cure mental illness but to ease its painful or debilitating symptoms. That permits the resident to function in school and to adapt in the home's program while the underlying disturbance receives appropriate treatment. Examples of conditions that are sometimes alleviated by drugs are depression, tension, debilitating anxiety, recurring headaches, lethargy, hyperactivity, and excessive weight or weight loss.

In all cases drugs should be employed only under the supervision of a medical doctor, usually a psychiatrist. Caution is required to avoid increased dependence on drugs by a resident as a means of adapting to the demands of everyday life, physical addiction to drugs, harmful side effects on health and personality, and the sharing of prescribed drugs with other youths.

GROUP THERAPY

Group therapy is indicated for youths who are seriously, but not grossly, disturbed and who can be helped toward greater self-awareness and self-understanding by intensive interaction with other youths under the guidance of a trained psychotherapist. It differs from group counseling in that leadership is always by a qualified psychotherapist and communication proceeds at a high level of emotional itensity. The therapist accepts the risks that accompany anger, confrontation, the stripping away of defenses and facades, the emergence of repressed feelings, and the questioning of habitual ways of relating to people and situations. Another difference is that sessions are often devoted to the most confidential areas of the participants' lives.

Like group counseling, group therapy lends itself to the setting of a small residential facility. The population of a home is about the right size for a therapy group. Residents share numerous activities and experiences that permit them to observe each other and that can serve as raw material for analysis. Living together, the residents form a group that exerts a strong influence on its members. For those reasons, homes that purchase group therapy from a group practice or other organization should insist that their residents be kept together in a group of their own, rather than being scattered among groups of other participants.

Group therapy is far less costly than individual psychotherapy, yet comparatively few homes provide that service. Many social workers do not feel qualified to provide group therapy. If a home turns to an outside therapist, it usually finds that the cost of group work is not reimbursable by the Medicaid program. In addition, the technique is not practical in homes with a high turnover of residents.

There are many variations of group therapy, ranging from game playing to encounter sessions. There are differences in theoretical orientation, procedures, and intensity. Numerous publications are available on the subject; see, for example, Raubolt (1983).

Probably the simplest forms of group therapy are best for group homes, given the characteristics of their residents. Parents and the placement agency are likely to object to techniques involving physical contact between participants, uninhibited ways of expressing feelings, marathon sessions, or verbal attacks on a resident. Familiar forms of group work are more easily understood and accepted.

Typically, group therapy is provided once a week in facilities employing that service. However, in some facilities groups meet more often and may be viewed as the central element of the treatment program.

COUNSELING PARENTS

Counseling for parents is an essential service in the treatment of troubled youths. The reasons include the following:

1. The need to understand family relations and practices in order to address the causes of a youth's disturbance.
2. The need to gain the parents' support for the group home's program. Otherwise, their negative attitudes can affect adversely their child's adaptation and response to services.
3. The need to help parents resolve guilt, anger, despair, and anxiety aroused by the out-of-home placement of their child.
4. The critical need to strengthen the family's ability to provide a supportive milieu for the youth when he is ready to leave the group home.

Despite the acknowledged importance of parent counseling, that service is often missing or inadequate for the families of group home youths. Placement agencies lack sufficient staff members to work intensively with parents. After the placement has been made, agency caseworkers may be limited to sporadic contacts to update information or handle emergencies. Group homes lack the resources needed to provide parent counseling on their own. There are other practical obstacles. some parents live far from the facility, lack money for transportation, and/or lack time for regular counseling sessions. They may have inconvenient working hours or be unable to arrange for babysitters to care for their younger children.

Family disorganization hinders parent counseling. The parents may have neglected or abandoned their child and now decline further responsibility. Spouses who have separated may refuse to cooperate. They may have remarried, moved into a house full of stepchildren, or relocated to a distant area.

Parents of group home youths suffer a high incidence of psychological problems themselves. Not infrequently, they are mentally disturbed, retarded, alcoholic, depressed, or enduring other psychic handicaps. They may be physically ill, unemployable, in jail, or in mental hospitals.

Sometimes the placement agency can arrange for the counseling of parents by a guidance service in the parents' own community. However, communication between the parents' counselor and the group home may be minimal, so the treatment of parents and child is conducted without coordination. Family arrangements may change or parents may simply drop out of the counseling program without the knowledge of the placement agency and the group home.

Within their limited resources group homes can meet at least part of the need for parent counseling. Counseling can begin during the parents' preplacement visit to the facility. Thereafter the social worker should try to schedule periodic sessions to update the home's knowledge about the family's status, inform the parents about their child's progress, respond to their concerns and suggestions, and evaluate the youth's visits to and from the family.

In some cases the social worker may wish to include the resident in a family counseling session. That enables the worker to observe the relations between family members, and it may help the participants understand and improve their relations as well. The technique is particularly helpful as the time for the youth's return to the family draws near.

In addition to individual counseling, it is strongly recommended that all homes offer group counseling for parents who are willing and able to attend. Such a technique is economical, requiring only 1 or 2 hours of the social worker's time for each session. It enlists the interaction among parents as a therapeutic tool, encouraging them to exchange information and experience in a supportive way. Homes serving compact geographic areas are in a particularly good position to assemble at least some parents at regular intervals for that activity.

To enable parents to participate in counseling, the home should help with transportation if possible. Sessions should be conducted during evenings and weekends when employed parents are most likely to be available. The serving of refreshments is a special help for parents who have had to skip dinner to meet this commitment.

The home's social worker should accept some responsibility for contacting outside agencies that are providing counseling or other services to the parents. The objective is to exchange information about the progress of family and youngsters. In particular, preparations to terminate a youth's placement should be coordinated to ensure that the family is capable of providing a supportive environment for the child.[1]

[1]For more information on work with parents, see Horejsi, Bertsche, and Clark (1981); Krona (1980); Littaur (1980); and Maluccio and Sinanoglu (1981).

Chapter 11

EDUCATION, RECREATION, AND
HEALTH SERVICES

Continuing the discussion of structured treatment services begun in Chapter 10, this chapter covers three other essential components of group home programs: education, recreation, and health services. Not only do those services contribute directly to the welfare and development of the young people but, by influencing their self-concepts, relationships, and attitudes, they affect the outcome of all other program activities. If health problems are not resolved, for example, they may aggravate psychological distress and impair a youth's relations with peers. Similarly, an untreated learning handicap, an insensitive teacher, or failure at school contribute to psychological problems and may lead to negative behavior in the group home.

The chapter also includes a section on the use of volunteer workers to strengthen education and recreation services in group homes. It is suggested that volunteers, properly selected and trained, can enrich and enliven group home programs.

EDUCATION

Many group home youths did poorly at school prior to their placement. Low grades, bad conduct, truancy, and dropouts are common problems. To a large extent, difficulties at school may have reflected psychological disturbance, physical and cultural deprivation, and the devaluation of education by the peer group. It falls to the group home to counteract such negative influences and to help its residents adapt to life at school.

The schools also must accept responsibility for combating the youngsters' alienation from formal education. Because most group home residents continue to attend public schools after admission, the home depends on the school to identify their learning handicaps, offer supportive services, provide stimulating and relevant courses, and maintain a positive social environment. There is not much a group home can do to overcome the learning handicaps and negative attitudes of its residents if the local school is of poor quality.

It is the school itself that determines what will be taught and how. The school may be chaotic or regimented, stimulating or monotonous, sensitive or indifferent to individual needs—and there is not much the home can do about it. In fact, school officials may blame the group home for their own deficiencies, attributing all truancy, inattentiveness, and lack of progress to inadequate discipline or services in the home.

Fortunately, group homes do not have to remain passive bystanders. There are important things they can do to support the education process. The resources expended for that service are repaid amply by the improved behavior and attitudes of the residents and by the enrichment of their knowledge and interests.

There are at least four ways in which group homes contribute to the schooling of their residents: (a) enrolling the youths in an appropriate school; (b) helping residents make the most of their school experience by reducing psychological barriers, providing incentives, and offering remedial services; (c) correcting negative behavior at school; and (d) conducting educational "enrichment" activities to supplement the school curriculum. Those four areas will be discussed below.

Arranging Appropriate Schooling

At first thought, this function of a group home seems simple. The home merely enrolls each new resident in the local public school, which is required to provide adequate education for all youngsters living in the area. In some localities, however, group homes must be prepared for serious obstacles. The quality of local schools may be inadequate. They may have low standards, unappealing curricula, limited extracurricular activities, and standards of discipline that are either too permissive or too rigid. Special education classes may be absent or inadequate. The student body may include a relatively high proportion of tough or streetwise youths who devalue education while drawing prestige from violent and/or illegal behavior.

Problems are not confined to inner-city schools. Although suburban school districts are likely to have more resources, they are not always a comfortable place for group home youngsters. Those who come from culturally deprived backgrounds or who have limited potential for higher education may feel inferior in that environment. The school may emphasize preparation for college enrollment rather than for immediate employment after graduation. Vocational education for manual trades may be limited. Some student social activities may be too costly for group home residents. Also, experimentation with alcohol and drugs is popular in many suburban high schools.

Delays in enrolling residents are not uncommon. If the family of a new resident lives in the local area, a group home usually has no difficulty in enrolling the youth in the local school. Such youngsters may even remain in the very school they attended prior to their placement. Problems can arise, however, when a group home admits a youth from a different geographic area. The local school may be reluctant to accept outsiders who are labeled as disturbed or maladjusted, and who will probably require special education, intensive counseling, and other expensive services. Local school authorities may object to paying for the education of out-of-area youths. They may resist an enrollment by demanding excessively detailed records and evaluations of the youth's learning handicaps, or by denying that he requires the special services requested by the placement agency. Once admitted, the youngster may be suspended or expelled on the slightest pretext, such as a minor disciplinary incident.

The local school is less reluctant to admit an out-of-area youth if it is reimbursed by a state agency or by school authorities in the youth's home area. Even under those circumstances, however, admission has been delayed while questions such as the following are resolved:

How much money should the school be paid?

Who pays for the youth's education if the parents move to still another geographic area?

What extra services does the youth require, and at what cost?

Which agency is responsible for reimbursing the local school if a child last lived in a residential institution or in foster family care?

What happens if the "sending" school district is dilatory in making payments to the group home's school district?

In recent years states and localities have enacted laws to clarify the responsibility of public schools for the education of children in residential care. Generally, new rules have facilitated school enrollments for group home youngsters. However, even the most precise laws cannot overcome the resistance of uncooperative school officials.

Prejudice presents still another problem. By the time youngsters have been enrolled, evaluated and, where necessary, placed in special education classes, their status as inhabitants of a group home may become widely known in the school. Their frequent meetings with school counselors and the special attendance forms that some homes ask teachers to fill out also help to label them as "different" from other students. Unless school personnel are sensitive to that problem, the young people may become victims of prejudice that interferes with their adaptation at school.

Prejudice can be expressed in subtle ways. It leads teachers to expect group home youths to do poorly and to treat them unconsciously in a manner that invites poor work and bad behavior. A teacher may, for example, demand less work of, or apply lower standards to, a group home youngster. His bad conduct may be dealt with in stricter or more tolerant fashion than similar conduct by other youths. The school may show a readiness to expel group home residents for minor infractions or to relegate them to "home instruction." Fellow students may avoid labeled youths, leaving them to gravitate toward antisocial or marginal peers who are willing to accept them. Prejudice can make school an unpleasant or forbidding place and dissolve a youth's motivation for learning and behaving in a positive manner.

Faced with the reality that they must rely on public schools, what can group homes do to make sure the young people receive appropriate schooling? The best approach is a preventive one; that is, homes should be established only in areas served by high-quality schools capable of assimilating their residents and meeting their educational needs. The schools should have available special education classes and a range of remedial and counseling activities. The social and economic characteristics of their students should comprise a supportive social milieu for the group home's residents. Preferably, the school should be racially integrated, and it should not serve a student body that is drawn exclusively from high- or very low income neighborhoods.

In view of potential problems, group homes must inform themselves about state and local school enrollment and reimbursement policies, which have to be taken into account in selecting residents and setting admission dates.

It is usually a good idea for the director and social worker of a new group home to meet with school officials before they begin enrolling residents. That provides an opportunity to explain their program and to solicit the school's cooperation. The school's anxieties may be alleviated by describing the supportive services and incentives the home plans to employ to combat truancy and to encourage good schoolwork. Arrangements for continuous liaison between the school counselor and the home's social worker are another objective of the meeting.

It may sometimes be advisable to invite the principal or another school official to join the group home's board of directors. However, that is not a good policy in cases where school authorities perceive their interests as different from those of the home. An antagonistic school representative may, for example, insist on the exclusion of youngsters with difficult educational problems and demand excessively rigid punishments to control truancy and bad conduct at school.

Some homes enroll their most maladjusted residents in experimental "alternative" schools, where they are sure of acceptance, individual attention, and flexible curricula. Although that approach may be necessary to serve a few severely handicapped youngsters, there are drawbacks as well. In an alternative school a resident's contacts are limited to other individuals with learning and behavior difficulties. Students of alternative schools are labeled as "problems" by the community, making it more difficult for them to gain social acceptance and to find a job after graduation. Also, homes may find it a hardship to pay the fees required by some alternative schools and to arrange transportation for their students.

Group homes affiliated with larger residential treatment facilities often assign problem residents to private on-grounds schools operated by the parent agencies. That policy may be the best course of action for youngsters who would otherwise wait a long time for enrollment, evaluation, and special education in the public schools. However, in the long run it is inconsistent with the group home concept, under which residents are expected to share community services and mingle with the noninstitutionalized population to the greatest possible extent.

Helping Residents Make the Most of School

After their residents have been enrolled, group homes must help them adapt to the structured school environment and meet academic standards. The youths face the task of making new friends and finding a place in the life of the school. Some may lack adequate motivation to attend school regularly and to break away from patterns of negative behavior. Without assistance, such residents are likely to fail in both the school and group home's program.

There are at least four ways in which group homes can directly support adaptation at school. They are motivation, logistical support, combating truancy, and tutoring. The importance of such activities is underscored by the fact that they are conducted in virtually all homes to a greater or lesser degree. Each is discussed in turn, below.

Motivation   To help youths who lack adequate motivation for schoolwork, staff members should show interest in the residents' progress at school. They should take time to listen to residents who want to talk about their teachers, exams, term papers, achievements, and problems. Where appropriate, the residents' schoolwork can be displayed on a bulletin board in the home. Staff members should visit the school during "open school week" and attend plays, concerts, and other events in which residents participate.

Negative attitudes and values concerning education should be addressed in counseling. The receipt of school grade reports and other school communications can trigger a productive counseling session. Through group counseling, an effort should be made to enlist peer support for good conduct and conscientious work at school. Relevant subjects for counseling sessions include the value of education, choosing friends at school, ways to improve schoolwork, coping with prejudice at school, causes and cures for truancy and other negative behavior, and the consequences of dropping out of school.

Incentives should be made available to encourage good effort at school. They may range from simple praise to material rewards, expanded privileges, and recognition at ceremonial events. The staff should be aware, however, that incentives for schoolwork may have injurious effects if not planned with proper care. For example, rewards given to educational achievers may discourage or anger residents who have tried hard, but unsuccessfully, to improve their schoolwork. Rewards for schoolwork may disrupt peer relations in the home, stimulating jealousy, creating hostile cliques of those who do and do not value education, and threatening existing status relationships. Youths who do not receive rewards are likely to try to influence other residents to take a cynical view of the incentives and to denigrate hard work at school.

The key to planning an incentive system is careful consideration of how the incentives will be perceived and valued by the residents. To be effective, incentives should be valued by all residents, even those who fail to win a reward. Also, they must not impair positive peer group relations in the home. Perhaps the best approach is to distribute equal rewards to all youths who have demonstrated good conduct and effort at school during a specified period, regardless of their grades. Those objectives are attainable by even slow learners and youths alienated from schoolwork. Awards for good school attendance also give all youngsters an equal chance for recognition. To encourage group acceptance of the proffered incentives, the residents themselves might be invited to nominate individuals to receive awards for effort and cooperation.

If the home offers gifts as incentives, it is a good idea to select gifts that contribute to educational achievement. For example, a youth doing well at science is likely both to enjoy and to benefit from a magnifying glass or chemistry set. A good reader benefits from a book of short stories; an athlete might find a book on sports to his liking.

Logistical support.   Group homes can help their residents meet school requirements by providing necessary materials and facilities. They should provide school supplies required by the youths, arrange transportation after regular school hours to permit residents to engage in extracurricular activities, and provide clothing that does not distinguish residents from their schoolmates. A daily "quiet period" should be set aside for homework and reading. Some basic reference materials, such as a dictionary, thesaurus, and atlas should be available in the home. A lucky group home may receive a dog-eared set of encyclopedias from some charitable donor. Encyclopedias also can be purchased at low cost at stores selling used books.

Residents with learning problems should be enrolled in summer school, if necessary, to help them keep up with their studies.

Combating truancy.   Getting their residents to attend school regularly is a difficult task for group homes. Truancy reflects not only the attitudes of the resident but the quality of the school. The former can be modified by the home's treatment program, but the latter is not within the control of the home.

By punishing or withholding rewards from truants, the staff is in a position to compel them to attend school, however reluctantly. However, compulsion alone is likely to give rise to hostility toward schools and study. Youths forced to go to school may vent their frustration by exerting negative peer pressure against fellow residents who try to meet school requirements. It is important to supplement compulsion with more positive measures: exploring the reasons for the truant's behavior, working with the school staff to meet individual needs, and providing services to support the education process.

The factors that contribute to truancy are so varied that substantial flexibility is required in working with different offenders. A youth might stay away from school for the following reasons, among others:

a desire to gain or retain prestige and acceptance in the peer group;

boredom and failure to see the relevance of courses at school;

inability to grasp the schoolwork and to keep up with the class;

fear of hazing and bullying at school;

exaggerated fear of failure in examinations and class recitations;

physical problems, such as poor sight, impaired hearing, and insomnia that interfere with learning and' attentiveness;

embarrassment about physical defects such as unusual height or obesity, nudity in the locker room, physical exams, poor grades, inability to speak English clearly, and the like;

family problems, homesickness, and harmful personal relationships that prompt visits to ailing relatives, the old neighborhood, and friends of the opposite sex;

use of mind-altering drugs.

Within the constraints that limit the group home's influence there are steps the home can take to alleviate the truancy problem. The school should be requested to notify the group home promptly, by telephone, of the unauthorized absence of any resident. Otherwise it may be days before the staff learns about a youth's truancy. Immediate notification requires special arrangements with the school. However, every effort should be made to avoid labeling the residents and stirring the latent prejudices of teachers and fellow students.

Some homes have required their residents to carry cards that teachers sign daily to certify that the youths have attended their classes. That is an effective policing technique, but it identifies in an obvious manner pupils who live in a group home and presents them as individuals who bear watching—thus contributing to the labeling process.

Problems contributing to a youth's truancy should be explored in individual counseling. If possible, counselor and resident should reach an agreement specifying the actions that the youth and the home will take to combat truancy in the future. The staff, for example, might agree to step up tutoring and to contact the school concerning possible transfer into a work–study program. Extra family visits, speech therapy, or new eyeglasses might be indicated. The youth, in turn, might agree to such steps as accompanying another resident to school each morning; accepting another student as a "buddy" or mentor at school; refraining from visiting friends during school hours, inviting them to visit at the group home instead; altering modes of dress and behavior that irritate peers at school.

In group counseling, residents should be encouraged to discuss the value of education in enriching personal life and achieving career goals. Where appropriate, the group may focus on the truancy of one of its members—exploring its causes and consequences for the individual, discussing alternative ways in which he can improve attendance, suggesting action that the group home might take, and providing support and approval for the offender's efforts to improve.

The home's social worker should maintain close liaison with the school counselor to combat truancy. Nonpunitive actions that the school might consider include testing for sight and hearing defects; testing of intelligence, aptitude, and scholastic achievement; transfer to a special education class or a different course of study; enrollment in a work–study program; tutoring; advancement to the next school grade or other grade adjustments; alerting the youth's teachers to his special needs, with suggestions for providing support or attention.

For some chronic truants, punishment may be a therapeutic response. That is particularly true of youths who could do satisfactory schoolwork if they tried but who absent themselves because they derive prestige and/or material gains from truancy.

Tutoring.   Apart from its educational value, tutoring yields important psychological benefits. By helping slow learners keep pace with good students, it motivates them to attend their classes and do their schoolwork. It bolsters self-esteem and confidence as schoolwork shows improvement. And it offers opportunities to develop supportive relationships with the adults or peers who serve as tutors.

Tutoring should not be limited to subjects in which the resident is receiving low grades. Just as important are general scholastic skills that help students analyze, learn, memorize, and present their thoughts effectively. Many group home youngsters are handicapped by their lack of these capabilities. Examples of general scholastic skills that lend themselves to tutoring are proper study techniques; clear and rapid penmanship; reading with speed and comprehension; clear and grammatical speech; effective writing; research techniques, including how to select topics for term papers, use library facilities, collect and organize data, and analyze research results; how to prepare for and take exams; how to write and "package" school reports; how to make oral reports in class.

Child care workers are more likely than other staff members to serve as tutors. With or without a planned tutoring schedule, the youngsters may be expected to ask workers for help with homework and problems at school. Unfortunately, child care workers have other pressing duties and may not be able to spare an adequate amount of time with each individual. Moreover, workers may lack some of the technical knowledge needed for tutoring teenagers. Not all of us remember our high school mathematics, physics, sociology, or computer science. We may have been taught such subjects in now outmoded ways.

To provide adequate tutoring, some group homes have tapped outside personnel. Arrangements fot tutors have been made through local schools and federally funded work programs such as CETA, VISTA, and Foster Grandparents. University students majoring in education, psychology, or related subjects are usually willing to serve as tutors in return for course credit or research data. Often unaffiliated volunteers can be recruited from the surrounding community.

It is useful to experiment with peer tutoring, in which youths who are having trouble at school are coached by more capable residents who volunteer for the job. That not only improves a youth's schoolwork but provides benefits to the tutor as well. The latter gains status in the peer group, self-esteem, an opportunity to demonstrate leadership qualities, and even a better knowledge of the material being taught.

Peer tutoring has obvious limitations. The youths lack tutoring skills. They can base their instruction only on their own routine experiences at school. They cannot supply the illustrations, stimulation, or generalized scholastic skills that contribute to long-run achievement. Still, the advantages of peer tutoring suggest that it is a worthwhile supplement to tutoring by adults in many cases.

Correcting Negative Behavior at School

Sooner or later school personnel are likely to complain about a resident's behavior. Negative incidents at school are to be expected from disturbed or maladjusted youths. The school probably will insist on corrective action by the group home and may even expel or suspend the offender until the misbehavior is brought under control.

To plan appropriate responses it is helpful to distinguish three kinds of misbehavior. One form may be termed learning-related; it includes lack of attention or sleeping in class, failure to turn in homework, and minor mischief during class or study periods. A second form consists of violations of rules regarding the maintenance of order and safety in the school. Examples of such misbehavior are disobedience to teachers, smoking in unauthorized places, hazing weaker youths, or smearing grafitti on the walls. Such actions are disruptive and violate the rights of others but are not likely to involve law enforcement authorities. Most serious is a third form of misbehavior—activities that are significant violations of the law. Examples are assaults on a teacher or student, theft from a fellow student's locker, destructive vandalism, and use of illegal drugs on school property. Distinguishing among those three types of negative behavior makes it possible to plan remedial action geared to individual needs.

In all cases the first step is to learn the facts surrounding the school's complaint. If necessary, the home's social worker or director should discuss the problem with school personnel. A private counseling session should be scheduled to get the resident's side of the story. Sometimes the incident may merely be the result of poor communication, inadequate information, or prejudice.

In cases of negative behavior that is learning-related, the staff should try to identify and alleviate the problems that led to the misbehavior. Poor health may be a factor; e.g., inability to see the blackboard or hear the teacher. Simply moving a youth to the front row in class, fitting him with new glasses, or procuring a hearing aid may lead to long-run improvement. Sleeping in class may be due to a youth's lack of sleep at night. That might be corrected by advancing the home's curfew or "lights out" hour, assigning a less garrulous roommate to the youth, encouraging more physical exercise, and extending the "cooling off" period before bedtime. Fatigue caused by excessive physical activity during nonschool hours also may be the cause of sleeping in class. A youth may be working too hard at a paid part-time job or spending too much time at football practice.

An overcrowded schedule of activities in the group home may be responsible for a youth's failure to turn in homework. In such a case it would be advisable to cut back on scheduled activities and to extend the daily "quiet hour" to provide more study time.

Family or other interpersonal problems in and out of the group home may leave a youth tense and preoccupied at school. Sensitive counseling may ease that situation.

School courses that are uninteresting or that exceed a youth's capabilities contribute to behavior problems. The school may be able to arrange a change of courses; e.g., from an academic to a vocational program. Some youths may find new motivation in a work–study program. Learning disabilities might be overcome by tutoring, transfer to a special education class, or other remedial services.

Intensive fact-finding is also important in addressing disruptive and antisocial behavior at school. The causes and meaning of such incidents vary from youth to youth. A disrespectful "wisecrack" to a teacher, sneaking out of the chemistry lab for a smoke, or circulating pronographic pictures in the lavatory may reflect efforts to maintain a "tough guy" image, compensate for failing grades, express sexual anxieties, or act out resentment against adult authority. Counseling may bring to the surface the meaning that negative behavior holds for the offender and factors that contribute to its persistence.

Group counseling can be particularly effective in this area because participants share school experiences and can identify aspects of their fellow resident's activities at school that may be unknown to the staff. Where punishment is called for, a well-informed staff is in a position to select the penalty most likely to outweigh the psychological or material gains that the offender receives from his misbehavior.

The most serious forms of misbehavior—illegal activities—obviously require a more stringent response. If a law has been violated to a significant degree, the police have to be involved. However, a school that has a cooperative relationship with a group home may agree not to press charges against a youth for relatively minor episodes of vandalism, fighting, or small-scale theft —provided that the home takes remedial action to prevent future incidents.

If illegal activity has been relatively minor, not likely to be repeated, not physically dangerous to self and others, and unlikely to impair the group home's program, the staff may agree to retain the offender and take corrective action on its own. There is room for flexible judgment; nobody is anxious to stigmatize and lock up a remorseful teenager for smoking "pot" in the school lavatory or gambling in the schoolyard during lunch hour. Fines, restrictions, and restitution may be adequate punishments that impose no lasting harm on a youth's development. On the other hand, if a resident exhibits a continued pattern of illegal behavior, it is best to remove him from the home.

Educational Enrichment in the Home

Most families supplement the formal education of their children with stimulating activities that add to their knowledge and skills. The typical family takes trips to historic sites, plays parlor games, and discusses current events. The curiosity and intelligence of the children are stimulated as they help adults perform tasks around the home, accompany them on walks and shopping trips, and talk to them over the dinner table. Parents send their children to Sunday school and enroll them in music and art classes. Often there are books, magazines, and records around the house. Young people exposed to those sources of educational enrichment are more likely to do well at school than those who grow up in culturally deprived, intellectually drab settings.

Like the family, group homes can supplement the education of their residents—helping them become achievers at school and improving their social and economic opportunities after graduation. Homes can help to offset the cultural deprivation experienced by many of their residents while stimulating new interests that divert youthful energy from negative behavior.

One way to enrich the education of the young people is to expose them to reading materials. A bookcase full of books and magazines should be maintained in all homes. If possible, light fiction should be supplemented by some of the classics, poetry, and other nonfiction works. Often books and magazines are donated by charitable individuals or can be purchased at low cost in used-book stores.

Homes should subscribe to at least one good newspaper. Access to the public library should be facilitated, using the home's vehicle for transportation if necessary. Residents should be encouraged to apply for library cards.

Weekly group discussions on educational topics expand the knowledge and interests of the youngsters. Guest speakers, such as health specialists, marriage counselors, businessmen, athletes, and community officials might be invited for short talks. Perhaps someone who has traveled can be prevailed on to show slides of the trip.

Residents should be invited to suggest discussion topics that interest them. An endless array of potential subjects includes current events; local politics; the presidential election; conservation and environmental issues; budgeting, credit, and money management; consumer rights and skills; buying and maintaining a car; etiquette and proper dress; good marital relations; parenting; speaking in public; your philosophy of life; choosing a career; a thought-provoking play, movie, or television show seen recently by all residents.

Like good parents, the group home staff should be alert to identify and encourage residents who have talents in the arts, crafts, or other special areas. The home should facilitate extra learning opportunities for interested youngsters; e.g., by arranging for lessons in piano playing, drawing, or singing. Placement agencies should accept the cost of lessons, transportation, instruments, and materials as appropriate child care expenditures, and they should reimburse group homes accordingly. Art and craft activities demand an investment of time and money, but it is repaid amply by the diversion of youthful energy into positive channels and by gains in personal growth.

RECREATION

The best recreation activities are fun. They emerge spontaneously from the interests and feelings of participants. Why then should they be included among the planned, structured services of group homes? The answer is that recreation not only provides fun and relaxation but offers opportunities for influencing the character and growth of young people. It becomes, therefore, an important therapeutic tool in the group home program.

A group home's recreation program has the following objectives:

1. Providing fun and relaxation that improve the residents' state of mind and receptivity to other services. Activities should help to reduce depression, anxiety, passivity, and withdrawal.

2. Diverting residents from self-harming behavior and encouraging them in a nondirective way to spend more free time in positive activities.

3. Improving health through exercise and exposure to the outdoors.

4. Providing opportunities for informal and pleasant interaction with the staff.

5. Encouraging group cohesion through shared experiences.

6. Providing residents with opportunities for achievement, group acceptance, and leadership.

7. Providing opportunities to learn how to compete, win, lose, cooperate, be assertive, and apply other social skills.

8. Providing opportunities for boys and girls to become acquainted in a safe, natural way.

9. Identifying and encouraging talented youngsters.

10. Providing opportunities to learn lifetime recreational skills, e.g., swimming, bridge, birdwatching, dancing.

11. Expanding cultural horizons and interests.

12. Making constructive use of free time during the summer months when residents are not in school.

Recreation activities guided by those objectives require thoughtful planning and coordination with other services. As an essential program activity, their cost should be reimbursed by the placement agency.

The supply of potential recreation activities is bounded only by imagination. A group home's choices are influenced, of course, by the characteristics of its residents, the interests and capabilities of the staff, the physical facilities of the home, its financial resources, and the mix of services available in the community. Even a low-budget home, however, can develop a creative program by drawing on the avocational skills of its own staff, free community facilities and events, donated equipment, and the labor of adult volunteers. Some suggestions follow.

Spontaneous Activities

Recreation equipment and materials should be available around all homes for spontaneous use by residents. A rack full of bats, racquets, and balls, a net for volleyball and badminton, bicycles, weightlifting equipment, and a basketball hoop on the side of the garage encourage wholesome physical activity. A Ping-Pong table in the recreation room and some popular records for dancing keep active youngsters busy on rainy days. Access to shelves containing Monopoly and Scrabble games, jigsaw puzzles, and playing cards facilitates quieter, more cerebral recreation.

Membership in Organizations

Group homes should enroll their residents in organizations that offer recreational opportunities. The local YM/YWCA is an excellent resource. So are local swim clubs, hiking clubs, the Police Athletic League, and the Boy/Girl Scouts. In addition to giving access to recreation facilities, such organizations help residents meet new friends of both sexes in a positive setting and contribute to their social skills.

Community Resources

Group homes should encourage youths to participate in community programs. Youngsters may be interested in singing with the choral society, attending a dance sponsored by a local church, running in the Park Department's annual marathon, or playing in a bowling or baseball league. Lists of community happenings are available in newspapers and from local recreation departments.

Outings

Recreational outings are conducted by all homes. Some are simply spectator activities—watching a ball game or movie or taking a boat ride. To stimulate cultural interests, an occasional outing to a museum, play, concert, dance recital, or historic site is added to the schedule.

Perhaps most beneficial are outings that involve active participation by the young people. Examples are canoeing, swimming at the seashore, fishing, hiking, and cross-country skiing. Such activities teach the youngsters lifelong recreational skills and satisfy their adventurous urges.

Generally, residents should not be taken on outings more than once a week. Greater frequency tends to make them blasé and unappreciative and may interfere with other activities. The youths should be consulted on the choice of outings. The staff will not get far in trying to impose its own interests, as anyone knows who has shepherded a glum, reluctant group of teenagers around a museum all afternoon.

In some populations there may be a persistent difference of opinion on the choice of outings. Older and younger youths often have divergent interests, and a resident who likes concerts will always be outvoted by those who prefer ball games. Where reasonable compromises cannot be worked out, it is a good idea to split the group from time to time, to satisfy the special interests of its members. If the home does not have sufficient staff members to escort more than one group at a time, it may be able to recruit adult volunteers for this task.

Occasionally a resident prefers to remain at home rather than participate in an outing. Although that may inconvenience the staff, it is unwise to force the youth to come along. Rather, patient counseling may uncover significant reasons for the youth's decision. There may be some rational justification; e.g., the need for time to complete a school project or the onset of a bad cold. The youth may be experiencing tensions in relations with other residents, feel embarrassed about revealing a physical disfigurement at the beach, or dread showering in the nude at the swim club. He may be ashamed to admit never having learned to dance or swim, a fear of high places, or claustrophobia. An older youth may be embarrassed about being herded about in public with much younger residents. Or refusal to go on an outing may simply be an expression of resentment about some unrelated aspect of group home life. Such problems are better handled by private counseling than by cajoling or compulsion.

It is not wise to plan outings that some youngsters may find threatening. The staff should keep in mind the needs of phobic residents who are afraid of deep water, snakes, horses, heights, crowds, getting lost in the woods, and the like.

Long trips not only consume time and money, but they invite boredom, restlessness, and mischief. In turn, that negative behavior leads to disciplinary measures, wears out the staff, and spoils everyone's fun. To avoid problems, therefore, outings should be limited to short periods of travel. Longer trips undertaken on rare occasions should be planned to minimize sources of possible friction.

As a general rule, the duration of outings should not exceed the participants' span of interest. In activities such as camping, interest may be sustained for several days. On the other hand, a couple of hours is likely to be the maximum for a trip to the art museum, and that probably includes a visit to the snack bar, to boot.

Group Adventures

Many young people seek adventure and new experiences that contrast with the safe humdrum routines of daily life. If they cannot satisfy that tendency within the boundaries of the home's program, they may satisfy it in secretive and dangerous ways outside the home. It is suggested, therefore, that group homes provide opportunities for adventure and the testing of personal limits—but in a controlled setting that holds risks to a minimum and maximizes the therapeutic benefits of such activities. Examples of group adventures are camping trips, moonlight hikes, rock climbing for beginners, ski lessons, canoeing, rafting, "tubing," a day of sailing, a sightseeing visit to a nearby metropolis, and a visit to an amusement park.

The availability of legitimate outlets for risk-taking and excitement is likely to reduce peer pressure to engage in more dangerous or harmful activities. It enhances the cohesion of the group; the youths have done something together that outside friends cannot share. It may lead to a gain of self-confidence for some youngsters. Sometimes participation in venturesome activities opens a crack in the protective facades with which residents face the everyday adult world and helps them form more open and trusting relationships with the adults who have shared their outing.

From a treatment viewpoint the gains of "controlled adventure" outweigh the risk of an occasional sprain, bruise, or spill. Seeking excitement, independence, and the admiration of peers, disturbed youths can get into much greater trouble on their own.

Planned Activities in the Home

Recreation activities need not involve a trip from home nor payment of admission fees. Group homes can draw on their own resources to provide recreation within the facility. That approach is rooted in an old American tradition: the gathering of family and friends around the fireplace, piano, or Christmas tree to share good times. The tradition includes the sharing of holiday rituals, festive family dinners, joining in song and instrumental performances, reading aloud, and playing group games—from building a tower of matchsticks to "pin the tail on the donkey."

Whether that is myth or reality in the dispersed and fragmented family of today, in-home group recreation can have worthwhile effects. It helps to convert the group home from a drab impersonal dormitory to a warm and vibrant community. It fills dull intervals caused by bad weather, canceled outings, and the closing of school for holidays. It builds cohesion among the residents. Planned recreation in the facility provides residents with opportunities to display their talents, assume responsibilities, and learn social skills. It develops interests and tastes that youngsters may carry over into their family life when they leave the group home. In a nondirective, nonconfrontational way it keeps the youngsters close to home and out of trouble during their free time.

Some activities that should be considered for an in-home recreation program include the following:

1. The celebration of Christmas/Chanukah, New Year's Day, the Fourth of July, and other holidays with parties and appropriate ceremonies.
2. Play readings in which residents take specific roles.
3. Group singing.
4. Demonstrations and performances by local artists, and lessons by experts in judo and aerobic dancing.

5. Mentally stimulating team games such as charades, Scrabble, "What's My Line?" or spelling bees.

6. Group projects such as sewing a patchwork quilt or painting a mural on the rec room wall.

It is not easy to squeeze planned in-home recreation into the busy schedule. If time cannot be found on a regular basis, the activity may have to be limited to special days or undertaken spontaneously whenever rain keeps the residents indoors, they are overcome by lassitude or depression, or there is a spontaneous surge of interest in the activity.

Like other forms of recreation, in-home activities cannot be forced on unwilling youngsters. They should be consulted about the type of activities they prefer and given a hand in the planning process. The activities should be something they look forward to and are proud of. Enthusiasm may increase if residents are permitted to invite a few outside friends to observe or participate.

Extracurricular Activities at School

Participation in extracurricular activities at school can be enjoyable and at the same time help young people make new friends and develop social skills. In many group homes there are youths who engage in school-sponsored athletics, play in the school orchestra, and participate in school clubs.

Unfortunately, the proportion of residents who participate in such activities is usually small. Some youths do not remain in the facility long enough to establish roots in their school. Others are hindered by psychological problems. Transportation difficulties and inadequate funds may make it difficult for the youngsters to join in certain activities. Generally, extracurricular school activities are underutilized as a recreation resource.

SUMMER ACTIVITIES

Planned recreation assumes special importance during the summer months, when youths are out of school. In the absence of daily school routines, there is ample time for idleness, depression, and negative behavior. On the other hand, the summer offers opportunities to enrich the lives of the young people with outdoor activities, trips, paid employment, and avocational projects. Tensions may decline as residents go further afield for work, recreation, and companionship.

An effective program for the summer requires extra money and staff. There are more activities over longer periods, and they are more expensive. A "summer activities leader" may have to be hired. The cost of transportation, a week in the country, dancing lessons, camping supplies, and such can exceed a home's resources. Placement agencies should recognize that summer recreation activities are essential and provide extra funds to support them.

Suggestions for planning summer activities are presented below.

Employment of a Summer Activities Leader

It is recommended that at least larger group homes employ a summer activities leader to plan and implement a recreation/education program for the summer months. Generally, child care workers and other regular staff members are too busy to assume that responsibility, and they may lack the necessary skills.

There is enough work to be done to keep the summer activities leader busy on a full-time basis. Tasks include (a) planning activities in consultation with the staff and residents, (b) exploring and arranging access to community recreational resources, (c) seeking summer jobs and volunteer opportunities for the residents and supporting their adjustment on the job by counseling both the youths and their employers, (d) identifying and arranging educational opportunities for youngsters with special talents and interests and for those who need help keeping up at school, and (e) leading recreational and educational activities both in and outside the home. In addition to assuming those responsibilities the summer activities leader meets the practical need for an additional hand to help supervise the residents during the extra hours that they are out of school in the vacation period.

Because the summer activities leader is employed in the interval when schools are closed, vacationing teachers and graduate students are likely candidates for this job. Some homes have been able to acquire summer workers at no cost from their parent agencies or from federally funded employment programs.

Homes serving only a few youngsters may find it practical to share the services of a summer activities leader with another small facility located nearby.

Summer Jobs for Residents

A good way to use the summer constructively is to work at a paid job. In addition to earning money, employed youngsters can learn good work habits and how to cooperate with supervisors and co-workers. A job helps them test their career preferences and develop confidence and independence. Idleness, boredom, and the temptation to engage in negative behavior are reduced.

Group homes should try to arrange paid summer employment for their teenage residents, and the youths should be encouraged to seek jobs on their own. The choice of jobs depends on local employment opportunities and the age, interests, and psychological handicaps of the residents. Jobs may be full-time or part-time. The young people may work for private employers at such tasks as making deliveries, caring for lawns, selling ice cream, baby-sitting, and clerical work. Or they may be employed in jobs subsidized by government agencies; e.g., as aides in child care centers, nursing homes, parks, and libraries. Perhaps the home's parent agency may have summer openings for one or two youths. If no paid work is available, it may be possible to arrange interesting jobs as volunteers in community health and welfare agencies.

After placing a resident in a job, the group home's staff cannot wash its hands of the youngster. There is a continuing need to follow each individual's progress to detect and deal with emerging problems. Conflicts and misunderstandings between youngsters and their supervisors and co-workers may have to be resolved. A resident may have difficulty in grasping instructions, experience anxiety, find the job monotonous and unproductive, or rebel against authority. Such problems often can be alleviated by counseling the youths and their supervisors, or by modifying work arrangements.

Earnings from summer employment, added to a resident's regular allowance, can amount to a substantial sum. The young people may be tempted to use that money unwisely. Also, large sums of money carried about the facility invite envy, borrowing, stealing, and extortion. It is a good idea, therefore, to require employed youths to bank a portion of their take-home pay in individual savings accounts.

Utilizing Community Resources

In most localities government and private agencies make available extra recreational activities during the summer. Often, it takes some digging to identify the resources and to solicit access to them, but the effort is repaid by the exposure of a home's youngsters to stimulating activities at low cost.

The following are examples of benefits that are provided by some private organizations and government agencies:

1. A week or two in a summer camp, donated or subsidized by businessmen's groups, the YM/YWCA, or other sources.

2. Day camps operated by the local recreation department, the Y, or others.

3. Scholarships provided by health clubs, dancing schools, and modeling schools.

4. Free or discounted tickets to ball games, bowling establishments, plays, swim clubs, and museums.

5. Invitations to dances and picnics sponsored by local churches.

6. Guided tours through wildlife sanctuaries and other nature settings.

Outdoor Recreation

During the summer outdoor exercise and exploration partly displace the sedentary televison watching of the winter season. To encourage outdoor activities, it is helpful if at least some staff members have skills and interests related to the outdoors. Sometimes adult volunteers can be recruited to lend a hand in that area. Members of the local bird-watching group or a vacationing science teacher may turn a stroll through the park into a great learning experience. Local athletes may offer to provide tips on their specialty, and a retired forest ranger makes good company on a camping trip.

Expanded Educational Activities

Summertime also opens new opportunities for educational enrichment. Activities can be undertaken that require more effort and time than can be spared while school is in session. A resident may wish to enroll in a 6-week art class or work with the local amateur theatre. Another may use extra time to rehearse with a musical group or to start guitar lessons. Time can now be found for the in-home discussion groups, guest speaker, "amateur hour," and baking demonstration that were squeezed out of the schedule by the pressures of the school year.

Some residents can use the vacation period to improve their achievement in school. Summer schools are operated in many school districts for students in need of extra help. The group home itself can intensify tutoring by the staff, fellow residents, and/or adult volunteers.

HEALTH SERVICES

Health services must be a planned component of every group home's program. The home assumes responsibility for providing suitable health care for all youths placed in its charge. That is a matter of deep concern to the placement agency and, in most cases, to the parents of residents.

Poor health affects adversely the youngsters' adaptation in the home and school. Many examples of the effects of physical health problems on social/psychological adjustment can be suggested:

1. A vitamin deficiency or other chemical imbalance may be linked to lethargy, depression, hyperactivity, and irritability.
2. Susceptibility to colds and other infections impairs school attendance and curtails participation in beneficial activities.
3. Hearing, speech, and sight defects handicap schoolwork and the ability to interact with other people.

4. Chronic headaches, backaches, ulcers, bad teeth, and other painful maladies make it difficult to concentrate at school, join in peer group activities, and benefit from treatment services.

5. Physical disfigurement may affect adversely an individual's self-image and the way he is viewed by others. Youths who suffer from obesity, acne, an unsightly mole or scar, or badly formed teeth may fear or experience rejection and ridicule. They may respond by isolating themselves from peers, developing a tough-guy facade or other self-harming behavior.

The group home's responsibility for nurturing the normal sexual development of its residents is another aspect of health services. Serving adolescents simmering with sexual urges and curiosity, the home is responsible for helping them understand their feelings and learn to express them in ways that are appropriate for their age and level of maturity. Troubling questions and decisions about sexual activity, birth control, pregnancy, abortion, and venereal disease must be anticipated.

Health services are too complex to be left to improvisation. They require advance consideration of costs, funding, and objectives. Sources of medical care need to be arranged. Staff training is required, covering first aid, prevention of illness, identification of health problems, and action in emergencies. There is also a need for coordination between staff members and outside health professionals who work with the youths.

Suggested Services

Preventive health care is an important function of group homes. Physical and dental exams should be arranged for all residents at least annually. Tests of sight and hearing should be included.

Balanced meals at regular hours are an aspect of preventive health care. Homes also must take into account the needs of youths on special diets and make available healthful snacks to reduce the consumption of junk food.

With the cost of medical and dental care usually covered by Medicaid or placement agency funds, group homes are in a position to arrange high-quality health care for their residents. The home can choose competent doctors from those in individual practice, group practice, and health maintenance organizations. Resources may even permit special treatment to correct disfigurement that affects adversely the psychological adjustment of a youth.

It is helpful to select a health care provider who is within walking distance, so that the staff will not have to drive residents to all of their appointments. During their initial examination for a particular illness, however, most residents do appreciate the supportive company of an adult.

The home should choose health care providers who are sensitive to the feelings of troubled young people. Many youths are unfamiliar with medical procedures and have unrealistic conceptions of illness and treatment. They may fear gynecological checkups, blood tests, injections, dental procedures, anesthesia, and surgery. Doctors and dentists patronized by the home should be patient and sympathetic people who take time to listen, explain what they are doing, and try to relieve undue anxiety.

Health education should be a component of every home's program. Most youths are ignorant about proper nutrition, opting for candy bars, french fries, and sugar-rich beverages at every opportunity. They do not brush their teeth regularly. Insufficient exercise is a problem, particularly in the winter months. The young people lack adequate information about the symptoms and treatment of common ailments, patent medicines, and common health appliances like thermometers and vaporizers. Facts about harmful practices such as drug abuse, drinking alcoholic beverages, and smoking are also not universally known. Group homes can help to fill the information gap.

Health care is a good subject for group discussions. Useful topics include hygiene, nutrition, and drug abuse. A qualified staff member or guest experts such as doctors, nurses, and dietitians can serve as resource persons. In some areas local health departments, drug and alcoholism clinics, local chapters of voluntary health organizations, or other community groups may furnish speakers and audiovisual aids.

Supporting Healthy Sexual Development

Like teenagers elsewhere, those in group homes are under peer pressure to explore sexual relationships and many are sexually active. Their sexual experimentation is normal, and efforts to eliminate it are unrealistic and counterproductive. Rigid controls breed evasion and a breakdown in open communication between staff and residents. They surround a natural biological/social development with ignorance, shame, and anxiety.

The group home does, however, have legitimate concerns and responsibilities with respect to sexual development. The sexual beliefs, attitudes, and feelings of the young people, and the relationships they form must be taken into account in the treatment of their emotional disturbances and maladjustment. The home has to guide the youths to form positive and realistic conceptions about their own sexual nature and about relations with the opposite sex. It must monitor their outside contacts to become aware of self-harming relations and to influence them in positive directions. There is also a practical need to prevent venereal disease and pregnancy. Some suggested steps are listed below:

Sex education.   Sex education should be provided by all homes. Even the most sexually active youngsters are often ignorant about the physiology of reproduction, health hazards, and the emotional aspects of relations between boys and girls. Their knowledge is based on folk myths, exaggerations circulated in the youth subculture, television shows, destructive experiences in their own families, and superficial adventures with atypical partners. Factual description of the processes and structures of sex and reproduction help to undermine beliefs that they are dirty, evil, or something to be ashamed of.

In group counseling and discussions the staff should guide residents to a view of sexual relations as not only an expression of natural instincts but as an intimate emotional experience shared by people who care for each other. The responsibility of sexual partners to each other should be highlighted. Distorted views about the opposite sex and myths about masturbation, menstruation, nocturnal emissions, and changes in body characteristics that accompany adolescence can be dispelled.

The prevention and detection of venereal disease is another topic for sex education, with particular relevance in an age when herpes, AIDS, and other sexually transmitted diseases have reached epidemic proportions.

Birth control information.   Serious religious and philosophic questions have been raised about the treatment of birth control as a topic for sex education. It can be argued on moral and health grounds that teenagers should be persuaded to abstain from sex until marriage and that the provision of information on birth control encourages promiscuity. In practice, however, there is nothing a community-based group home can do to prevent determined youths from pursuing sexual relationships. If the youths do not receive reliable information about birth control, there is the risk of unanticipated pregnancy, perhaps inflicting lifelong social, psychological, and economic harm. Worse, it may lead to secret, dangerous efforts to terminate the pregnancy. It seems reasonable, therefore, to make available reliable information about birth control.

The need for information is not limited to girls. Boys too should be counseled about the mutual responsibility of sexual partners.

Group counseling and discussions on birth control should be led by adults who are knowledgeable and comfortable with the subject. It has been suggested that instructors be of the same sex as the residents, to encourage a franker exchange (Mayer, 1958, p. 85). In addition to staff members, outsiders such as doctors, nurses, and local representatives of Planned Parenthood may be available to give instruction.

Supplying birth control materials.   A more sensitive question is whether group homes should make available birth control devices and substances to sexually active youths. Often the young people and their partners are too ignorant, embarrassed, or apprehensive to purchase condoms, spermicides, and other over-the-counter materials on their own. Diaphragms and birth control pills, which require contacts with medical personnel, are even more out of reach. If the home does not help residents acquire and learn how to use those items, it is likely that they will trust to luck in their sexual encounters —with a high risk of getting into trouble.

Before making available to a resident means of preventing pregnancy, the youth should receive counseling concerning the motives, feelings, and consequences associated with his or her sexual relations. The group home should check with the youth's caseworker to be sure that it is in conformity with placement agency policies. The age of the youth, the characteristics of the sexual partner, and the duration and effects of their relationship must be taken into account. In extreme cases, youths who insist on pursuing self-destructive relationships may have to be transferred from the group home to a treatment center capable of providing more intensive controls.

The group home, in consultation with the placement agency caseworker, will have to decide whether to notify the youth's parents that he is involved in sexual activity and whether the parents' permission to provide birth control materials should be requested. It is probably best to decide each case on an individual basis. Some overly rigid parents may inflict cruel punishments, demand an end to long-term and supportive relationships that are actually of therapeutic value, and even remove their child from the home. They might file complaints with the placement agency, elected government officials, and the news media, alleging that the facility is a hotbed of immorality.

A reasonable principle is that group homes should notify parents about a youth's sexual activity or ask their permission to provide birth control materials only when it is in the therapeutic interest of the resident to do so.

It is suggested that the youngsters be required to pay all or part of the cost of birth control measures. The objective is to compel them to decide how much of their limited financial resources they are willing to assign to that aspect of their lives relative to the claims of competing interests and needs. It is to be hoped that the expense, accompanied by sensitive counseling, will lead youths to evaluate the rewards and disadvantages of teenage sexual relationships and to clarify their values and priorities.

Dealing with Pregnancy

Sooner or later, a pregnancy will occur among girls who pass through group homes. The home's response must reflect concern for the welfare of the pregnant girl. The staff has other responsibilities as well: to prevent the incident from affecting adversely the state of mind of other residents, to protect the home's reputation in the community, and to satisfy the requirements of the placement agency. The role of the girl's parents also can become an issue. Although the needs of individual girls differ, a few general suggestions for supportive action can be offered:

1. Scolding, moralizing, and punishing are counterproductive. These merely aggravate the emotional problems of the young girl, adding rejection, shame, fear, and resentment. They create barriers to open communication between staff and residents. In extreme cases the girl may run away from the home, attempt a back-alley abortion, or engage in other self-destructive acts.

2. An immediate priority is competent medical care. In addition to an appropriate examination, the doctor should provide information on the pro-

cesses of pregnancy and birth and tell the youngster about the physical and psychological changes she can expect. Instructions on nutrition, exercise, and other aspects of prenatal care should be furnished.

3. The group home and placement agency caseworker must decide, in consultation with the youngster, whether her parents should be notified. Among the factors to take into account are placement agency regulations, the age and legal status of the resident, her relations with the parents, and the likelihood that the parents will play a supportive role. Sometimes it may be a good idea to notify another relative, such as an aunt or older sister, rather than the parents.

4. In counseling, the pregnant girl should be helped to clarify her feelings about her male partner and the prospect of bearing a child. The counselor should help the youth evaluate the options open to her and provide information she needs to develop a realistic plan for managing the situation.

5. If, after counseling, the girl decides to continue her pregnancy, she will probably have to be informed that she cannot remain in the group home for the full term. There are several reasons for that policy. The youngster may require special health care, food, and instruction that the home is not equipped to provide. School authorities may require her to transfer to a special school when her condition becomes obvious. The girl's condition can affect the attitudes of other residents adversely; they may view her pregnancy as "grown-up" and glamorous or, on the other hand, respond with envy and derision. Finally, a pregnancy may affect adversely a home's reputation and thus stigmatize unfairly all of the facility's residents.

Among possible alternatives available to the resident if she chooses to give birth are (a) return to her parents; (b) living with another relative; (c) transfer to a residential care facility for unmarried pregnant women; (d) placement with a foster family; (e) independent living arrangements if she is of sufficient maturity.

6. During the transition period that precedes the girl's departure, her placement agency caseworker and the home's social worker can provide information about the eligibility requirements of government welfare programs, Medicaid, sources of prenatal and postnatal care, adoption agencies, and the small number of residential care facilities that admit unwed mothers with their babies. If the girl plans to live independently, the workers may be able to help her find a suitable dwelling, employment, and supportive services.

7. If the prospective father wishes to participate in the planning and counseling process, he should be permitted to do so unless that is countertherapeutic for the pregnant girl. Needless to say, the girl should not be pressured to continue her relationship with him if she does not wish to.

8. These days abortion is increasingly accepted as an alternative to bearing an unwanted child. If, after counseling, the pregnant girl prefers an abortion, the group home should consult the placement agency caseworker about agency regulations, requirements for parental consent, and sources of funds

to pay for the operation. A gynecologist should be consulted to ensure that an abortion will not be hazardous, to provide information about procedures and postoperative care, and perhaps to identify a reliable health facility. A staff member of the home should accompany the girl to her medical appointments to lend support at that difficult time.

Staff Training in Health Care

Staff members should be helped to acquire a knowledge of the everyday essentials of health care. Subjects for discussion include the following:

1. First aid (a first-aid kit should be kept in an accessible place).
2. What to do in emergencies (telephone numbers of the fire department, rescue squad, doctor, group home director, and others to call in emergencies should be posted prominently).
3. Sanitary food handling and dishwashing.
4. Good nutrition and cooking procedures.
5. The symptoms and treatment of common illnesses such as allergies, colds, influenza, sinus infections, athlete's foot, and stomach disorders. An important topic is the management of contagious diseases in the facility.
6. The home's policy governing the dispensing of nonprescription medications for common ailments, e.g., aspirin and antihistamines for colds, and nasal sprays for sinus trouble.
7. Questions about health asked frequently by young people.
8. Identifying and treating drug abuse and alcoholism.

VOLUNTEERS

It is obvious that a full education, recreation, and health program places a severe strain on the tiny staff of group homes. The director, social worker, and child care workers will have trouble finding time for all of the recommended activities. They also may lack requisite skills and knowledge; not all people who work in residential facilities are campers, athletes, artists, and experts in remedial education or health care. It seems reasonable, therefore, to supplement limited staff resources with adult volunteers recruited in the community.

Unfortunately, relatively few homes make extensive use of volunteers, for which directors offer various reasons. Volunteers are said to have trouble adapting to group homes because they bring unrealistic expectations and their own unresolved emotional problems to the job. Often they are not available to work during the hours of greatest need: evenings and weekends.

Some are unreliable or quit after a short while. Their training and supervision requires excessive staff time. In short, many group homes feel that volunteers are not worth the effort needed to recruit, train, and employ them productively.

In spite of such widespread skepticism, the potential contributions of volunteers are so substantial that they deserve consideration. Volunteers can free staff members from routine work so that they have time for rest, informal interaction with residents, and training. The presence of volunteers improves supervision and safety on field trips and in the home. Volunteers can enrich the home's education and recreation programs. Properly selected, they can help to balance the age, sex, racial, and ethnic composition of the staff.

Drawing workers from the community tends to improve public relations. Volunteers are a source of recruits for membership on the home's board of directors and for regular staff jobs when openings occur. The value of their labor can be counted as part of the home's share of a matching grant sought from a foundation or government agency. Overall, the advantages may well outweigh the problems associated with unpaid manpower. For a more detailed discussion of the contribution of volunteers, see McCroskey et al. (1983).

Some people who volunteer for work in group homes have had experience in child care; others have helpful skills for other program activities. Still others are just nice folks who want to be helpful. Fortunately, the activities available for volunteers around a home are so varied that assignments can be tailored to individual capabilities.

There are tasks for volunteers that involve close and frequent interaction with the residents, individually or in groups. Other tasks require only scattered and superficial contacts, or no face-to-face contact at all. Similarly, some volunteer work requires art, craft, and other specialized skills; other jobs require only a generalized ability to relate to youths for short periods. Almost anyone who is intelligent, emotionally mature, and motivated can lend a hand.

Some specific activities for volunteers are suggested below:

1. Tutoring in reading, grammar, math, proper speech, and other subjects.
2. Instruction in arts, crafts, athletics, and nature appreciation.
3. Accompanying residents on outings such as camping trips, hikes, and museum visits to provide extra supervision and safety.
4. Providing extra manpower to make it possible to divide the group during outings. This permits residents of different ages and interests to engage in activities that they most enjoy.
5. Helping residents shop for clothes and supplies.
6. Serving as a Big Brother or Big Sister for individual youths.

7. Chauffeuring residents to and from medical appointments, the bus station, and extracurricular activities.

8. Replacing child care workers for short periods while they attend staff meetings or training sessions, and while they take a brief respite from their duties.

9. Appearing occasionally as a guest speaker or entertainer.

10. Providing legal or accounting services.

11. Maintenance work such as painting, gardening, and repairing furniture or cars.

12. Clerical work such as typing and duplicating.

13. Public relations tasks such as preparation of a newsletter, planning an annual open house, representing the home at civic group meetings, or communicating the needs of the home to legislative committees.

14. Fund raising; e.g., soliciting donations, organizing benefit performances, selling raffle tickets, and arranging an annual dinner party.

When recruiting volunteers, it is not a good idea to advertise in the mass media. Such ads may yield a large number of applicants who lack suitable qualifications. Better results are obtained by asking the home's staff and board of directors to recruit informally among their acquaintances, and by contacting organizations such as civic groups, schools, art groups, and professional associations with which individuals who possess needed skills are likely to be affiliated.

Applicants should be interviewed carefully. Objective characteristics to note include their employment and family status, health, avocational skills, previous experience with troubled young people, and the days and hours they have available. Beliefs and attitudes concerning residential child care should be explored, including the applicant's motives for volunteering in the group home, preconceptions about the qualities and treatment of disturbed and maladjusted youths, and expectations about the nature and results of the job.

The interviewer should try to evaluate relevant personality traits: whether the applicant is flexible or rigid in dealing with people, is emotionally stable, has a sense of humor, shows good judgment, is open to direction, and can serve as a positive role model for the residents. At least two references should be requested from responsible people with firsthand knowledge of the applicant.

Applicants who pass the interview should receive an orientation to help them evaluate realistically whether they would feel comfortable with the home's personnel, activities, and milieu. The duties of volunteers should be explained, and they should be invited to tour the facility, talk to staff and residents, and even share a meal with the group before making a final commitment. The orientation period provides opportunities to observe the way prospective volunteers relate to staff and residents. The opinions of both of those groups should be taken into account in deciding whether to add the volunteer to the rolls.

Sometimes altruistic law enforcement personnel, such as policemen and prison guards, volunteer to work with troubled youths. Those worthy individuals must be evaluated with special care because the discipline and authority to which they are accustomed may not conform to the reality of small community-based child care facilities. Homes also must consider whether the frequent presence of law enforcement officials will affect adversely the way in which they are perceived by neighbors, parents of residents, and the placement agency.

In selecting volunteers it is often advisable to aim for a varied mix of ages, sexes, and races. That increases the likelihood that each resident will find at least one adult with whom he can establish a special rapport. The presence of both men and women helps the youngsters learn to think about and relate to the opposite sex in a realistic and natural way.

Initially, volunteers require a heavy investment of staff time. They must be trained, supervised, and given continuous support to enhance their competence and longevity. They should be informed about the facility's history, objectives, and staff, the characteristics of its population, and relevant policies and procedures. Lines of authority and communication should be indicated. The duties of volunteers should be explained carefully, and they should receive appropriate background information about any individual youth(s) they will be working with. Training also should include constructive ways to interact with troubled teenagers.

Volunteers donate their time in what are often frustrating jobs. They gain little in the way of immediate gratification; there are few miraculous changes of character or outbursts of gratitude among the young people. Under such circumstances the group home owes its volunteers respect and appreciation.

One way to show respect for volunteers is to use their time efficiently. No more than an essential number of volunteers should be recruited and they should never be assigned to "make-work" tasks. Staff members should minimize their periods of idleness by being on time for appointments, having the residents ready on time for tutoring and other volunteer activities, and letting volunteers know in advance if their services will not be required on a given day. Difficult as it is to find extra time, workers should spare a few minutes to chat with volunteers and give them counseling and encouragement.

Group homes can show their appreciation by providing coffee and other refreshments to volunteers on duty, awarding certificates of service annually, and calling attention to volunteers at meetings of the board of directors and other occasions. Residents also should be encouraged to express their appreciation in such ways as making small gifts and greeting cards for volunteers at Christmas.

Chapter 12

TERMINATION OF PLACEMENTS

Unless the home serves only a long-term custodial function, its services are in-tended to expedite the departure of each youth as soon as the objectives of his treatment plan have been achieved. Despite the universal acceptance of that goal, most homes have found that the termination of residents in a systematic and therapeutic manner is one of the most difficult phases of their program.

The problems are numerous. To cite a few: Some youngsters are with-drawn by their parents before their social/psychological problems have been alleviated or their families have developed supportive capabilities. A substan-tial number of youths are expelled, transferred to more restrictive facilities, or leave under other negative circumstances. Services are withdrawn from older youths as soon as they reach the age of emancipation (usually eighteen years) and little is done thereafter to ease their transition to independent adult life. In some areas the responsibility and criteria for deciding when a youth is ready for termination are so vague that residents may remain in placement longer than necessary.

Not enough is known about how placements in group homes come to an end. There are only fragmentary data on how long youths remain, why they depart, and where they go after leaving. We know very little about where they are 1, 2, or 5 years later and whether they have adapted successfully in their new settings. Experience indicates, however, that there is a need to strengthen the termination process—to ensure the timely evaluation and

188

preparation of residents, to prepare parents for the return of their children, and to provide support in the post-termination period.[1]

This chapter discusses various types of terminations and suggests policies for managing terminations in a therapeutic manner. It considers such issues as who decides when a resident should be separated from a group home; when a resident is ready for termination; what new living arrangement is best for a departing youth; what services are needed by residents and their families to facilitate a positive termination.

TYPES OF TERMINATION

Termination policies must take into account the different circumstances under which residents can leave a group home. At the very start a distinction can be drawn between positive and negative terminations. In the former, residents are discharged after they have improved to the point where they are ready to join their own or an adoptive family, move on to a less restrictive placement such as foster family care, or live as independent adults. Negative terminations, on the other hand, are those in which a youth's departure is not in accord with his planned course of treatment. The youth may be expelled or transferred by the home, arrested by law enforcement personnel, committed for emergency treatment to a mental health facility, or simply may have run away.

Nationwide, nobody knows the proportion of group home youths who are terminated for positive or negative reasons. Local data on termination are inconsistent and usually combine group homes with other forms of residential care. Even the comprehensive survey of group homes conducted by the Citizens Committee for Children of New York (1976) in the mid-seventies was unable to ascertain fully the circumstances under which residents left the surveyed facilities. In most homes for disturbed or maladjusted youths, negative terminations are a significant proportion of the total. It would not be surprising to find that negative terminations outnumber positive ones in some facilities.[2]

Positive Terminations

Return to the family. Of all the positive options, the return of youngsters to their families is probably the most common type of termination. That is, of

---

[1]Helpful data on terminations are reported in Fanshel (1978). However, the study presents no separate data for group homes.
[2]In a study of three Ohio group homes Simone (1985) found negative terminations averaged about one-third of all terminations. In 18 New Jersey group homes surveyed by the author in 1975, a majority of terminations over the preceding year were negative —mainly expulsions. However, almost all of the surveyed facilities were comparatively new and still learning the business of residential child care.

course, the most desirable outcome from society's point of view. However, sending a youth home is not always a positive solution for parents and child. Family stresses may not have been resolved by the time that the youngster is ready to leave the group home. Families with a history of neglect, alcoholism, violence, incest, and other symptoms of disorganization are likely to exert a harmful influence. Parents who abused or abandoned their children in the past may resist their return. The mother or father may have remarried or be living with someone who does not want the youth to come home.

There can be problems even when the parents wish to cooperate. They may be unable to provide proper care because of illness, unemployment, and poor housing. They may be unable to supervise their child adequately because of frequent on-the-job travel, long working hours, and the absence of a spouse in the household. There may be a lack of supportive services in the family's community; e.g., counseling, psychotherapy, and parent effectiveness training at prices that the parents can afford.

A boy or girl may resist a return to the family because of fear, hostility, continuing differences in values and lifestyles, or a desire to live independently. In some cases, there is a danger that a youth may resume harmful peer relationships on returning to the former neighborhood and school. Reuniting the family, therefore, is not always the best alternative. It requires a readiness on the part of all participants and often the availability of post-termination services to strengthen the family.

Living with other relatives.   When it is not advisable to return a youth to the parents, living with other relatives may be a positive alternative. There may be an uncle, a married sibling, or a grandmother who can provide a suitable environment and maintain a supportive relationship with the youngster.

Probably the number of such terminations is small but significant. Some subcultures attach a special value to solidarity in the extended family and have a tradition of child care by relatives. However, the release of young people to relatives is not without potential difficulties. Well-meaning relatives may have unrealistic expectations about life with a troubled teenager. They may be unable to assert adequate controls over his behavior. In the absence of strong commitment, the relative, the youth, or both may simply change their minds about living together, leaving the youth in a perilous limbo.

It is a good idea to provide counseling in advance for relatives to whom a resident is to be released. Where needed, supportive services should be arranged for the post-termination period.

Foster families.   Another group of terminees is assigned to foster parents who are paid and supervised by placement agencies. Providing a less restrictive and less institutional environment, foster families serve as a transitional step to normal family life or independent adulthood.

There are several reasons, however, why foster care has been only a limited resource for youths leaving group homes. Age is probably the most important obstacle. Foster parents generally prefer preteen children, who are thought to adjust flexibly to a family setting, respond to the approval and disapproval of parent figures, and to be amenable to parental control. Group home terminees, on the other hand, are usually teenagers who are at an age when they seek new experiences and resist the authority of parents and other adults. Prospective foster parents are apprehensive that youths of that age will resume harmful patterns of behavior, reject their guidance, and yield to harmful peer group influences.

For older residents nearing the age when they can live as independent adults, it may be disruptive to join a foster family for a short period before guardianship by the placement agency comes to an end. A short-term placement is likely to add new tensions to an already difficult transition. In addition, foster parents are usually less able than the group home to provide pretermination counseling and social services to prepare the youth to live on his own.

A third reason for the limited use of family foster care is a shortage of foster parents in some areas. That may be the result of inadequate reimbursement, lack of publicity, insufficient training and supervision, racial prejudice, or other factors.

Adoption. Despite the current emphasis on transferring institutionalized children to permanent family settings, only a small proportion of group home youngsters end up in adoptive homes. Most, of course, retain strong links to their natural parents and, with appropriate supportive services, can rejoin them after a period of time. Others cannot be placed because there are fewer adoption openings for teenagers—the most common age group in group homes—than for younger children. The scarcity of foster families further limits the number of adoptions because foster parents are potential adoptive parents for youngsters in their care. Finally, the long period of time required to terminate the rights of natural parents and to find and evaluate potential adoptive parents limits that option for group home terminees.

Independent living. Some group home youths live as independent adults after their departure. At age eighteen, or at a younger age under some circumstances, the young people are emancipated from the guardianship of parents and child welfare agencies. Some find jobs or continue their education. They may move in with relatives or friends, rent an apartment or room, or live in a college dormitory. A few may join the armed forces or the federal government's Job Corps. Unless they choose to write or visit friends and staff members at the home, most simply disappear from view.

The transition to independent living can be difficult. Youths need help in finding a job and a place to live. They need counseling in choosing a vocation, securing appropriate training, and adapting to the work place. To live independently, they must learn how to prepare wholesome meals, per-

form housekeeping chores, manage their money, use leisure time constructively, and take care of their health. Sometimes financial assistance is necessary until a youth becomes self-supporting.

The resources of a typical group home are too limited to provide all of
the services needed by residents preparing for independent living. Moreover,
homes are rarely in a position to help former residents after they have left the
facility. Fortunately, an increasing number of child welfare agencies are recognizing the need for transitional and aftercare services.[3]

Negative Terminations

The problems associated with the positive termination of residents are
of little consequence compared with the anguish and complications that often
accompany a negative termination. Unplanned departures, expulsions, and
the transfer of youths to more intensive care must be anticipated by all group
homes. Various types of negative terminations are identified and discussed in
more detail below.

Runaways. Eighteen New Jersey homes studied by the author some
years ago reported a total of 20 runaways in the preceding year; that is,
youths who left for good or were absent without leave for more than a few
days. Residents ran off for a number of reasons, including:

> homesickness and discomfort during the first few weeks of
>   placement;
>
> concern about family problems such as the illness of a par-
>   ent;
>
> concern about the fidelity of, or need to be with a girl or
>   boy friend;
>
> harmful relations with peers in the group home; e.g.,
>   scapegoating, ridicule, hazing, racial friction, or ostra-
>   cism;
>
> anger at staff members;
>
> psychological disturbances such as depression, delusions,
>   and paranoia;
>
> failure at school;
>
> health-related problems such as pregnancy, fear of an im-
>   pending physical examination, or fear of surgery;
>
> a conviction that, in any case, they would be expelled or
>   transferred in the near future.

[3]Issues and practices in preparing residents for independent living are explored in Citizens Committee for Children of New York (1984).

With all runaways it is important to notify the placement agency and the police promptly because failure to meet legal requirements may open the facility to criticism and adverse legal action. The staff can help the authorities locate the missing youngster by contacting relatives and friends and by checking places where he has been spending time.

If the youth returns, the group home must decide whether readmission is advisable. There is no simple answer; each case can be reviewed in the light of the reasons for running away, the duration of the absence, and the youngster's age.

In deciding its response a group home may wish to take into account whether youths have run away on previous occasions and whether they have run away alone or with fellow residents. Youngsters who go off to their families without permission must be distinguished from those who simply wander off in search of adventure or engage in self-harming activities during their absence. Perhaps the best criterion for readmission is the ability of the runaway to benefit further from the home's program without exerting a harmful influence on other residents.

If a youth is readmitted it is, of course, essential to identify the factors leading to the incident and to take corrective action. After evaluating the problem, the staff can decide on steps to reduce the youngster's motivation to run away. Examples of steps that might work in particular cases are extending the curfew to a later hour, facilitating family visits, changing roommates, counseling to improve peer relations, improving overnight security in the facility, and helping a youth do better at school.

Removal by parents.   Since most group home placements are "voluntary" in the sense that they are based on the consent of the parents rather than ordered by a court, parents are generally in a position to withdraw their children. Even if there are legal limitations on withdrawal, placement agencies are reluctant to retain children over the objections of their natural parents. Therefore, a significant number of residents are removed before their psychological and social problems, and those of the parents, have been resolved.

Among the reasons parents withdraw their youngsters are relocation of the family to another state or area; a change in family circumstances, such as the remarriage of a parent; dissatisfaction with group home services; complaints by the resident; a specific negative incident, such as a theft or fight involving the resident; racial prejudice directed at the home's staff members or population.

In some situations placement agencies may be in a position to resist the premature withdrawal of a youngster. The agencies, for example, may have legal authority to retain children who are victims of parental abuse or neglect. The agreements signed by parents may provide for a waiting period during which they have an opportunity to reconsider their decision. Some nominally voluntary placement agreements are signed by parents to keep their child from being charged and processed as a juvenile delinquent. In those cases parents are likely to be hesitant about withdrawing a youth from residential care.

In general, it is in the best interest of all parties to enlist the cooperation of parents, rather than using compulsion to retain a group home resident. Keeping parents informed about their child's progress, consulting them on the choice of a placement site, and encouraging them to accept counseling and other supportive services help to secure their backing in the treatment process.

Emergency hospitalization.   On rare occasions a resident may experience an acute psychological crisis requiring temporary emergency hospitalization. Suicide attempts, a loss of contact with reality, a drug overdose, uncontrolled violent behavior, and other crisis symptoms require prompt removal to a psychiatric facility where intensive round-the-clock care is available.

It is important for the group home to learn in advance the emergency procedures for transferring a youth to a psychiatric facility. The staff should identify treatment facilities that are able to accept crisis patients and discuss commitment procedures with the physicians who serve the home's residents. Placement agency rules for transferring a youth to a psychiatric facility also must be consulted. Jurisdictional disputes, financial requirements, and placement agency restrictions that might complicate emergency transfers should be ironed out before actual emergencies present themselves.

In the excitement of arranging an emergency hospitalization the staff should not forget to notify concerned persons and organizations about the youth's temporary absence. Notice is required by the placement agency, parents, and the school. Employers, the dentist, a baseball coach, and others who are expecting the youth to show up also require notification.

Transfer to a long-term intensive care facility.   More common than emergency hospitalization is the transfer of a resident who is not benefiting from the group home program to a facility providing more intensive long-term care. The youth may have engaged in self-destructive behavior, been a threat to the welfare of fellow residents, disrupted the home's program, displayed a serious psychological disturbance, or failed to meet school requirements—all to a degree that exceeded the home's treatment capabilities.

Transfers to more appropriate institutions are in the best interests of the young people involved. They are listed here as negative terminations only in the sense that they involve the termination of residents whose psychological handicaps have not been treated successfully by the group home. Even when a youth is transferred, however, the group home deserves credit for having evaluated his needs for additional care and often for laying the groundwork for more successful adaptation in the youth's next placement.

Expulsion.   Most group homes have the option of expelling residents who engage in disruptive behavior, violate the rights of staff and residents, break the law, or are otherwise likely to cause serious harm to self or others. Depending on the circumstances, expulsion may be the right response to frequent fighting, attacks on staff members, persistent stealing, and sexual asaults. Continued abuse of drugs or alcohol, chronic truancy, and persistent flaunting of staff authority also justify expulsion. It is in the interest of all concerned to move serious offenders without delay to more appropriate placement sites.

Expulsion of a resident is a worrisome experience in group homes. Staff members sometimes feel guilty or inadequate. The youth's fellow residents experience distress as well. The placement agency may conclude that the home is not competent or that it is seeking to serve only youngsters who are easy to care for. The expulsion leaves a vacant bed for which the home may receive no reimbursement, creating financial strains until the vacancy is filled. Despite such difficulties, there are times when an expulsion is in the long-run interest of the expellee and the home, and it must be undertaken in a supportive but firm spirit.

A group home may encounter serious administrative prbblems if there is a need to expel a particularly difficult youth without delay. The youth cannot simply be thrust out-of-doors and told to go away. A logical first step is to ask the placement agency to remove the offender. Often, however, placement agencies require days or weeks to review the case and to find an alternative placement. In the meantime the youngster may be left in the group home, sullen, angry, anxious, and disrupting the social milieu.

When the prompt transfer of a dangerous or disruptive youth cannot be arranged in any other way, a home may, as a last resort, file a complaint with the police. If the police agree that the resident should be charged as a delinquent or status offender, they can remove him to a detention facility pending judicial review of the case. Group homes are often reluctant to take that last-ditch step, which may exacerbate the resident's psychological problems and evoke a negative response from the youth's parents and the placement agency. However, a short stay in the structured environment of the local shelter for delinquents or status offenders sometimes has a therapeutic effect, reassuring the youth that his impulses are not beyond the control of adult caretakers and stimulating constructive self-examination. Parents too are compelled to face the reality of their child's behavior and to reassess their views of his treatment needs.

RESPONSIBILITY FOR TERMINATING PLACEMENTS

From time to time one hears complaints that youths remain too long in residential care facilities or "get lost in the system." That is attributed, in part, to a lack of alternative placement opportunities with foster families and adoptive parents. However, placement agencies and residential care facilities also are blamed for failing to keep track of each resident's progress and delaying unnecessarily the reassignment of youths in their care.

Placement agency caseworkers, who are officially responsible for terminating or changing placements, are burdened with heavy case loads. Of necessity they tend to concentrate on youths who present the most urgent problems. Other youths, who do not complain or present overt difficulties requiring immediate action, may temporarily be overlooked. Even when a youth has been placed in residential care by court order, there may be similar delays because the courts too are short-handed and rely on the placement agency's caseworkers for advice on when a youth is ready to be discharged.

Sadly, not all parents can be counted on to press for the return of their children. Some have neglected or abandoned them in the past or simply feel unable to cope with their problems.

In states and localities that have established an independent review system to assess the appropriateness of each residential placement and to follow the progress of the youngsters, the review agency shares the responsibility for ensuring that placements are terminated in timely fashion.[4] Review systems have their limitations, however. They are likely to be overloaded and understaffed, so most youngsters cannot receive intensive consideration. Reviewers necessarily rely heavily on records and recommendations submitted by the placement agency rather than on independent sources of information. Reviews are conducted at annual or other long intervals, limiting their value in determining the current readiness of youngsters for termination or new services. Despite such handicaps, independent review systems are a worthwhile check on whether each youth's placement continues to meet his changing needs.

In those difficult circumstances a large share of responsibility for identifying residents who are ready for termination must be assumed by the residential care facilities themselves. They must review the status of each youth at frequent intervals and plan their services in a manner that prepares the young people for a safe departure as soon as feasible. And certainly group homes should never allow financial considerations, such as the loss of income that may result from the departure of a resident, to influence their termination decisions.

In addition to the adults who are officially responsible for a youth's care, it is important to note that the young people themselves are entitled to a voice in the termination or modification of a placement. They are no longer passive objects to be shifted about at will by adult caretakers, even their parents. Increasing attention is being given to their legal rights and to their role as partners in decisions that affect their lives.

Group home residents have a right to know why they have been placed in residential care and what changes in their behavior and circumstances must occur before they can leave the home. Otherwise they are at the mercy of unpredictable forces and are tempted to reassert control over their lives by sabotaging the program to which adults have consigned them. It is ironic that

[4]Independent review systems were described in Chapter 2.

juvenile delinquents can be sentenced to a correctional facility for specific terms or until they reach a specified age, whereas group home residents, who are not usually adjudicated delinquents, are in the anxiety-provoking position of being placed for indefinite periods of time that end whenever adult care-takers decide a termination is appropriate.

Involvement of youths in termination planning not only satisfies legal and ethical standards but is itself a therapeutic experience. It helps the young people overcome the anxieties of separation from the home and increases the likelihood that they will cooperate with termination arrangements. Involved residents are less likely to sabotage termination plans by regressing in their behavior, failing to meet commitments, experiencing psychosomatic illness, or running away.

READINESS FOR TERMINATION

There is no simple formula for determining when residents are ready for termination. That varies with each youth's needs, circumstances, and re-sources. It is possible, however, to suggest some general criteria that are rele-vant in most cases, as noted below.

Diminishing Benefits

Residents should not be retained beyond the point at which the services of the group home are no longer of any significant benefit to them. Group homes do not keep a youngster beyond that point unless their program is simply custodial in nature. Most homes are treatment facilities; they are too costly for use simply as a place to live. In addition, unnecessarily prolonged group care may have harmful side effects—fracturing family ties, weakening self-reliance, and possibly labeling the youths as deviants for the rest of their lives.

Alleviation of Psychological Disturbance

The alleviation of psychological disturbance to the point where a youth can function in a less institutionalized setting is an indication that he can be considered for termination. Readiness is suggested by the fading of self-harming behavior, compulsions, obsessions, depression, paranoia, volatile moods, passive withdrawal, temper tantrums, and proneness to violence. Ab-stention from drug abuse and other illegal behavior, the demonstration of problem-solving skills, and improvement of schoolwork are other good signs.

Capability for Positive Human Relations

Ability to function outside the group home is indicated by the ability to relate to peers and adults in a positive way. The trait is accompanied by improved self-awareness, self-reliance, self-esteem, and self-discipline. Acceptance of positive values, avoidance of harmful associates, and the ability to select and pursue realistic objectives are other related personality strengths.

Capacity for Rejoining Family

For youths whose objective is a return to the family, the emergence of positive attitudes and modes of relating to family members is an indication of readiness. For example, a youth may display a reduction of hostile attitudes and fears; a more realistic appraisal of the needs, feelings, and character of family members; more positive ways of relating to family members; improved communication with parents and siblings, as demonstrated during visits to and by the family; and an ability to manage more frequent and longer visits with the family, marked by satisfying feelings on both sides.

Age-Related Considerations

Placement agencies generally withdraw their supervision from youths who reach age eighteen or some other age plateau, regardless of their readiness to leave residential care. There is some flexibility in various jurisdictions; support may be continued for a short period if, for example, a youth requires additional care until the end of the school year.

Readiness of Parents to Receive Their Child

Among factors to consider under this heading are the following:

1. The stability of relations between the parents themselves. Sometimes this involves the completion of divorce proceedings, stabilization of relations with lovers, or a move into or out of a relative's home.
2. Parent interest in expediting the return of the child.
3. The tangible capabilities of the parents, including the adequacy of their income, job security, housing, and physical and mental health.
4. Parent cooperation in seeking and using supportive services to strengthen the family.
5. The extent of supportive communication between parents and child, and the frequency and quality of home visits.
6. The extent to which the parents keep in touch with the home concerning their child's progress and needs.
7. Improvement in the patterned ways in which parents relate to their child. One might look for a diminution of threats, violent punishment, authoritarian demands, rigidity, inconsistency, and un-

realistic expectations. Manipulation through tantrums, hypochondria, dependency, guilt, and other indirect means should have become less frequent.

8. The elimination of pathological behavior in the family, e.g., alcoholism, drug abuse, prostitution, incest, and dependence on criminal activity for a livelihood.

9. The suitability of older siblings or other relatives as parent surrogates if the parents are unable or unwilling to facilitate their child's return.

10. The availability of necessary post-termination support services in the family's home area.

Capacity for Independent Living

A different set of factors must be considered for older youths preparing to live as independent adults after leaving the home. One may ask whether these residents have (a) realistic vocational and educational objectives; (b) adequate vocational training, job prospects, and the ability to seek and keep a job; (c) appropriate living arrangements; (d) essential skills for housekeeping, money management, use of public transportation, use of health and welfare services, and identifying wholesome recreation and social opportunities; (e) a supportive network of family members and friends.

THE TERMINATION PLAN

There are so many participants in implementing a youth's separation from a group home that it is very helpful to prepare a written plan to coordinate the process. Such a plan should be made whenever a review of a resident's progress indicates that he may soon be ready to leave the facility. The plan is not necessarily a new document but simply the final updated version of the youth's regular treatment plan. It is best prepared by the home's social worker or director, in consultation with the placement agency caseworker, the youth, the parents, and others, such as court officials, who may be involved in the placement.

A termination plan spells out the post-termination objective of the youth and proposes a tentative time period for ending the placement. It identifies what remains to be done to effectuate the youth's separation, and it specifies the steps that will be taken by each participant. The plan helps to systematize termination activities and ensures continuity in the event of turnover among caseworkers or group home staff members. It also may motivate parents and youngsters to work harder at resolving their problems by indicating clearly what they can do to expedite a termination and setting a tentative target date for departure.

The contents of a termination plan should include at least the following elements:

1. The youth's post-termination objective, e.g., return to the family or independent living.

2. A target date for termination. That must take into account such constraints as the beginning and ending dates of the school year, the date on which freshmen are admitted to college dormitories, and the starting date of a terminee's new job. If the departing youth is moving into a foster family home, a transitional program, or another residential facility, the termination date must be geared to the availability of a suitable opening. For other youngsters the departure date may depend on the time needed to arrange an adoption, a change of guardians, or a transfer to an out-of-state placement agency. Group homes should be aware of such time limits and try to plan each termination well in advance to minimize disappointing delays.

3. Remaining services to be provided. Those might include, for example, correction of residual personality problems. It may be advisable to retain a youth until some medical or dental work is completed. There may be a need for further preparatory work with parents. Older youths may need additional training in vocational or social skills or help in locating a place to live as independent adults. The conditions to be corrected should be as specific as possible, to provide well-defined and measurable objectives for all participants.

4. Action required. This section identifies the steps that each participant will take to implement the termination. The approximate timing of each step should be indicated so that the combined efforts of all individuals can proceed in a coordinated manner. Although the actual steps required for each youth vary, some examples may be helpful.

Action to be taken by the placement agency caseworker include the following:

> Conduct pretermination counseling session with the parents.
>
> Initiate a search for a new placement if that is the post-termination objective.
>
> Initiate required official documents.
>
> Prepare any notices required by a court or independent review system.
>
> Arrange specified post-termination services for the family.
>
> Assist in finding housing, a job, a scholarship, or other aids for a youth nearing the age of emancipation.

Action by the group home staff:

> Contact therapists and outside agencies that have served the youth and family to coordinate termination plans.

Schedule parent counseling sessions.

Provide pretermination counseling for the youth.

Discuss the prospective termination with other residents in group counseling.

Provide instruction in skills for independent living; see Furrh (1983) and Mauzerall (1983).

Arrange a farewell party, gift, and certificate.

Plan follow-up contacts after the youth's departure.

Action by the parents:

Participate in pretermination counseling sessions with caseworker and group home staff.

Make specified changes in living quarters, life-style, and family arrangements.

Practice specified ways of relating to the youth during his visits to the family.

Enroll in service programs; e.g., Alcoholics Anonymous, a community therapy group, or a parenting class.

Arrange post-termination supportive services for the youth; e.g., psychotherapy, tutoring, health services.

Notify local school and welfare authorities prior to youth's return.

Action by the resident:

Participate in one or more termination planning sessions with the home's social worker.

Achieve specified short-term goals such as remaining on the highest level of the home's incentive system for at least 2 months, completing the school year with passing grades, and spending several consecutive weekends with the family in a comfortable manner.

Demonstrate independent living skills such as cooking, housecleaning, shopping, budgeting.

Achieve a savings account balance of $100.

Begin job search or, if preparing for college, submit timely applications to selected schools.

Transitional Programs

For older residents who reach the age of emancipation the transition from life in a group home to full independence can be very difficult. In addition to success stories, group home directors tell of terminees who keep returning for support, who revert to self-harming life-styles, and who fail in other ways to cope with the unfamiliar demands of adulthood. A troubled eighteen-year-old may readily be overwhelmed by the challenge of finding a place to live, keeping house, keeping a job, managing money, developing supportive friendships with both sexes, and using leisure time constructively. There is increasing recognition, therefore, that transitional programs are required to strengthen the capabilities of group home "graduates."

Some placement agencies are experimenting with new services. In one approach several young people preparing for termination are transferred to an apartment near the group home, where they practice independent living. They are expected to meet housekeeping responsibilities, attend school regularly, look for a job, use their leisure time constructively, and handle other commitments with a minimum of adult supervision. The group home, reimbursed by the placement agency, continues to provide counseling and financial support until the final termination of such residents-in-transition.

Such programs are of great potential value but face practical problems. Because most placement agencies withdraw support from the young people by age eighteen, individuals who have not yet fully matured by that age must be dropped from transitional programs before they are ready for independent living. Another problem: placement agencies are likely to pay less for transitional care than for conventional group home care, thus limiting available supervision and services. Overall, however, transitional programs are an encouraging addition to the spectrum of residential services.

REFERENCES

Adams, M., & Baumbach, D. J. (1980). Professional parenting: A factor in group home programming. *Child Care Quarterly, 9*, 185–196.

Adessa, S., & Laatsch, A. (1965). Therapeutic use of visiting in residential treatment. *Child Welfare, 44*, 245–251.

Adler, J. (1981). *Fundamentals of group child care.* Cambridge, MA: Ballinger.

Adler, J. (1979). The child care worker's leadership in group process. *Child Care Quarterly, 8*, 196–205.

Adler, P. M. (1985). Ethnic placement of refugee/entrant unaccompanied minors. *Child Welfare, 64*, 491–499.

Association for Children of New Jersey (Written by C.A. Scalera & P. Yuen) (1979). *Survey report on implementation of the Child Placement Review Act.* Newark, NJ.. Published by author.

Baker, N. G. (1982). Substitute care for unaccompanied refugee minors. *Child Welfare, 61*, 353–363.

Beckham, C. O., Johnston, L., & Beckham, E. (1979). Sex education for children in a residential center. *Child Welfare 58*, 393–402.

Bramhall, M. & Ezell, S. (1981). How agencies can prevent burnout. *Public Welfare, 39*, 33–37.

Burmeister, E. (1967). *Tough times and tender moments in child care work.* New York: Columbia University Press.

Chappell, B., & Hevener, B. (1977). *Periodic review of children in foster care: Mechanisms for review.* Newark, NJ: A Policy Information Paper of the Child Service Association.

Cherniss, C. (1980). *Staff burnout: Job stress in the human services.* Beverly Hills, CA: Sage Publications.

203

Child Welfare. Two special issues on group care: 44 (May 1965) and 51 (October 1972).

Child Welfare League of America. (1980). *ORPSCCA Newsletter* (September & October). Published by author.

Child Welfare League of America. (1978). *Standards for group home service for children.* New York: Published by author.

Child Welfare League of America. (1964). Group homes in perspective. New York: Published by author.

Citizens Committee for Children of New York. (1984). *The foster care exit —ready or not.* New York: Published by author.

Citizens Committee for Children of New York. (1976). *Group homes for New York City children.* New York: Published by author.

Connis, R.T. et al. (1979). Work environment in relation to employee job satisfaction in group homes for youths. *Child Care Quarterly, 8*, 126–142.

Cutler, J. P., & Bateman, R. W. (1980). Foster care case review: Can it make a difference? *Public Welfare, 38*, 45–51.

Dore, M., & Kennedy, K. (1981). Two decades of turmoil: Child welfare services, 1960–1980. *Child Welfare, 60*, 371–382.

Dore, M.M., Young, T. M., & Pappenfort, D. M. (1984). Comparison of basic data for the National Survey of Residential Group Care Facilities, 1966–1982. *Child Welfare, 63*, 485–496.

Edelwich, J., with Brodsky, A. (1980). *Burnout.* New York: Human Sciences Press.

Empey, L.T., & Lubeck, S. (1971). *The Silverlake experiment.* Chicago: Aldine.

Euster, S.D., Ward, V.P., Varner, J.G., & Euster, G.L. (1984). Life skills groups for adolescent foster children. *Child Welfare, 63*, 27–35.

Fanshel, D. (1978). Children discharged from foster care in New York City: Where to—when—at what age? *Child Welfare, 57*, 467–483.

Festinger, T.B. (1976). The impact of the New York court review of children in foster care: A followup report. *Child Welfare, 55*, 515–546.

Freudenberger, H. (1977). Burnout: Occupational hazard of the child care worker. *Child Care Quarterly, 6*, 90–99.

Furrh, P.E., Jr. (1983). Emancipation: The supervised apartment living approach. *Child Welfare, 62*, 54–62.

Gordon, T. (1970). *Parent effectiveness training: The no-lose program for raising responsible children.* New York: Wyden.

Gula, M. (1965). *Agency operated group homes.* Washington, DC: U.S. Children's Bureau.

Harstad, C.D. (1976). Guided group interaction: Positive peer culture. *Child Care Quarterly, 5*, 109–120.

Henry, N. (1972). *When mother is a prefix.* New York: Behavioral Publications.

Herstein, N. (1983). The children's agency executive as political practitioner. *Child Welfare, 62*, 213–220.

Hirschbach, E. (1976). Memo to child care workers on their role in group homes. *Child Welfare, 55*, 681–690.

Hirschbach, E. (April 1975). The Role of the Child Care Worker in Group Homes. Paper presented at the Association of Child Care Workers Conference on Group Homes, Sparkhill, N.Y.

Hirschbach, E. (1973). Structure and program in group home care. In Federation of Protestant Welfare Agencies (Eds.), *Group homes for children and youth—a report on the Group Home Conference*, New York.

Horejsi, C.R., Bertsche, A.V., & Clark, F.W. (1981). *Social work practice with parents of children in foster care*. Springfield, IL: Charles C. Thomas.

Jewett, D. (1973). The group home: A neighborhood-based treatment facility. *Children Today, 2*, 16–20.

Kahn, R. (1978). Job burnout, prevention, and remedies. *Public Welfare, 36*, 60–63.

Konopka, G. (1976). The needs, rights, and responsibilities of youth. *Child Welfare, 55*, 173–182.

Krona, D. (1980). Parents as treatment partners in residential care. *Child Welfare, 59*, 91–96.

Krueger, M. (1978). *Intervention techniques for child care workers*. Milwaukee, WI: Franklin Publishers.

Krueger, M.A., & Nardine, F.E. (1984). The Wisconsin Child Care Worker Survey. *Child Care Quarterly, 13*, 72–73.

Lambert, P. (1977). *The ABC's of child care work in residential care*. New York: Child Welfare League of America.

Leahy, M., & Barnes, M. (1977). Private social welfare agencies: Legal liabilities facing employees. *Public Welfare, 35*, 42–46.

Leeman, W.A. (1978). Third party purchase of voluntary agency services. *Child Welfare, 57*, 497–504.

Levine, T. (1977). Community-based treatment for adolescents: Myths and realities. *Social Work, 22*, 144–147.

Littaur, C. (1980). Working with families of children in residential treatment. *Child Welfare, 59*, 225–234.

Maloney, D.T., Timbers, G.D., & Maloney, K.B. (1977). "BIABH project: Regional adaptation of the teaching-family model group home for adolescents. *Child Welfare, 56*, 787–796.

Maluccio, A., & Sinanoglu, P. (Eds.). (1981). *The challenge of partnership: Working with parents of children in foster care*. New York: Child Welfare League of America.

Mattingly, M. (1977). Sources of stress and burn-out in professional child care work. *Child Care Quarterly, 6*, 127–137.

Mauzerall, H. (1983). Emancipation from foster care: The independent living project. *Child Welfare, 62*, 46–53.

Mayer, M.F. (1972). The group in residential treatment of adolescents. *Child Welfare, 51*, 482ff.

Mayer, M.F. (1958). *A guide for child care workers*. New York: Child Welfare League of America.

McCorkle, L., Elias, A., & Bixby, F.L. (1958). *The Highfields story*. New York: Henry Holt.

McCroskey, J., Brown, C., & Greene, S. R. (1983). Are volunteers worth the effort? *Public Welfare, 41*, 5–8.

McInnis, E., & Marholin, D., II. (1977). Individualizing behavior therapy for children in group settings. *Child Welfare, 56*, 449–463.

McLaughlin, J.E. (1981). Monitoring children in juvenile court. *Family Life Developments*. (Newsletter of the Region II Child Abuse and Neglect Resource Center). Ithaca, NY: Cornell University.

Meyer, M., Odom, E.E., & Wax, B.S. (1973). Birth and life of an incentive system in a residential institution for adolescents. *Child Welfare, 52,* 503–509.

National Council of Jewish Women. (1973). How to set up a group home. In *Justice for children* (Vol. 2). New York: Published by author.

Olin, R. (1978). Linking the group home and the community school. *Child Welfare, 57,* 513–518.

Phillips, E.L., Phillips, E.A., Fixsen, D.L., & Wolf, M.M. (June 1973). Achievement place—Behavior shaping works for delinquents. *Psychology Today,* pp. 75ff.

Pierce, L., & Hauck, V. (1981). A model for establishing a community-based foster group home. *Child Welfare, 60,* 475–482.

Piliavin, I. (1970). Conflict between cottage parents and case workers. In H.W. Polsky et al. (Eds.), *Social system perspectives in residential institutions* (chapter 18). East Lansing, MI: Michigan State University Press.

Pines, A., & Aronson, E. (1981). *Burnout—From tedium to personal growth.* New York: The Free Press.

Pizzatt, F. (1973). *Behavior modification in residential treatment for children.* New York: Behavioral Publications.

Polsky, H. (1962). *Cottage six.* New York: Russell Sage.

Polsky, H., Claster, D. S., & Goldberg, C. (1970). *Social system perspectives in residential institutions.* East Lansing, MI: Michigan State University Press.

Rabinow, I. (1964). Agency-operated group homes. *Child Welfare, 43,* 415ff.

Raubolt, R.R. (1983). Treating children in residential group psychotherapy. *Child Welfare, 62,* 147–155.

Redl, F. (1959). The concept of a therapeutic milieu. *American Journal of Orthopsychiatry, 29,* 721–736.

Ross, A.L. (1984). A study of child care staff turnover. *Child Care Quarterly, 13,* 209–223.

Scallon, R. J., Vitale, S., & Eschenauer, R. (1976). Behavior modification in a residence and school for adolescent boys: A team approach. *Child Welfare, 55,* 561–571.

Schwartz, M., & Kaplan, I. (1961). Small group homes—placement of choice for adolescents. *Child Welfare, 40,* 9ff.

Seidman, A. (1965). The caseworker's role in small group homes. *Children, 11,* 19–22.

Shostack, A. L. (1978). Staffing patterns in group homes for teenagers. *Child Welfare, 57,* 309–320.

Shostack, A. L. (1977). The Experience of Group Homes for Teenagers in New Jersey. Unpublished report of a statewide survey sponsored by the New Jersey Association of Children's Residential Facilities.

Simone, M.V. (1985). Group home failures in juvenile justice: The next step. *Child Welfare, 64,* 357–366.

Sinanoglu, P., & Maluccio, A. N. (Eds.). (1981). *Parents of children in placement: Perspectives and programs.* New York: Child Welfare League of America.

Solomon, P. (1983). Analyzing opposition to community residential facilities for troubled adolescents. *Child Welfare, 62,* 361–366.

Trieschman, A.E., Whittaker, J.K., & Brendtro, L. (1969). *The other 23 hours.* Chicago: Aldine.

Turner, C. (1980). Resources for help in parenting. *Child Welfare, 59*, 179–188.

Vander Ven, K.D. (1979). Developmental characteristics of child care workers and design of training programs. *Child Care Quarterly, 8*, 100–112.

Wald, P. (1976). Making sense out of the rights of youth. *Child Welfare, 55*, 379–393.

Weber, D.E. (1978). Neighborhood entry in group home development. *Child Welfare, 57*, 627–642.

Werner, R.M. (1976). *Public financing of voluntary agency foster care: 1975 compared with 1957.* New York: Child Welfare League of America.

Whittaker, J.K. (1979). *Caring for troubled children—residential treatment in a community context.* San Francisco, Washington, London: Jossey-Bass Publishers.

Wolins, M. (Ed.). (1974). *Successful group care.* Chicago: Aldine.

Zischka, P. (1981). The effect of burnout on permanency planning and the middle management supervisor in child welfare agencies. *Child Welfare, 60*, 611–616.

INDEX*

*Authors cited in footnotes or references are not listed.